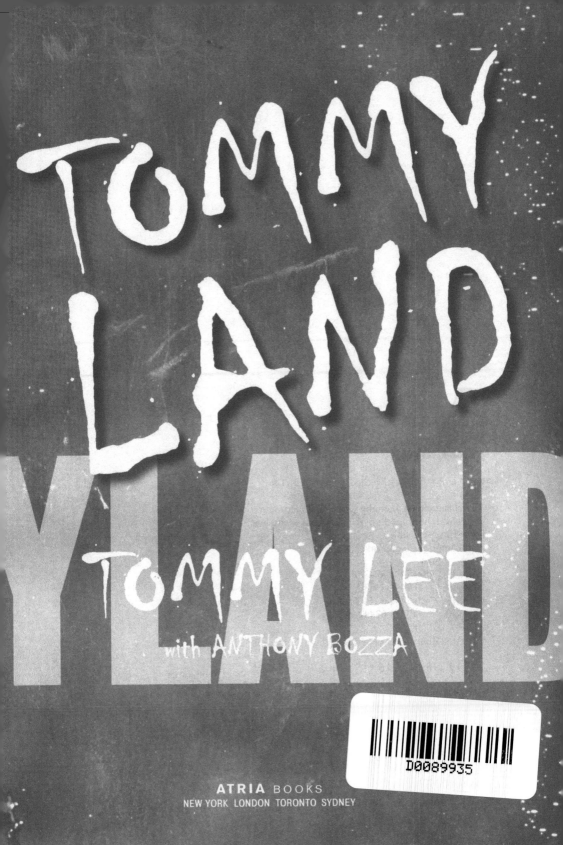

TOMMY LAND

TOMMY LEE

with ANTHONY BOZZA

D0089935

ATRIA BOOKS
NEW YORK LONDON TORONTO SYDNEY

ATRIA BOOKS

1230 Avenue of the Americas
New York, NY 10020

ISBN-13: 978-0-7434-8343-8
ISBN-10:   0-7434-8343-X
ISBN-13: 978-0-7434-8344-5 (Pbk)
ISBN-10:   0-7434-8344-8 (Pbk)

First Atria Books trade paperback edition September 2005

20   19   18   17   16   15   14

ATRIA BOOKS is a trademark of Simon & Schuster, Inc.

For information regarding special discounts for bulk purchases,
please contact Simon & Schuster Special Sales at 1-800-456-6798
or business@simonandschuster.com

Designed by Joseph Rutt

Manufactured in the United States of America

CONTENTS

CONTENTS

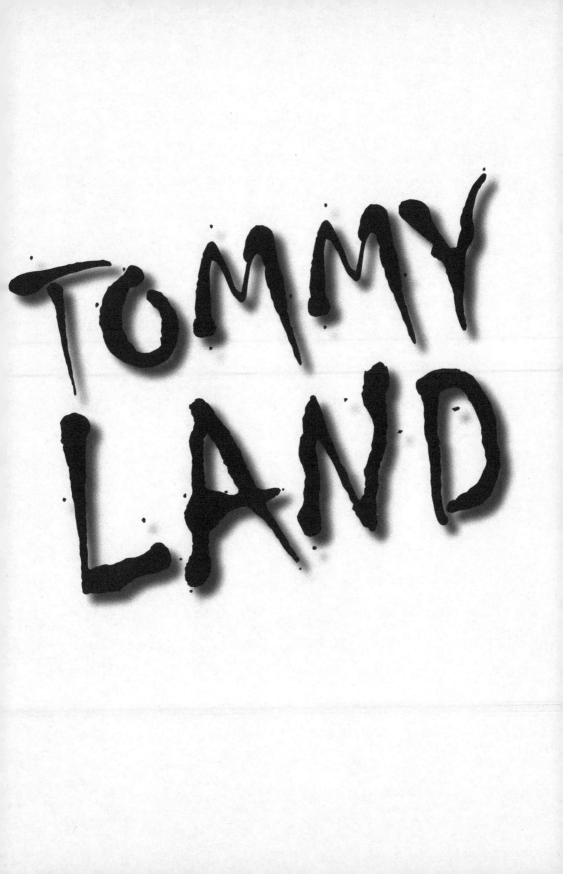

TOMMY
LAND

INTRODUCTION: STATE OF MIND

a.k.a.
STRAIGHT FROM
THE DOME

Tommy: Good morning, my man.

Dick: What's up? Well, besides me? I've been up for a while. I'm always up before you.

Tommy: You got that right. Fucking go back to sleep, would ya? Why do you have to wake me up every morning? You know I like to sleep in.

Dick: I'm up because I *want* to be up. It has nothing to do with you. You're just attached to me, bro. This life you're living, it's not about you, Tommy, it's about me. From your first trip to the bathroom in the morning to your last orgasm at night, it's all about me. I'm the *man*, bro. You're the copilot. If it weren't for me you'd sleep all day, and then where would you be?

Tommy: I'd be nice and rested.

Dick: You'd be rested without a life. Listen, I'm busy enough, but you know what? You should make me your road manager, Tommy. I am the only one who can wake you up on time.

Tommy: This is insane. My own dick is busting my balls. *Dude!* You can't be my road manager, you're a *penis!* Well . . . maybe you're right, a lot of road managers are dicks.

Dick: See what I mean? Well, now that you're awake, what are we doing today? Are the strip clubs open yet? I can't see the clock from here. Can we visit Hef up at the Playboy Mansion and see what honeys are lying out at the pool? I could use some sun.

Tommy: Sorry bud, no strip clubs, no mansion. I'm writing my book today.

Dick: Oh really! So are you going to come clean, tell the truth, the whole truth, and nothing but the truth, so help you God?

Tommy: Yes, your Honor. This book is going to be all truth, I promise you, whether the world can handle it or not. But dude, you're bringing back bad memories with that court talk. Don't you re-member jail? Go easy, I haven't even had my coffee yet.

Dick: Okay, but I'm glad you're going to be honest, amigo. I'm glad you're ready to publicly admit that I'm *way* more famous than you. We both know that I'm the star and you're the personal as-sistant, that I'm Batman and you're Robin.

Tommy: Bro, that is so wrong.

Dick: Oh yeah? We all have God-given gifts, and I'm yours. Do you re-ally think people want to read a book revealing what you think about every day? Those romantic notions you have concerning life and living? Right. All they want is me, me, and more me. If your body were a band, I'd be the front man. And the front man always does the interviews. So start taking dictation. I'll write this book myself.

Tommy: What the fuck? Have you lost your mind? You're in my pants most of the day! I talk to the public, my man, and people want to hear what I have to say. I'm the one up here making the moves, you just starred in the movie. I've had a fucking crazy life and yes, you've definitely done your part. There's no denying that, but you're not all there is to me. There'll be plenty of sexy stuff you can cowrite with me. I could use your help recalling some of our finer collaborations over the years. But my man, I'm forty-one, I've lived a full life, and there's a lot to tell, a lot of which has nothing to do with you. I'm the captain of this ship.

Dick: Whatever, skipper. If that helps you get through the day, hold tight to that notion. Just be sure to include this bit of truth: You owe your entire life to me. I made it all happen for you.

Tommy: Are you crazy?

Dick: No, *you're* crazy. I'm the cool, rational one in this relationship. I know what I want and I know how to get it. Fuck, I know what *you* want and I know how to get it. Tommy, my dear friend, you're old enough to know this by now: I have been behind every decision you've ever made since second grade. I got you every-thing and everyone you've ever had. Think about it. Heather Locklear? Pamela Anderson, and way too many others to list? Joining your first rock band? Picking up a drumstick? That was all me, my son. I planted those seeds and I sowed plenty of them too. Fact is, I knew how to get us what we wanted. There was no way I was going to wait around for you to figure it out.

Tommy: Dude! I'm going to put a fucking rubber on you if you don't shut up.

Dick: Whatever, tough guy. No matter what you write in this book of yours, I promise you, people will buy it for one reason: to find out how long I really am.

Tommy: Dude! Please shut up, I gotta do some work. It's hard enough just remembering the details of my life without you yappin' at me. I'm not exactly the kind of guy who's kept a journal all these years. Listen, I'll write about you, I'll even write with you, I promise. You'll get your props, you'll get your airtime. When I'm out doing my book tour, promoting this thing, doing signings, trust me, you'll be with me, and they'll be asking me all about you. And don't even think about asking Jay Leno for some couch time, because if you do, I'll catch you in my zipper right there in the greenroom during my preshow piss. But listen, while I'm on the couch and you and the balls are sweatin', I'll make sure I shift you into a comfortable position so the camera captures your good side.

Dick: Bro, don't disrespect me. I've always been a fan of yours.

Tommy: Yeah, I've always been a fan of yours too. But let's get one thing straight. I am the face man in this circus. This is *my* life, this is *my* story. You're a big part of it, but there is so much going on all the time. Life hands me new insanity every day. Some of it is good, some of it is very, very good, and some of it is pretty fucking bad. But, you know, I wouldn't have it any other way. I've had the highest highs and the lowest lows that you can have in life. I've done some great things and I've made some really big mistakes. And I take responsibility for all of it. I'm telling you, people are going to learn the truth about me in this book. They're going to learn that when I do something, anything at all, I always go big.

Dick: Uh-huh. Are you done yet? You really can ramble. So let's start this book off right, with a chapter about groupies.

Tommy: Unbelievable! Just go down, would you please? Let me start writing already. We'll cover that—don't worry, you'll have your chance to brag. Let's get this straight, I drive the boat, you just honk the horn, remember?

Dick: Whatever, captain.

THIS IS MY LIFE,
THIS IS MY STORY.

1

THE STATE OF THE UNION ADDRESS

a.k.a.
CHAPTER JUAN

Hi there, my name is Tommy Lee, and there's a couple of things you should know about me right away: I don't like to do the easy thing and I don't believe that there's ever just one way to do anything. If people tell you no or assure you that you only have one option in any situation, trust me, they're lying. There are many doors to your destiny, people. Please believe it.

Anyone who knows me won't be surprised that this book isn't a typical journey in a straight line from day one to day now. I can't really do that because I'm really not into history. I'm going to rail on my high school history class in a few minutes. Right now, though, you have to know that I'm more interested in revealing what's most important about my life, like how I cook my steaks; what I think of the tabloids, the truth, my ex-wives, my ex-band, my music; and what an innocent observer might find hanging around my house on any given Sunday. You'll see, just sit back — you'll get plenty of facts and I'll tell you my story, but my real mission is that I want you to know how my memories smell.

I don't like to leave anyone out of my party — and sometimes that's a problem—but in this situation, I'm going to tell all of you fact-and-figure-loving readers where to find what may be missing here: Head into cyberspace. I suggest starting with Google and I'll tell you what you'll discover there if you type in my name: lots of pictures, porno sites, links to shitty tabloid talk shows—what I call my Untrue Hollywood Stories—crazy fan sites (you guys rule!), plus a recurring Tommy Lee Jones theme. Somehow it's true, but I don't mind because I've been getting awesome fan mail about the kick-ass roles I've played in films like *Men in Black* for years now. It's crazy because, to tell the truth, I didn't even know I could act well enough to carry a feature. If no one minds, I'd like to take a moment to send a message to Mr. Lee Jones if he's reading.

Mr. Lee Jones,

Sir, I'm sorry if any unusual mail intended for me, Tommy Lee, has arrived at your house. I've received plenty of it over the years, so I know what my fans are capable of. Again, my apologies, and if any of the packages included amazing Polaroids that you've grown fond of, please keep them for your trouble. And good luck to you, sir!

T. Lee

Readers, would you like to know why I've named this ride *Tommyland?* The word means many things to me: It is the name of my studio, my home, my hard drive, and the place where my nerves and pleasure centers freak each other inside my skull. Tommyland is where my boys were born, it's a playland that my ex-wife Pamela Anderson built for my thirty-third birthday, it is where I lose myself most days making records, having sex, and sleeping. It's the only word I've found to describe what makes me up and what makes up my state of mind.

All right, it's time to start the ride now, so please take your seats. I advise you to keep your arms and legs inside the car at all times. If you have a pacemaker, a heart condition, or if you are pregnant or too damn short to reach the safety bar, I ask that you turn back immediately. Same goes for those with weak stomachs, strict morals, or chronic indigestion. In fact, you people might want to just put this book down now and slowly back away or return it to your local bookstore.

I hope those who remain enjoy their tour through *Tommyland*. If all goes according to plan, expect that you'll leave with side effects including pure fear, a perma-grin that requires corrective surgery, and a true whiff of me. Consumption of *Tommyland* may create the urge to get all "woo-hoo" with your friends.

Hallo, Tom, I must implore you not to ask people to return this book! We're in the business of selling, aren't we?

Sorry, dude. I thought you chaps had a sense of humor. This line stays in, mate.*

Be warned, *Tommyland* may cause involuntary tears and infrequent vomiting, because *Tommyland* is a loop-de-loop corkscrew brain masher that Six Flags wished it had.

I am Tommy Lee, born Thomas Lee Bass in Athens, Greece, on October 3, 1962, and raised in a California suburb by an American father and a Greek mother. At seventeen, I joined Mötley Crüe and we became one of the baddest-ass rock bands in his-

What does all "woo-hoo" mean? In England, it's the guy whose soccer, I mean "football," team just won the World Cup and has just slammed fifteen pints with his blokes. In America, it's the sunburned guy without a shirt who had lunch at Hooters before driving his rented Winnebago (that's an RV, or camper, Percival) over to watch his favorite NASCAR team haul ass. Again, this line stays.

---

* Hello readers, Anthony Bozza, Tommy's cowriter, here. I'm going to do my best to provide you with all the salient facts and figures you'll need to make sense, as best you can, of your stay here in Tommyland. Right now, I'd like to direct your attention to these editorial notes that you will find throughout your journey. They capture the dialogue that ensued between Tommy and our British editor at Simon & Schuster during the creation of this book. My heart goes out to that poor bloke, as should yours.

tory. We sold more than forty million albums, we wreaked havoc, we scared parents, and we titillated too many fathers' daughters. We drank oceans of liquor, snorted and shot mountains of drugs, crashed cars, watched people die, and watched one another fight, make up, break up, reunite, and break up again. I've been married three times: once for just a few weeks to a *Penthouse* centerfold, once for seven years to Heather Locklear, and once for five years to Pamela Anderson, with whom I have two beautiful sons. I've gotten in a lot of fights and I've been to jail a few times, the longest for four months, in 1998, after pleading no contest to spousal abuse. In 2001, a beautiful young boy named Daniel tragically drowned in my pool during my son Brandon's birthday party.

If you've watched *Entertainment Tonight* in the last ten years or glanced at the "newspapers" on the racks by the supermarket checkout line, you have an idea of what has happened in my life. If you believe those stories, that's fine. If you believe that there is no more to me than what they say, that's fine too. That kind of "entertainment" is the status quo today. I don't even know anymore if that's what the public craves or if it's just a brand of societal therapy. Do people really feel better watching strangers feel bad? Or is it watching famous people feel bad? Whatever. Just remember that information is like clay: It's easy to get and those with a good hand can bend it into whatever shape they want to. Believe me— I've seen statues of myself I don't even recognize.

Listen, I'm not complaining, I'm just fascinated by this shit. I don't know if you all can relate, but it's weird, it's interesting, and it's fucking frustrating to watch your life become a play that, for the most part, you're not even in.

After years of fighting the shit, and winning and losing all kinds of battles, I've learned one thing: I see the cult of celebrity as a test. You might follow your dream to make art, but it comes with a price. I think what you do, how you act, and who you are after you've made it is the test of your mettle.

I'm not going to get all spiritual guy on you — the books I've read and the religions I've learned from are my business. I'll list them later if you care to check them out, but I'm not going door-to-door with this shit. What works for one person sure as hell might not work for anyone else. But there's one truth that's real across the board: What you send out is what you get back. Send out the good, people, and it will come back to you. There's another thing I've learned over the years: In court, in fights, and in arguments with people I love, there isn't one truth, there are many. This book is my truth. Actually, I've got one more tenet to add to my state-of-the-union address. It's a saying I found in an unlikely place: on a refrigerator magnet that I don't even remember buying. What matters is what it says and where I've placed it. It's in the heart of Tommyland, in my studio, behind the bar, stuck to my Jägermeister machine, and it says it all: We do not stop playing because we grow old, we grow old because we stop playing.

2

STATE OF SEDUCTION

a.k.a.
DR. LEE'S LOVE TIPS

> Tommy, we've discussed this before and I maintain that this chapter is way out of place. We're just getting started and this is really jarring. You need to replace this chapter with the next one, State of Origin.
>
> Listen Algernon, I've been way out of place and in the business of jarring people since I was seventeen. If that's how you feel, that's cool. But dude, it's only chapter two, don't go south on me this early. God, I feel like we're breaking up before the honeymoon even started. C'mon! Learn to love it, let's jar some people! People love getting jarred! That's why they're gonna buy this book. Again, mate, this stays.

If you want a
woman and you're looking for
one, then stop, because in love, you only find what you
want when you're not looking. If you're on the prowl, think about your
attitude: It's clear that you're trying too hard. And where do most people
prowl? Clubs and bars. Trust me, if you're digging for treasure in a
Dumpster, you might find some, but you're gonna get pretty fucking
dirty rootin' through all that trash. I shouldn't say shit because, aside

from Heather, I've met just about every woman I've ever been with in a club. But that's because I don't go anywhere during the day. Hey, maybe that's my problem: I never meet the women I date in normal places like supermarkets or bookstores or kids' soccer games. Whatever.

Dr. Lee has learned a few things about sex and love over the years and here's the first: Big girls are the hottest, craziest fucks ever. I'm talking about big girls—and I don't mean tall. They are a screaming, fucking crazy hot, big yummy time, trust me. Big girls need love too, so be there for them, bros, and be prepared for them to go fucking nuts on you. I hate dudes who hate on big girls. Don't hate on any girl because she's anything. She's a girl, dude. I'm proud to say that this Doctor does not discriminate. The girls in my life have come in all shapes and sizes. Diversity—that's what the Doctor orders.

A good idea to fire up your relationship is to drive down the highway at about sixty-five miles per hour and have sex with your girl. Now if that doesn't excite you, you must be dead. But please believe me, you've got to be careful.

I like danger, always have. I like feeling that good and knowing that I could die at any second. There are rules though. Never use cruise control if you plan to try this because you'll end up cruising along like, "This is rad," and then, *boom!* And there's no bigger bummer than crashing your car midfuck. That is the worst wake-up call: If you don't die, you've made your car into an accordion up the ass of an eighteen-wheeler. You'll nurse your blue balls and broken bones on the side of the freeway waiting for the cops and the tow truck to show up—if you're lucky. (Not to mention the damage an air bag will do.) You have to watch it when you cum too, dudes, because the rules of the road become completely irrelevant for a minute there. I don't know about you, but when I'm cumming, I'm screaming, my eyes are closed, and I have no idea where I'm at. Not to mention how all us guys become stiff as a board from our ankles up when we have an orgasm, which can be lethal when one foot is on a gas pedal and you can't see because there are tits in your face. And that is *no* way to drive down the freeway.

But never fear. Some sex-maniac engineer at Mercedes has figured out a way around that problem. In the two-seat convertible I have there's a computer that monitors how close you are to the car in front, behind, and to the sides of you. When you put on the cruise control you can tell it how many feet to stay away from the car ahead of you. I haven't taken full advantage of it yet, but when the time is right, it's on. Sometimes you just can't wait until you get home to get some, you have to rock shit right where you are. Thank God for tinted windows. Oh yeah, don't even think about trying this without tinted windows.

* * *

To turn up the heat even more, the Doctor recommends a company called Jungle Roses if you've got the love and the cash. It's owned by Rodney Dangerfield's wife and it specializes in exotic flowers. You can order petals from them—just rose petals—and completely rock your girl's shit by covering your bed or whatever else you want with them. But you gotta go big. The pathway of petals must start in the front yard and lead into the house, up the stairs to where the bathtub is filled with warm water and more petals and then the bedroom, where the bed has to be covered with petals too. Lose the covers and top sheet, though. You don't want to fuck with sheets when you get out of the tub and dive into bed. Making love with the smell of roses in the crack of your girl's ass? It doesn't get any better.

While we're on the subject of smells that inspire love and sex, Dr. Lee would like to recommend the gardenia, one of his favorite flowers. They are planted in my yard and I pick them all the time and leave a flower or two in bowls of water all around my house. If it were cool to walk around with a gardenia duct-taped to each nostril I would so that I could smell that scent all day long. I could smell that odor of horniness while I went about my business. I'm serious about gardenias. When I've been with women who wear perfume that has a trace of gardenia, I end up spraying it on myself. The Doctor doesn't believe in gender-specific scents, and neither should you. You are allowed to smell like a flower if you are a man, don't worry. Citrus smells are good too, my students, fresh and clean. If something smells like you can eat it, I'm down. Chocolate, fruit, certain spices—it's all good. But if a girl walks by me smelling like a gardenia, I'm done. I have to go up to her to tell her that she smells fucking amazing. Smell is key, so remember this: If you're into a girl and you want to know whether it's really on or not, smell her. Just walk up to her and fucking inhale her, it'll set it off or turn it off real quick.

* * *

Now Dr. Lee often hears from people chasing the dream, those hoping to land the ultimate dude accomplishment: a three-way with two girls. I have been with two chicks many, many times and it isn't all it's cracked up to be. Something drastic happens when you've got one person left out in the cold. There are only so many things you can all do together and there are a few lovely things you can do to both of them at the same time and them to you. But when it comes time for fucking, unless there's something out there that I don't know about, you've only got one dick. You can only give it to one girl at a time, so there's always someone waiting. You can touch the other girl and watch her touch herself while you fuck the other one, but c'mon, you know she isn't quite where she wants to be.

The Doctor has the answer: The thing to do is have foursomes: three chicks and just you. Now *that's* what I'm talking about. It's an easy way around the threesome problem I kept running into. If you have three chicks as into one another as they are into you, you can fuck one and watch the other two go at it, which adds to the overall horniness. Everyone's happy, everyone's playing, and everyone has someone to do. Then you switch.

After I did that once, that was it: The Doctor was converted. He will never agree to anything less. He may increase the number of girls, but he will never be with fewer than three. One last note: To make the foursome work you have to have your bull's-eye, your anchor girl, you know, and then she's got to bring in her wing-women. Don't try to mix that cocktail yourself—you probably can't.

* * *

Here's a word to the dudes. Think about how much maintenance women do to look good. Dudes, listen to me: Mow the front lawn and the backyard too. Trust me, the right woman—fuck that, *any* woman will appreciate it. Keep the pubes in control, shave the hair off your arms, but you can leave the legs alone. Leg shaving is weird. And if you have back hair so that your girl can knit a sweater up your spine, it's all bad—do something about that. Buy a Weedwacker or Nad's,* or fuck—go to a salon and get your shit waxed. If you're all scared, feeling like hair removal ain't macho, look at that pair of high heels you like your girlfriend to wear. You think that's easy? Walk a mile in her shoes, dude. Fuck it, walk down a flight of stairs in her shoes and you'll realize that the least you can do is keep your unit trim.

Dr. Lee would like to take a moment to discuss a related item, that is, going south on a lady. I refer first to comedian Sam Kinison, who suggested that men trace the alphabet on their girl's clitoris. It's a good idea. It gives you a focus and it keeps you engaged. Of course if you don't know the alphabet, you're fucked. I do, and I like when I get to the letter "i" because I just grab the clit and suck on it to dot that fucker. But I don't only do the alphabet, I mix it up: a little hard, a little fast, a little nibbling, and a lot of licking. My favorite thing to do when I'm in the southland is to pull my girl's lips all the way back so that her little Gummi Bear just pops out at me. Dude, I love Gummi Bears! You do that and there she is, saying "*Heeeay*, I'm here! I'm sensitive, please be careful with me." It's good to bite her a little bit, but not too much. A lot of people forget that air is good too. When you're down there and your girl is all wet and you've got her lips pulled back and her clit sticking straight out, send in some air, dude. Air is good. Just pull back and send a little breeze over it, just a little subtle blast in to cool Mama Bear off. Trust me.

---

* Anthony here once again to enrich your stay in Tommyland. The Nad's Tommy is referring to is the hair-removal gel advertised regularly on late-night television, not the slang term for gonads. If you're in need of a reliable hair-removal product, you can purchase the Australian-made pube eliminator online at www.nads.com or through the 800 number: 1-800-653-9797.

A little throat vibration is good too. Say after me, "*Hmmm.*" Tell your girl to return the favor—that's why it's called a *hummer*, people. Water is always a good thing to have around too. If you're in a bathtub—which is, of course, an awesome place to partake—and you have one of those spray attachments: Use it. Ladies like it, please believe. A lot of girls masturbate by getting all up under the faucet. If you don't have a tub, use the shower. If you're in a pinch and you don't have a shower, it's okay, urine works too. She can play Fireman while you play the Hose.

The doctor has some practical advice for you too, kids. Dudes, actually, this is serious—fucking listen up. Do you guys know Peter North? He's a porn star and if you've seen him even once you know who he is. He's the guy who sandblasts every single girl in his scenes with a gallon of man juice. He is ridiculous. It's like the guy has a hose with some tank full of stuff that you can't see and a trigger in his dick that lets loose a fucking blast that could hit your grandma from here, no matter where she lives.* When I had a party at my house that he came to, I wasted no time with small talk and asked him straight up how the fuck he made that happen each and every time he did a movie. I mean, I've had my good days, but, *dude,* this guy is consistently on some other shit that's not even human.

Peter's real cool, he just told me what he does like it's no big thing. Which it isn't if you think about it—busting nuts is that guy's office job. That's fucking awesome! So here you go, a secret from the Jizzmaster: The day before Peter North shows up to shoot a scene, he eats an entire bunch of celery. He told me that there is a ton of water in celery, which gets shit started down there. There's also a lot of other stuff in celery that, like, triples your supply somehow. I believe it—and if you've seen his movies you probably do too. But aside from the androsterone that celery releases in your body and the mild aphrodisiacal qualities that that chemical has

---

* Tommy's statement here, as far as I know, is not true, but he is not exaggerating much. With nearly 1,000 credited movies, among them *Carlito's Backway* (1993), *Pump Friction* (1995), *Battlestar Orgasmica* (1992), and *Anal Hounds and Bitches* (1994) under his, eh-hum, *belt,* Peter is, to say the least, a well-oiled machine. And all who have seen his work would concur that his distance and achievements precede him.

on the opposite sex, the Doctor can't verify the effects of celery on the wad supply first-hand. A bunch is a *lot* of celery, bro. Pete's not talking about a stalk or two, which is all that I'd be able to scarf down. He is talking about the whole fucking bunch you get at the store. If you're thinking about Viagra, I'm telling you, try this first. It's a cheap over-the-counter alternative — and it's all natural! Man, I wish I could get that big green bunch down in a day. I wish I would fucking remember to try that the day before I want to coat a lady. Celery . . . that's *crazy*. Big props, Pete. And good luck.

Let's not forget to drink our pineapple juice every morning either, fellas. A glass a day will do ya — an hour before you get it on is even better. It'll make your cum sweet and your girl will definitely love you for that. That's one for you, ladies!

* * *

You guys need to know that Dr. Lee is pretty much always "in" unless I'm working, stressed, miserable, or in a fuckin' load of trouble. That means that the female anatomy is consistently on the Doctor's mind, please believe. The longest time that it wasn't was the four months I was in jail.* When I got out, I celebrated my freedom in the best and worst way: a visit from a pair of cheap hookers. I've done a lot of shit, I've been low, I've been high, but that night, when those girls left, is one of the times I can easily say I felt worse than the lid on a rancid can of fuck. It was fucking terrible. I'm totally not a hooker kind of guy at all. But I was so out there, so tweaked by solitary confinement, that I had totally forgotten how to relate to anyone or anything. Fuck, I had a hard time just holding up a conversation. It sucked.

I thought getting laid was the answer. Boy was I wrong. The hookers came over and got the pent-up sex out of my system but it made me feel worse. After that, sex grossed me out for a long while — and that was weird

---

* That was in 1998. Tommy's arrest and sentence occurred after an incident with his then-wife, Pamela Anderson. It's not a time period that can be summarized easily in a half inch at the bottom of the page — and it won't be. Stay tuned, but know this now: If it is possible to narrow down one event as the turning point in an individual's life, his time in jail would be Tommy's.

as hell. There had never been a time in my life when a sexual experience had not made me just want more sex.

PLEASE, DON'T GO THERE.*
I BARELY SURVIVED.
I HAD LOST THE WILL TO LIVE.
LIFE WAS A CLOUDY DAY
WITHOUT END TO ME.

Listen, don't get me wrong. The Doctor isn't just a doctor of sex, he's also a doctor of love. Here's a relationship tip for you: If you want drama in your life, marry an actress. That should be a bumper sticker. Please believe, I know this is true because I've done it twice.† The Doctor is over that. The next girl I marry is going to be selling purses in Zimbabwe or

---

* Sorry to interrupt again, readers, but for the sake of clarity I must have you know that these, um, eruptive insertions you will find throughout *Tommyland* were spewed forth by a prominent, erm, member of Tommy's inner circle—namely, his penis, a.k.a. Dick. Thankfully, said individual added his takes on the text while I was not present.

† I'd just like to point out that the two actresses whom Tommy married, as he mentioned a few pages ago, are Heather Locklear and Pamela Anderson. Heather is best known for playing incredibly sexy, powerful, and generally bitchy characters on two major TV shows. From 1981 through 1989, she played Samantha Josephine "Sammy Jo" Dean Reece Carrington Fallmont on *Dynasty*, where she broke hearts, chronically married, and made all kinds of trouble. From 1993 to 1999 Heather played Amanda Woodward Blake Parezi McBride Burns on *Melrose Place*, and through that character redefined the concept of blond ambition. She also played a hot cop named Stacy Sheridan alongside William Shatner in *T.J. Hooker* from 1982 to 1986. Pamela Anderson, the quintessential *Playboy* Playmate and international icon, first came to acting fame as Lisa, the "Tool Time" girl on *Home Improvement* from 1991–1993. Next, Pamela became truly famous via a red one-piece bathing suit on *Baywatch* as Casey Jean "C.J." Parker from 1992 to 1997. Pamela then moved on to her third most-notable role, playing a bodacious private eye named Vallery Irons on the despicably entertaining *V.I.P.* from 1998 to 2002.

working at the mall, or even better yet: a nymphomaniac who owns a liquor store. I'm done with drama—I've overdosed on it too many times. I don't want a famous girl anymore, I just want a normal girl with a job, please. It would be great if I could get involved with a chick who doesn't even know who I am. Maybe she'll be some babe who lives on a compound in Boise, Idaho. Maybe she'll be Amish—one of those girls taking her break to figure out if she wants to be Amish or not.* I hear there's a town in Amish country called Intercourse. My dream girl awaits me. I can tell you how it would end too. On our first date out of Amish territory, out in the real world, she'd be so freaked out by what she'd hear about me that she'd run home and be Amish forever. If the Amish had a convent, she'd go join it. I'd love to meet a woman who is like, "Tommy Lee? Who is that?" But the Doctor is realistic. He knows that this is probably not possible. It would be fun to try though. We might have a good run of anonymous love until the first time we took a walk somewhere. She'd be like, "Why does everyone know you? What do you do? Why are you always looking over your shoulder?" Um . . . I don't know.

Sometimes the good Doctor is jealous of his friends who are able to meet normal girls and just hang out with them. One of my favorite things in the whole world is watching two old-as-fuck people walking down the street, still kissing or holding hands at lunch, not doing anything but looking into each other's eyes and having a conversation. You just know they

* Tommy is referring to *rumspringa*, an Amish word that translates as "running wild." As soon as Amish adolescents turn sixteen, they are allowed to take a break from living as Amish to experience the rest of the world. All of their restrictions are lifted: They may wear modern clothes, drive, drink alcohol, date, consume modern culture, and all else that piques their fancy. Most sow their oats at huge parties called "barnhops" or "hoedowns" thrown in fields by their rumspringing peers, others form Amish rock bands that converge for an annual summer concert (an Amishpalooza, if you will), and even others run drugs (two brothers were indicted in 1998 for running mountains of cocaine bought from a neighboring biker gang all over Pennsylvania Dutch country). Amazingly, 85 to 90 percent of all Amish teens return to the Amish way of life. For a clear-eyed peek into Amish life and *rumspringa*, see the award-winning documentary *Devil's Playground*, available at Amazon.com.

still love each other. Think of that visual the next time you see a young couple together with so much ahead of them and absolutely nothing to say to each other. You know who I'm talking about: They're both on their cell phones, one is clicking away on his Crackberry, emailing whoever-the-fuck. My favorite is when one of them is sitting there reading and the other isn't. That's tight.

When I see people who still have something to talk about and they're old, I get so happy just knowing that it's possible. I watch my buds play with chicks they meet and I see them go do normal shit, which, hello, is what makes the world go round. Dr. Lee has had dreams of doing stuff like going down to the beach, meeting a rad surfer chick, and feeling how excellent it is to take her out for a hot dog. He has also thought about what he would need to do to make that situation happen. He's thought about buying a wardrobe of long-sleeved shirts and shaving his head. That's as far as he will fuck with his appearance for a lady.

I guess meeting new people is always a form of rolling the dice. You never know what you're going to get, even when you seem to be rolling a winner. And if I look at the hands I've thrown, I'm thinking the dice are already loaded, usually on both sides.

I have one more subject to cover before I make my house calls. Dr. Lee has very strong opinions on the subject of porno. It's all about sex, so why are there always so many things wrong with your average porn movie? Why does the music suck? Why does the cameraman always focus on the wrong thing? Why do they even make porno that doesn't show penetration? What the fuck is *that*? That's what the Playboy Channel serves up. C'mon, Hef, let's rock the shit! Show those fine-ass girls takin' it in the ass through a fish-eye lens. What the fuck do you think we're showing up for? To be *teased*?

NO, WE SHOW UP TO TEASE,
THEN TO PLEASE, MY MAN.
AND PLEASE AGAIN.

The Doctor must bid you good night, but first, a toast: "May all your ups and downs be in bed" and remember, no matter how fun you think it is going to be, don't ever, ever, EVER pull out your video camera and film yourself bumpin' fuzz. Trust me, it's all bad. You don't even want to try to explain that one to the kids. And if you think you're in the clear because you don't have kids, imagine how you'll feel explaining it to your parents. Just ask Paris.

3

STATE OF ORIGIN

a.k.a.
OPA!

Tommy, this is similar to the chapter on you and Pamela. Can you be more explicit here?

For the first time I agree with you, Sir Tippets. Yeah, this is similar to the chapter on Pamela and me—but hey, we're talking about my parents. Like father, like son, my man. And there's no way in hell I'm gonna get all explicit about my mom and dad, dude! Paging Dr. Freud?

My parents met in Greece, with the help of a translation dictionary. My mom, Vassilikki, was Miss Greece in 1957 and my dad, David, who was born in St. Paul, Minnesota, and therefore didn't speak a word of Greek, met her while he was an army sergeant stationed in Athens. They met at my grandmother's house when her sister was having a christening for one of her kids. A friend of my mom's sister asked if she could bring an American guy along so that he could see how the Greeks celebrated their christenings. My dad was winking at my mom all night long and even told her right then and there that he wanted to marry her. She thought he was crazy and kept wondering when the American was going home. He never really did. The next day he showed up with a ring and that was it—my mom ditched her boyfriend, and decided to marry my dad and leave Greece. First though, my dad had to have a long chat with my mom's brothers. He passed that test, and when her family talked it over to decide if the marriage was the best thing to do, they figured that my mom would have a better life in America than she could in Greece. My mom didn't even speak English, so when they weren't pointing at words on a page, my parents communicated by drawing pictures for each other. It's hard enough to make a relationship work when you speak the language. What they had was *love*.

After my parents got married, they lived in Athens. Exactly one month after I was born, my dad was relocated to Thailand briefly before we left for America and moved to Covina, California. During his time in the army, my dad was in both World War II and the Korean War. My mom gave me all of his medals after he died. He was a Mason too. To all the Masons out there, don't worry, he wouldn't tell me a thing about it. He'd go to the meetings and I'd ask him all the time what being a Mason meant and what Masons did at those meetings, but he wouldn't tell me a fucking thing. So the secret is safe.

My sister, Athena, was born in 1964, two years after I was, and when we were very young, my parents would take us to visit my mother's family in Greece during the summer. Later, when we were a little bit older, when I was about ten and she was about eight, they would send us over there as if it were summer camp. It was much better than lakes and log cabins. Let me tell you, spending those summers in Greece was the most amazing experience a kid could hope for. The roofs in Greece are flat and in the summer everyone sleeps outside on them because it is so hot. Even though my relatives lived in Athens, which is a huge city by any standards, it was so dark there that you could see thousands of stars. Back then, in the early seventies, Athens had no streetlights to block the night sky and I couldn't believe how beautiful it was. I'd lie there every night taking it in until I fell asleep because the night sky sure as hell didn't look like that in Covina. I would look forward to going to bed—and what kid ever looks forward to that? Every night was like going on a camping trip. Each member of the family—my sister, cousins, my aunt and uncle—would be tucked away on their cots, under the sky.

I was just as happy when morning came. The sun would wake me up slowly as it lit up the sky and so would the aroma of fresh bread floating up from the bakery down the street. When everyone was out of bed, my grandma would give me some money and send me out to buy these delicious little loaves of bread for our breakfast. That was my job and, unlike most kids and their chores, I was all about it.

Those summers taught me early on that the world is a big place. I loved being somewhere so completely different from home. I loved walking to the bakery and tripping out on all the old men sitting at sidewalk cafés, sipping their muddy Greek coffees while they played dominoes and cards. Even then I recognized that life there was way more laid back than at home. Those summers on my own also forced me to grow up quickly. Our mother taught us the language back home, but without her there to help me, I had to figure it out on my own because no one spoke any English.

But it wasn't all idyllic. The second summer we were there my sister and I made serious friends with this cute little rabbit they had at my uncle's house. We had a spider monkey named Nitnoy for a pet at home that my dad brought home for us one day. He was rad, he'd jump all over the chandeliers and wear diapers. But a rabbit—this was a whole different story. We loved that little fuzzy white guy and spent every day with him for nearly a month. Then one day my uncle reached into the cage, grabbed the rabbit by its back legs, and karate-chopped it in the neck. I fucking freaked. I had no idea why he did it, so I asked my sister if it was because he didn't want it anymore. We just started crying and ran away to hide in a closet. We didn't come out until dinnertime, which was a big mistake because there was the rabbit, all stretched out and cooked, lying on a platter on the table. My sister and I watched as the adults dug into it like nothing was wrong while we tried not to start crying again.

I wasn't scared of my uncle after that and I didn't hate him or anything, I just thought, "Wow, he killed the rabbit, just like that." He didn't even think twice about it being a pet to us. It was really simple: It was time to eat, so *wham!* And that was that.

My uncle spoke maybe a word or two of English and had this big furniture factory in Athens. He'd take me to work with him and let me varnish furniture or send me out to buy Cokes for everyone. I cleaned up the shop, and he'd let me fuck around with the wood and tools if I wanted to. The only job I've ever had aside from playing music is painting houses, and I got my first taste of it in that factory. By the way, I can still paint a room like a pro—and fucking quick too. I painted a friend's house as a housewarming gift this year and rocked it—trim, molding, everything. No drips, no mess. I've still got skills, please believe.

4

STATE OF FAMILY VALUES

a.k.a.
OH, SHIT,
PARENTHOOD—HERE
WE GO!

My parents were totally supportive of everything my sister and I did. If they saw that we had an interest in something, whether it was tap dancing or playing accordion, piano, drums, or guitar, they found a way to nurture it. We were a middle-class family and my dad worked very hard. My mom sometimes worked too. She'd clean houses part-time for a few families and she's very embarrassed to admit it (sorry, Mom).

My dad was the shop superintendent for the L.A. County Road Department. He ran the division that maintained all those big crazy tractors and dump trucks that repair the roads. My dad was amazing; he could fix *anything*. In the army he had been a staff sergeant in the motor pool and was trained as a diesel mechanic. My dad was so mechanical that we never needed a repairman in our house. When the washing machine broke, my dad took it apart, spread the pieces across the floor of the garage, fixed the broken part, and put it back together. You'd turn the switch and there you go—it worked again.

My parents knew early on that only a few things mattered to me and the first in line was music. They supported my interest but they were strict about it too: They wouldn't let me get out of practicing whatever instrument I wanted to learn. Piano was the worst. I was like, "Fuck, man" because I had to practice all these scales and be tested each week at my lesson. It got pretty boring, pretty quick, let me tell you. I wanted to fucking rock. I'd be plunking along, thinking, "This blows." I wanted to play songs, and although I did soon enough, I found out that piano wasn't going to get that much more rocking. Sure, I learned "Mary Had a Little Lamb," but I wanted to play "Stairway to Heaven." Now, of course, I've learned to appreciate the piano for the beautiful instrument that it is, but back then it seemed to me that unless you were Jerry Lee Lewis, a piano wasn't going to rock shit as hard as a guitar or a drum set.

Growing up, my sister and I did everything together, even tap dancing and ballet lessons, which was fucking bizarre. I hung with dance as long as I could because I liked dancing with the girls, but ballet ended all that. Aside from dancing with the chicks, everything else about it was wack and it freaked me out way too much to really go for it. Tap dancing was cool because it was rhythmic, something I took with me when I started drumming and that I'll always have. Nothing changed much in high school—I just wasn't one of those guys who was all about football or hanging out with the guys. I played baseball a little bit; I did the Little League thing for a minute. I was really more about coed volleyball and

SEE? HERE'S ANOTHER EXAMPLE OF
MY STELLAR LEADERSHIP.

spiking was my forte.

NO DUDE, IT WAS MINE.

It's pretty simple: I always felt more comfortable around girls. I was friends with girls who were juniors and seniors when I was a freshman. They'd pick me up in their cars in the morning and drive me to school. It ruled. I was a fucking freshman, dude, riding in the backseat, cranking the Rolling Stones on the way to school.

From the start, I really wasn't interested in academics. History, in particular, bored the fuck out of me. I was like, "Wait a minute, who cares? I wasn't here when this happened anyway." I didn't care who the first president of the United States was. I mean, I know the answer—it was George Washington—but what does that matter to me? Nothing is going to change about history, and that's the truth. If I can't do anything about it, I don't see much point in being interested in it.

History was like a root canal without novocaine, but math was cool. I liked figuring out problems, so math interested me until it became too complicated. When I started doing algebra and trigonometry, I was like, "Whoa, hey, whoa. Wait a minute. Take it *easss*."

I felt pretty lost in high school until later on when I got into the arts. Art class was great because I could make silk screens and soon enough the only thing I wanted to do was stay late to print rock-and-roll T-shirts. I made fucking Van Halen and Zeppelin shirts, and I spent a lot of my extra time drawing. It wasn't long before I skipped or lied my way out of every class except art and music. My music teacher, Mr. Dvorak, was the only guy I looked forward to seeing every day. My favorite thing to do was to go play drums and he'd let me. I don't remember having Mr. Dvorak actually teach me how to wail, but he did recognize how much I loved it and he let me go off. During the writing of this book, I went back to my old high school to see if Mr. Dvorak was there and I'm happy to say that he was.

As I drove up to the school that day, I wondered why everyone seemed so much smaller than what I remember them being when I was in high school, but then I realized that my old high school was now a junior high. I walked on the grounds and looked at the field where I used to run laps during PE and practice with the drum corps of the marching band. I looked at the parking lot where I used to roll up in my fucked-up blue Chevy van. The windshield wiper squirters on that thing were loose, so I turned them to the sides so that I could squirt people as I drove by. I'd come through, hit the button, *bzzzup*, and people would be like, "Dude!" After a while I drained all the water out and filled the reservoir with Jack Daniel's. When I pulled into the parking lot, my buddies who knew would be like, "Hit the switch, dude." They'd put their mouth over the sprayer and drink Jack windshield.

I walked around my old school, remembering where shop and music and gym were. There were kids running around everywhere, and I felt like I was doing something wrong and that at any minute I would get in trouble. I wasn't sure if I actually *was* doing something wrong by visiting my school or if I just remembered how many things I'd done wrong when I actually went there and felt bad about them. Whatever. I kept watching all the little guys run around, wanting to be them instead of the guy who is completely tattooed and who looks like he's gonna hurt some children.

The only thing that mattered to me when I was in that place was music; I didn't care about anything else or anything that anybody ever told me. When I got a piece of music to learn, I did that and no other homework really mattered. When I saw a girl with a flute, I said hello and asked where the office was—that's when I found out Mr. Dvorak was still working there. Mr. Dvorak used to throw erasers at me. He'd get mad because I'd always be doing rolls on the drums. He'd take the eraser off the chalkboard, toss it, and say, "Stop on the drums!" He wasn't really mad though. He knew how much I loved playing and let me hang out in the music room, practicing as much as I wanted to.

Mr. Dvorak was preparing his last spring concert in the gym. After teaching for forty years, he was going to retire. I'm so glad I didn't put off going back to my school—if I had I would have missed him. When I found him, Mr. Dvorak came over and gave me a huge hug. My eyes filled up and so did his—he was more than just a teacher to me. We talked for a while and here's how our conversation went.

Mr. D.:   So, Tommy, what the fuck happened to Heather? I can't believe it, man. I see her at the Lakers game and I think, "What the fuck did you do, man?" The other one I could understand, she's bad news, but that one, Tommy? My wife had to take the poster off the ceiling. Anyway, I'm still here. I'm doing the spring concert in the last week of May. Come on out. I'd be glad to have you. You know, Tommy, I gotta tell you, you were a pain in the ass! No—you were a good student, and a good kid. A good kid because you didn't turn to that heavy stuff until you left me. You were made for drums, I knew that much. Put you down at that drum set and it was like magic. I could sit there and watch you, and it was weird. From the start, you just chopped at that drum set like it was milk. You had come from another school and always told me that I was the only one who allowed you to get on a drum set and play and express yourself. I was the only one. Remember?

T.L.:   It's true. I wanted to play a real drum set for so long.

Mr. D.:   You were possibly the only student I've ever had who I watched play and thought would actually become something in the music business. It is your talent. It is in your blood. It is your natural God-given gift. If anyone was ever looking for you they knew to check room 505. Every time they walked in looking for you, you were in there. Remember that one time we had Music Appreciation class and Frank and the guys came in and beat the shit out of you—right in front of me almost? I was out having a cigarette or something like that. And I came back and you're all fucked up, and I ask you what happened and you say, "I don't know—they beat the hell out of me." You were a good kid, a real good kid. You really hadn't come into your own yet, Tommy.

T.L.: No, I really hadn't.

Mr. D.: And the girls? You were shy. You weren't like the other guy in Mötley Crüe, the one from Charter Oak. He must have been the girl lover. What's his name, Vince? Tommy, you were very, very shy.

T.L.: Yeah, I was a little bit of a loner. I was always by myself.

Mr. D.: When I see you in trouble on the news, I always ask my wife, "What did he do wrong now?" When you left, you joined a band with Galardo, and John Kemp and all that.

T.L.: John Kemp was my bass player and Tom Galardo was a great guitar player.

Mr. D.: Poor Tom. Tom married Tara and they had a baby. Tom might have been in Mötley Crüe if he hadn't. I spoke to him five years ago and he told me that.

T.L.: Oh, yeah. He totally would have been in the band.

Mr. D.: And John Kemp. He used to write poems. He used to come to my house at three o'clock in the morning depressed about not being in the band. I'd say, "John, it's okay, it wasn't meant to happen." Then he'd tell me about talking you into getting your first tattoo because he had one. John is still so thrilled about that.

T.L.: It seems like yesterday now that I'm here, but it's been a while. I'm in my forties.

Mr. D.: Yeah it's about time you got your ass back on the ground and said, "You know something? I've got a family, I've got kids—let's get my head together before it's Social Security time." Your life has been up and down, peaks and valleys, peaks and valleys, every time. On the news it's not the good things you've done, it's what you've done wrong.

T.L.: I know. Is there anyone in your classes right now that you think might make it in a band or play professionally?

Mr. D.: I had a student, a young guitar player, last year who lived with his guitar. I think he could do something. But all these kids are

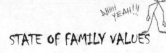

into this punk rock now. They're into the image more than the
music. They play the same Black Sabbath song over and over
again and that's it. This guy is well rounded in music and could
play licks on his guitar anytime. There has never been a drummer like you though. No one I've ever taught has become as
big as you, Tommy. Nothing like that. I did teach an actress
one year. She was on *90654*, or whatever that show was called. I
taught her singing for a year. But I've had no one in music who is
just there for music. There are dozens who come through here
who are doing other things like modeling. Talent scouts come
here on Friday nights for our performances to look at the kids.
Usually it's for modeling, commercials, stuff like that, never for
their singing abilities or anything musical. Tommy, you were
the only one I've had who I really knew would make it and who
really has. So, tell me, what are you doing with your life now?

T.L.:   I'm making a new record. I'm always writing music. I went on to
play every instrument: drums, bass, guitar, piano. I sing, I produce, I do everything now. I record everything, I've got a full-
blown digital studio in my house, I produce and mix it all with a
friend of mine, my coproducer, Scott Humphrey.

Mr. D.: That's like McCartney when he left the Beatles. He did everything. All the instruments, produced it himself. It's that album
with "Maybe I'm Amazed." It's still one of the top top things he's
done.

T.L.:   It's been a lot of fun. After a while you know what you want to
hear and you get tired of telling someone else what you want to
hear when you know how to do it yourself. I'm having a good
time musically and creatively right now. I think I'm finally at that
point in my life where I'm actually enjoying it all. It's not so
crazy and I'm not either. I'm just getting older, you know, I'm
starting to slow down a little bit. I lost my father the week of September 11, a few days after the tragedy in New York. It was the
most surreal week of my life.

Mr. D.: I'm sorry to hear about your dad. Remember how he used to carry your drums for you? I'm just happy that you're getting your life back together again, and I'm happy that no more of the bad stuff is gonna come on the TV again—the bullshit that you did this and you did that.

T.L.: No, it won't. That's all over.

Mr. D.: Well, Tommy, I've got to get back to practice, but I've got to ask you one more thing: What the fuck happened to Heather? I told you I saw her at the Lakers game, sittin' there with some dude, and I just prayed for them to keep the camera on her while I scooped up my saliva. . . .

* * *

Mr. Dvorak was the only one who thought I'd do something with music. And he had an idea even then that it would be something big. Thanks, Mr. Dvorak. I was a skinny kid in school, and I got fucked with by a lot of the bigger dudes. This one time at band camp, I mean in music class, the drum captain of the marching band achieved a new low. I was in the drum corps of the marching band, and each week, as part of our practice, all of us drummers tested and competed to determine our rank. There were skills you had to have: stick twirling (that came in handy later), the rudiments that strengthened your hands, the marching formations, and your overall showmanship. Each week, a drum corps member could rise or fall in the rank and it meant a lot to all of us. That captain guy was also a senior who was jealous and pretty fuckin' unhappy watching me, this freshman, rise through the ranks week after week. It was pretty clear to both of us that his job was on the line. So one day, after practice, he came up behind me, tapped me on the shoulder, and as I turned around, he sucker-punched me and relocated my nose to the other side of my face. What up, Mr. Drum Captain? How's your drumming going, bro? Played any arenas lately?

Other dudes took a different approach. I got snapped in the shower with towels during gym class and some fuckers picked on me whenever

they saw me in the halls. It was the typical bullshit: I'd be standing there in line at PE, freezing cold (it does actually get cold in California, people), and some fucking bully motherfucker would roll by and flick me in the ear. There was nothing I could do about it, because the guy would be there, looking at me, waiting for me to do something and give him a reason to shit down my neck. At those moments, I'd do the only thing I could do. I'd sit there, acting like I didn't care and thinking to myself, "You Fffffffffffffffffffffffffffffffffffffffffffffffffffffffffffffffffffffffffffffffffffffffffffffffffffff ffffffffffffffffffffffffffffffffffffffffffffffffffffffffffffffffffffffffffffffffffffffffffffffffffff ffffffffffffuck, you know what? One day motherfucker, one day you're going to be fuckin' coming to see me fuckin' play. And you're gonna want tickets and you're gonna wanna be backstage acting like you know me and shit, and know what? Sit your ass down in a lawn chair in the parking lot, bitch. You'll get nothin' and like it. Fuck *you*, fuck *you*, fuck *you*. And if you've got any friends, fuck them too." You don't have to believe me, but back then I knew that one day I was going to do something *really* big. I didn't know what it would be, but I knew what was coming would be something else. If I had to compare my attitude to anyone back then it would be to Spanky in *Our Gang* in that awesome episode about the go-cart race.* There he is, blazing down a hill in his little wooden car and one of the other kids asks him, "Spanky, where are you going?" He doesn't take his eye off the road for a minute and says, "I don't know where I'm goin', but I know I'm gonna get there." I had the same blind faith, and it was the only thing that kept me from going Richter every day at school when people picked on me. Fucking jerk-offs.

* * *

By the time I was a sophomore I was in a band. We didn't even have a name because we didn't play anywhere, but we fucking *ripped*. Here's the lineup: Tom Galardo, this Mexican guy, who was the shreddingest guitar

---

* "Free Wheelin'," 1932.

player anywhere local, this guy John Kemp on bass, and me on drums. We were all business—an instrumental power trio who didn't care about lyrics, singing, or anything but jamming. I am not at all lying, exaggerating, or coloring the past when I say that we fucking *crushed*. At least I thought so, and it seemed like other people did too at the backyard kegger parties we played. We also rehearsed regularly in my parents' garage, where anyone could catch us daily for no cover charge. When I turned that corner and headed full-on toward a rock-and-roll life, my dad definitely tripped out. He had been in the army, and it was obvious to everyone that it wasn't easy for him to look at his son's long hair. To his credit, he never really said shit about the hair—it was my earrings that freaked him out. By the time I was sixteen, I had pierced both ears and usually wore a long feather in one of them. One night, our family was at the dinner table chowing down and my dad stopped everything dead. He was like, "Is that an earring, Tom?" I usually tried to cover the feather with my hair when he was around but that time he saw that shit sticking out. He wasn't a yeller; my dad said what he needed to say with his looks. He sat there, pretty calm, his expression transmitting his message: "What the *fuck* is that?" I was like, "Dad, check it out, it's rad. Do you see this little feather hanging down?" Since he had been a diesel mechanic and a full-on army guy, he was probably thinking, "Great, my son's a fag." But he let me do my thang. Thanks, Dad.

At seventeen I got my first tattoo: Mighty Mouse flying through a bass drum at the top of my right shoulder, where it still is today. That was the clincher because by then my parents knew I was just going to go and do whatever I wanted. He might not have liked the direction I was heading, but my dad was so fucking rad. He did everything in his power to help me, including giving up his work space to fucking build me my first studio. We didn't have a big house—we had a two-car garage and pretty much the average middle-class suburban American layout. He started parking the cars in the driveway so that our garage could be my practice room. He soundproofed it and built a door so that my band and I could do our thing. It had everything you need in a garage studio: insulation, drywall, and a pressed-board door. It was the ultimate sacrifice for an engineer to give up the only place in the house where he could build shit. He just did it and didn't say much about it. He just told me, "Tommy, go nuts, play all day if you want. Just stop by ten o'clock."

When I started playing out with my first band my dad built us pyrotechnics. He had a little switchbox, four flashpots, metal pipe, and a piece of wood with spikes coming through the bottom, all tied together with guitar string. There was a little filament in the bottom of each flashpot, into which he poured gunpowder and then hit the switch. *Boom!* The neighbors must have thought he was fucking mad. He made us a lighting system too. It was made of cardboard and wood, and it was real Neanderthal — it only had an on/off switch, but it was something that the other high school bands did not have.

I can't say it enough: For a former army mechanic to give up his garage and tool area to build his hyperactive, hooky playin', maybe gay, wannabe rock star son a studio — that is a cool parent. If I can just be half the man my dad was I'll be all right. I've always realized the example he set, but after he died, like everyone else who loses someone, I started to see it more clearly. My dad was the silent type, but he sent me the right messages. As my life got crazy and as I got involved with the opposite sex, he was probably relieved yet also concerned that I'd get someone pregnant. Back when I was growing up, getting a girl pregnant was all you had to worry about. In the eighties everyone dropped their clothes and had sex when they wanted, how they wanted, where they wanted. No one thought about condoms, and no one was worried about diseases, though we should have been. It was about one thing: as much play as you could get. That's when Dad and I had "the Talk."

WORD! AHH, SEX, MY FAVORITE SUBJECT.
LET'S TAKE A BREAK
AND GO HAVE SOME.

He told me to be careful in such a beautiful way that I'm not sure any-one else but those of us who knew him can truly appreciate it. He said "Be careful, son. Be careful where you dip your wick. Your thing there, it's like a candle. And you can get burned."

BURNING BAD. SEX GOOD. MMM, YESS.

At my craziest moments, though, I've wondered how I could have grown up in my parents' wonderful, grounded household and become such a maniac. I always conclude that I'm still around, and that I'm happy and am what I consider to be some sort of a decent person simply because of them.

Now that I have two children of my own, I've tried to follow my par-ents' example as much as I can. I don't think parents should make rules; I think they should act as they wish their kids to be, as much as they possi-bly can. All parents want their children's lives to be perfect, and in this world that's a tall order no matter who you are or how much money, free-dom, or foresight you have. Do your best and remember that you are the living lesson they are learning from each and every day.

I'm lucky. It was so rad to grow up watching my mom and dad be-cause they were so in love with each other for their entire lives. I'd watch my dad pinch my mom's ass and blow her kisses across the room, or get up suddenly just to go over and give her a hug. Only one time during my childhood did I ever see my parents fight. Just once, and it was over money. (Hell, money will make anyone fight.) Times were tight and my mom thought my dad wasn't being straight with her about what he was earning. She thought he was spending his cash somewhere else instead of bringing it home for the family. When she confronted him, my dad pulled his wallet out, threw it at her, and told her to look in it and see how much money he had. He told her to take everything in there. I'll never forget it.

My parents were so in love and that's what I learned. They had the

kind of love that makes life worth living. I saw what a relationship between a man and woman could be and should be. It is what I've always compared my relationships to and I thank them for that. It is a lesson they never could have told me, but one they could have only showed me. And they did.

I miss you Dad. I love you Mom.

AHHH YEAH!!!

5

STATE OF VALEDICTORY

a.k.a.
MOM, DAD . . . I GOT IT

My parents were definitely cool about my passion for music, but soon they were fucking scared. It wasn't a good day when I told them I was going to split high school my senior year to be a musician full-time, as the drummer for Mötley Crüe. We had a record deal, yet it wasn't anything much—we were far from made in the shade. Maybe my parents sensed that, but it didn't matter to me. A record deal and a band that was ready to kick ass was all I needed. High school didn't stand a chance. They sat me down and said, "Tommy, just graduate. Why are you doing this?" And I said, "I *gotta* do this. I *gotta*. Because I *know* it's gonna happen. I don't *care* about a fucking diploma. I've got a *record deal*, and I'm gonna tour the world." They were being good parents, so they kept telling me I needed something to fall back on if it didn't work out. And all I kept saying was, "This *is* gonna work. Trust me, I'm goin'. Mom, Dad, *I got it.*"

My timing couldn't have been worse—I was two months away from my diploma and all that they saw was their son at a crossroad, choosing music as his only viable occupation. I'm sure in their minds they saw the worst-case scenario: me and my drum kit living in their garage for the rest of my life.

Again, my dad was supportive while all of this seemed like a hobby and I was still in school. I didn't play sports, I played music, so like a good dad watching all his son's games, he showed up at my gigs and was even a roadie for all my early bands. I was in a few bands—U.S. 101, Dealer, and my most successful outfit, Suite 19. None of those groups made any money. U.S. 101 was a cover band that played mostly at high school dances. The guitar player was a surfer and a huge Beach Boys fan, so our set was tons of that shit. Just think too much Beach Boys and all the horrible covers a band in the late seventies would play: Styx's "Come Sail Away," Frampton, ZZ Top—you get the picture. I just couldn't wait until it was drum solo time. I'd light my sticks on fire and enjoy myself for a minute.

Dealer was a better gig. When I went to audition, all of us took mushrooms before we jammed. I remember sitting there, trying my best to play while reminding myself that everything was okay and that what I was seeing was not what I was hearing. The entire world was jerky, there were trails coming off everything, and we sounded like shit. Anyway, I got the gig and thank God they played original music because I was into that. I hung with that band for a while and it was pretty good—until I fucked the keyboard player's girlfriend. Sorry, Mark.

I had to leave after that and she came with me. She showed me something that I'm a huge fan of to this day. She was a squirter—or I should say a female Peter North. She could really blast it out. I was bummed when I learned that every girl didn't do that. I was eating her pussy and pulling at her clit and then . . . it *happened*. It was like pee and cum at the same time—and I fucking loved it. When it was time for an explosion, she'd shoot it right in my face and when she was done, we looked like we'd entered a wet T-shirt contest.

I had my van by then, which is where we usually hooked up—a lot. You already know it squirted Jack Daniel's. It was also baby blue with a mural painted on the side and tinted teardrop windows in the back corners. That mural was wack: It was some Grand Canyon scene with horses running through rivers. It belonged on the side of Willie Nelson's tour bus—it was bunk as fuck. But it *was* the love machine, I'm telling you, man. It had Center Line rims on it and the whole back was a padded bed. I realized my girl's whole squirting thing was a problem though, when I gave my mom a ride one day. She was like, "Tom, it smells weird in here. What is that?" I said, "That's just the way the van smells, Mom." But I knew what it was. Fuck, everyone who set foot in that van knew what that smell was—except my mom. My ride reeked of sex.

The Squirter was my first real girlfriend and she was older than me—I was sixteen and she was twenty. Lucky for her the statute of limitations is up on that relationship.

Anyway, sorry I can't keep my mind off sex.

DON'T EVER APOLOGIZE FOR THAT. THERE'S NOTHING WRONG WITH YOU, TOMMY. IT'S THEM. THEY ARE ALL TOO UPTIGHT.

Where was I? Oh, yeah, music. After Dealer I joined Suite 19 and they were the best of my early bands. We were a power trio and had an amazing guitar player named Greg Leon, who was a little Eddie Van Halen. The music was cool, Greg wrote the songs, and since he was a huge Marc Bolan fan, we sounded like a heavier version of T. Rex and Slade. We used to do some covers like "Ray's Electric Farm" by Axis. We were a full-on hard rock trio who played loud as fuck. Suite 19 was my first experience playing real clubs—we played the Whisky A Go-Go, the Starwood, and the Troubadour, among others. We were good and had a lot of interest from labels. I felt like I'd finally found the group that I'd make it with.

During that time, Nikki Sixx was in a band called London* that was big on the scene. When their drummer left, Greg, who was friends with Nikki, told him to call me. I knew who Nikki was because I'd seen him play. I didn't know a ton about their music, but I thought London looked rad—they had crazy hair and they looked like the New York Dolls. I even had a poster of them in my room.

Nikki and I finally met in the front room of his Hollywood home where he played me some new music he was working on. It was harder than the poppy stuff that London was doing and he told me the other guys in his band weren't into it. I started pounding on his living room table to the music and everything just seemed to mesh. The rest is history. We found our guitar player, Mick Mars, through an ad he'd placed in the paper: "Loud, rude, aggressive guitar player. No bullshit. Call Mick." He came to Nikki's house and he didn't even have to play. We opened the door, and he's standing there looking like Cousin Itt from *The Addams Family*. I turned to Nikki and said, "This is our guy. He's perfect—he's disgusting and scary." Soon after that we poached our singer, Vince Neil, whom I'd gone to high school with, from another band on the scene, Rock Candy. It was simple: He looked rad and he did the best Cheap Trick covers of any singer we knew.

When we got the Crüe together, I knew it was *on*. I was a totally fucking insane seventeen-year-old maniac drummer and I was not going to be stopped. We played the circuit and got a devoted fan base real quick. We earned it: Nikki and I would drive around stapling posters on every fucking tree, telephone pole, and anything that didn't move in Hollywood. At the time, selling out the Whisky A Go-Go for three nights was the shit. I was so green that I thought we had made it and had no idea it could get bigger than that.

---

* London formed in 1979 and disbanded in 1988. Sixx and Lizze Grey formed the group after Blackie Lawless (best known as the leader of W.A.S.P.) supposedly kicked them out of the band Sister. According to Sixx, London's purpose was two-fold: to emulate the glam excess of the New York Dolls and annoy Rush fans.

From the start, we did everything ourselves to get the music to our fans. We got the money together to press a few thousand forty-fives—and instead of trying to sell them in a store, we'd throw them out into the audience at our shows. We had success in sight and did it our way.

In less than a year, we were selling out everywhere and soon enough the record companies came sniffin' around because they smelled a profit. They were like, "Oh, fuck, they're doing all this without us."

* * *

Our little world got bigger real quick at the dawn of the eighties. I'll take you back to the first whiff I got of it. I was still in high school at this point and I'm driving to rehearsal, and I hear our first single, "Live Wire," on the radio. I fucking freaked out, made my drum tech, Clyde, pull over, and I jumped out and ran to the pay phone to call my parents. I couldn't believe it—oh my God! That's me on the radio! My mom was home and I'm yelling down the phone, telling her to put on 94.7, KMET. She's all confused, but she finds it and says, "Oh, Tom, that's great." I hung up real quick because I could hear it in the car, because all I wanted to do was get back in there and fucking crank it. I can't tell you how much of a fucking rush it is to be in a car and hear yourself on the radio for the first time, and rock the fuck out. All of a sudden, there I was, on the radio, sandwiched between bands like Van Halen and Rush. It was completely surreal: It was everything I'd ever wanted, coming to me through the speakers in the doors. Be careful what you wish for.

I knew we were set to go right then—I *got* it—but for me, our success only became real when I saw my parents get it. Today, any parent can switch on MTV or VH1 or read *Time* magazine for God's sake and then tell their kid that the new White Stripes album is an instant classic. Whatever. It wasn't like that when I came up. The average adult was pretty alienated from what their kids were into. Youth culture just wasn't on tap, making money for all kinds of media outlets the way it is now.

I'd like to take a moment to apologize to all the parents I scared. I'm sure one day I'll be tripping about some band my kids are into. But I've already got the answer: I'll sit down with them and listen to the music. I'll do my best to understand it and I'll ask them what they like about it. Even if I think it's shit, who am I to tell anyone what to like? It's a personal choice that everyone is free to make. My parents felt the same way, so I'll follow their lead, with one difference—I won't ever tell them to turn the volume down.

My parents were encouraged when they heard my band on the radio, but they weren't convinced that it meant anything until they saw what they couldn't deny. I'm jumping ahead to prove a point but hold up and let me set the scene for you: When Mötley Crüe opened up for Ozzy Osbourne at the Long Beach Arena in 1984, it was at that very moment that I knew I'd made my parents proud, which is one of my greatest achievements. I was up on my riser at the back of the stage, and my parents were at the soundboard out in the center of the arena. They were out there, smack-dab in the middle of the crowd. They'd never been to a concert and had no idea that that world existed. When the bright lights came on, I saw my parents looking around, amazed, and their expressions said it all. I could tell that they knew it was all worth it: all their hard work making ends meet, all the music lessons they paid for and the life lessons they taught me, the garage my dad gave over to me, all their doubts, all their love, and, most of all, the wisdom they had to let me chase my destiny. They had given me everything, from life to feeding and bathing me, to letting me grow up my own way. And right then, all their worries about me making a living were blown away by what they witnessed.

That arena was full of 18,000 people going fucking crazy, pumping their fists and shouting along with us. At that moment, I remembered all those nights practicing in the garage, all those times my parents told me to turn it down and that when I got my own car I could listen to whatever I wanted to (I always hated that). Well, there I was: I was finally in my own car, with the volume on *stun*, my parents riding shotgun with their earplugs in, and 18,000 of my closest friends in the backseat going bananas.

Here's what happens at a big rock show when the aircraft landing lights get turned on: You can see everything. And I did. I could see all the way out to the soundboard in the middle of the arena. My mom is there wearing some rad little miniskirt looking like she's twenty years old, completely hot—just way too fine. She's doing her thing, she's got her hair all done up, and for a second I'm just like, "Mom, what *up?*" My dad is next to her, wearing this crazy Hawaiian shirt that he only wore for special occasions. He's smoking a cigar with Mom on his arm, just chilling. I am playing the fuck out of my drums that night and in the middle of all the insanity, there's my dad watching me with this look on his face that says, *"That's* my boy." I've had many moments of satisfaction in my life but that one won't be topped. My parents finally saw what I was talking about, and they were just like, "Whoa. Okay. He's *got* it."

6

STATE OF MATRIMONY

a.k.a.
MY DEAR HEATHER

I was married very briefly to a *Penthouse* pet from Canada, whose pet name was Candace.

Until Britney Spears was married and divorced in fifty-five hours, I thought I held the record for the shortest marriage ever. We were married and annulled in thirty days, and the easiest way to sum up why we were together is 1) I was nineteen, and 2) she was hot. Candace was the perfect wife for me then: She partied as hard as I did, she hung with the guys, and she always looked good. When I introduced her to my parents, my mother looked like she'd seen a ghost and my father just looked the other way.

> No, not that one!
> You lost me, buddy. Not that one? Well, which one are you thinking of? The OTHER Penthouse pet from Canada I married? I don't remember a lot of shit, bro, but I do remember who I married.

They weren't happy but they wished me the best. And everything seemed to be okay for the first and only month or so we were married—until Candace called my mother a cunt. It was obvious that my mother didn't like her, but Candace wouldn't let it go. I told her not to call my mother a name like that. But she did—again and again. And I won't stand for that. *No one* calls my mother a cunt. I kicked Candace to the curb like yesterday's trash.*

After getting my wedding feet wet and muddy that first time, I was totally against getting married again anytime soon. It wasn't hard to be single at that time in my life—in fact, it was the best way to be for a maniac in his early twenties whose band was starting to really make a dent in pop culture. By now I was twenty-three, and Mötley already had multiplatinum hit albums with *Shout at the Devil* in 1983 and *Theatre of Pain* in 1985. We'd toured the world two times over, committed what some call sins and others call fun, and turned the youth of America out on its ass like a cheap hooker. It was already crazy in our little world, but it got more insane before we drove it into the ground. Looking back now, 1985 was a turning point before we became a full-blown circus, touring constantly, partying hard enough to kill a family of elephants, and bedding more

---

* Canadian-born Candace moved to Los Angeles at seventeen years old and began dancing at strip clubs like the Body Shop under the name Candace Starrek. In 1984 she appeared in *Penthouse* and started dating Tommy. The relationship was volatile to say the least, fueled by youth and excess. Case in point: When Tommy returned to the couple's condo following the end of a tour supporting *Too Fast for Love*, he was proudly in possession of his first gold and platinum album awards. Candace, jealous of a photo of Tommy and a girl whom she'd seen in a magazine, threw a plate at him and smashed his two prizes by way of a greeting. During the first week of the couple's minimarriage, Candace stabbed Tommy with a butter knife as he made a peanut butter sandwich. She was jealous over a woman who was habitually phoning the house and hanging up with whom she was convinced that Tommy was having an affair. Tommy drove himself to the emergency room that night, with the knife protruding from below his right shoulder blade. The final straw to which Tommy refers took place in a limo ride en route to the Tropicana Club to take in some mud wrestling after an evening spent at WrestleMania.

women than a sultan in Saudi Arabia. It was during that circus of crazy that I met Heather Locklear.

Heather was my first taste of a world that was new to me, a world that has been nothing but headaches ever since. She was my first experience living with someone involved in the universe of television and tabloid popularity, which back then, even more than now, was a very, very different brand of fame. At the time, Heather was a star on two hit TV shows at once, *T.J. Hooker* and *Dynasty*. She'd work a few days on one show, then a few days on another. She worked all the time, and I wasn't used to having to schedule my time with someone either. Heather was a very big star in her world and she came with a lot of extras I wasn't used to. We'd step out for dinner and there was always a crowd of crazy people taking pictures. It was insane. I didn't know what the word "paparazzi" meant until I met Heather. As a rock guy the only photographers I ever saw were in the pit at the front of the stage during our show or on a set at a photo shoot—to which we were usually late, but that's another story. Heather couldn't bat an eyelash in public without someone taking a picture of it.

I was willing to deal with all of that and more though, because the first time we met I knew that there was something really special about her—and that I wasn't going to let her get away. I had seen her on TV, of course, and then one day when I was talking to my accountant about who I thought was hot, he told me that his brother was Heather's dentist.

I'D LIKE TO GIVE HER AN ORAL EXAM.

I perked up immediately, looked at him sideways a little, and said, "Dude, do you think there's any way your brother would cut loose with Heather's number?" He wasn't sure, but he said he'd work on it. He was very concerned that I'd tell people where I got it, which would land his brother in a pool full of shit for violating the sacred doctor-patient confidentiality pact. I told him he had nothing to worry about—I'd tell anyone who asked that I just found it. Remember, people, I was in my early twenties at the time.

I should have waited longer to get up the balls

ARE YOU KIDDING?
MY BOYS GOT THAT COVERED!

and prepare a speech before I called her, because when I did, I was such a fucking jackass.

BRO . . . WHY DIDN'T YA
JUST HAND ME THE PHONE?
I'VE GOT A LIST OF LINES.

When she answers the phone I just say, "Hey, what's goin' on? My name is Tommy Lee and I got your number, and I wanted to say hi." She's friendly as she ever is, but completely suspicious as she should have been. She says, "Oh, hi, how are you? How did you get my number?" Tommy, boy genius says, "Oh . . . I just got it." And she says, "Oh, really? You just got it?" I'm sitting there, going full speed ahead blind

IF WHAT THE PREACHER SAYS IS TRUE, DUDE,
WE'D BE BLIND A LONG TIME AGO.

and trying to set up a date with her. I say, "I'd love to take you out to dinner, you know, go bowling or whatever. I'm down for anything, anything you want to do." As I'm trying to make this thing work, I'm watching TV and see her, and of course use it as another way in. "Oh, shit, check it out," I say, "I'm watching you on TV right now." There's silence for a minute, then Heather says, "No, Tommy, that's not me, that's the other

Heather." It was Heather Thomas. I was watching a rerun of *The Fall Guy*, not *T.J. Hooker*. Open mouth, insert foot. . . . Idiot!

All I could think was, "Ah, fuck, I just blew it. This girl is never going out with me." I mumbled something about the two of them looking alike and Heather's just silent on the other end of the phone while I'm groveling. I could tell she's sitting there thinking, "This jerk-off doesn't even know who I am. He thought he was calling Heather Thomas. And how the hell did he get my number?"

I've thought about this many times, and I still can't figure out how I backpedaled out of that one.

DUDE, WHEN ARE YOU GOING TO LEARN? YOU DIDN'T DO IT. I DID. I CAN PEDAL FORWARDS, BACKWARDS, SIDEWAYS, UPSIDE DOWN, AND LOOP-DE-LOOP, MY MAN.

Our conversation must have either been spicy enough or Heather was curious enough to agree to a date, because a day or so later, there I was at her house to pick her up. I stood there in the entrance to her house with her sister waiting for Heather to come down the stairs, and when she did only one word came to mind: *Whoa!*

YOU GOT THAT RIGHT, PRIVATE.

I had a champagne-colored '82 Corvette back then and we went out for Italian food. I barely heard anything she said and I didn't taste my food at all. I was tripping! She was so beautiful and so out of my league. At the time, I was living in this kooky apartment complex, which is still around and still inhabited by actors but mostly musicians who need some kind of temporary living arrangement. It's like a flophouse and it's bunk as fuck: just gnarly one-bedroom apartments that far too many maniacs have worn into the ground. Heather, on the other hand, is this gorgeous, famous actress with a huge, crazy spread up in the hills in Tarzana. I was intimidated by her success and by her beauty. So weird that Samantha Carrington was having dinner with me and wasn't a bitch like she was on TV. Her smile paralyzed me—it was deadly. I sat at dinner, staring at her, and I kept saying, "I'm sorry, but can you just keep smiling?" If you met her then, she was so sweet that you'd never know that she was one of the biggest stars at the time—and I can tell you, she's just the same way today.

I dropped her off like a good boy that night and couldn't stop thinking or talking about her from the minute she closed the door until I saw her again. Our second meeting was a daytime date: She asked me to come over during the day to go swimming and hang out. I thought I'd won the lottery when I got over there and she was rockin' out by the pool lookin' hot floating around on some crazy inflatable lounger. We spent the day like it was adult summer camp: dancing, swimming, drinking champagne. It was amazing and I remember asking God what the fuck was happening because I was loving it all so much that I didn't think it could be real.

All that sun, fun, blond beauty, and bubbles went to my head though,

NOT MINE, BABY, I WAS IN PARTY MODE, READY TO POUNCE!

and after a few hours I told her I had to lie down for a minute and wandered upstairs because I was fucking toasty. I found her bedroom and sprawled out facedown on the bed like I always do when I need a power nap. While I was out like a busted lightbulb, Heather's dad, who was a dean at UCLA, calls to say he is stopping over for a quick visit. Heather's dad is a great guy who likes to drink wine and hang out, but that's after you've known him for a while. On first impression, it's safe to say that he's straitlaced. He isn't the kind of man who would be excited to see a half naked, tattooed rock guy come stumbling down his daughter's staircase.

Heather and her sister came upstairs to wake me up and later she told me that they had just stopped in their tracks. I was lying there at such an angle that my dick and balls

YOU TALKIN' TO ME?
HEY, YOU TALKIN' TO ME?
I'M THE ONLY ONE HERE!

were hanging out of my shorts.

I NEED SOME AIR SOMETIMES TOO . . .
AND SHIT I WAS LOOKIN' FOR BLONDIE.
WHERE THE HELL DID SHE GO?

Apparently, my big-ass balls were just dangling out there and she and her sister turned to each other in surprise when they saw my dick.

DAMN RIGHT THEY DID!
THE ANACONDA WAS TAKING A WALK.

They woke me up and put me into a long-sleeved white dress shirt that covered all my tattoos. They explained that their father was very conservative and that I needed to hide the ink and look a bit more presentable. I'm still not sure how presentable I looked in a dress shirt and swim shorts. Actually, I do have an idea. When I shook his hand and said it was nice to meet him, he looked like he'd just smelled raw sewage and his expression said, "What is *this* over here with my daughters?"

I had never been nervous to meet anyone's parents, but I was scared to meet Mr. Locklear. That was another sign that this was something new in my life: I cared in ways I didn't know I could. Heather and I started dating regularly and soon I was staying at her house all the time and being spoiled in ways I never thought possible.

ME TOO.

She bought me a dirt bike to ride into the hills behind her house. I was really happy, I couldn't believe it as our relationship grew into the kind of cool romance I didn't think existed.

YEAH IT DID, AND SHE . . .
OH, MAN . . . UH, SORRY,
I PROMISED I WOULDN'T TELL.

After about a year I asked her to marry me. We were in a limo, cruising down the freeway, and I opened up the moon roof, stood up, and asked her to come up there with me for a minute. My plan was to ask her to marry me once both of us had our upper bodies out there. It seemed like a great idea, but I hadn't really thought it through or taken wind velocity into account. It was definitely romantic, but if you want to get an idea of what it was like, stand on a tarmac while a jet is taking off and ask someone a question. I'm shouting, "Will you marry me?" Heather is shouting, "What? What?" It was awesome flying out there with the wind whipping in our faces, but she didn't understand anything until I pulled out the ring. I couldn't really hear her, but I knew by her expression that she'd said yes.

My dad had a few words for me when I married Heather Locklear. He was like, "She's a good one, Tommy, take care of her." He got quiet for a minute, then looked at me real hard and said, "Son, don't fuck this up." That was awesome. I'm still not sure if I followed his advice. I'll have to ask Heather.

Heather and I were married on May 10, 1986, and it was the whole deal: five hundred guests, massive cake, press coverage, a serious photo session, doves, a sky diver who delivered a magnum of Cristal, and then my favorite part—we jetted off to Fiji, one of my favorite places in the entire world. It's amazing how you get there. First you fly halfway across the world and then you hop on a seaplane, full-on *Fantasy Island* style. When you skim to a stop, people meet you out there on the dock with foofy drinks in coconuts topped off with pink umbrellas. (I kept snapping my head around looking for Tattoo and Mr. Roarke.) They never showed up, but we didn't care, we were in paradise, chilling in a hut on stilts directly in the water. Every morning we'd open our door, and Heather and I would jump into the clearest, bluest ocean I've ever seen.

It was the start of an amazing seven years together based on a deep, deep friendship and an incredible bond between us. Heather is such a cool, smart, bubbly woman that I was able to relate to her unlike anyone else I'd ever known. We were both kids when we married—I was twenty-four and she was twenty-five. We did so many of our firsts together, and everyone knows that you never forget your first.

We lived out a lot of each other's fantasies, but they didn't always go as planned. I hadn't been back to Greece since I was a kid so soon after we were married, when Heather was flown to Europe for a work engagement, we went by boat to a few Greek islands. We flew over on the Concorde and I'll never forget listening to the pilot announce that we were reaching Mach 2. When we did, our heads snapped back as we broke the sound barrier. That plane was fucking insane—we were flying at 80,000 feet, which is high enough to actually see the curvature of the earth when you look out the window. We landed in Nice, France, and hopped on the *Four Sails*, a beautiful, huge cruise ship with sails. The Greek islands are incredibly beautiful and untouched, and there are a ton of nude beaches I couldn't wait to get to. I wanted nothing more than to be naked on the beach with my wife, so as soon as we got to one, I was Naked Guy.

FINALLY, A VACATION THE WHOLE FAMILY CAN ENJOY! IS THIS SHIT ALL-INCLUSIVE? CAN I GET A MASSAGE AND A PIÑA COLADA? "THE NUTS": HEY . . . YA THINK HEATHER WANTS TO PLAY VOLLEYBALL??!

I looked at her, kissed her, and said, "C'mon, baby, let's get naked!"

DON'T WORRY . . . WHAT HAPPENS IN GREECE STAYS IN GREECE.

Heather isn't uptight, but she can be a prude sometimes, and there was no *way* she was taking it all off in public. She looked at me like I was insane and said, "No, No, NO. There are people from our boat on the beach." I said, "Yeah, so? Look, some of them are naked too. Fuck it, c'mon!" I already have my pants off, and I'm running down the beach, to the ocean, all "woo-hoo!"* while Heather watches me go, shaking her head. She's freaked because I was very tattooed and in Greece that attracted a lot of attention. But I did not care—did you expect me to? When I emerged from the ocean, I overheard these two local ladies talking about me in Greek and I had picked up enough of the language from my

---

* For those readers confused, as was our English editor, by the state of being known in Tommyland as "woo-hoo," I refer you to T. Lee's response to the line edit on page nine (Chapter Juan). As a handy rule of thumb, when someone says "woo-hoo" think cripplingly inebriated, inappropriately naked, sunburned spring breakers.

mom to know they were saying, "Oh my God, look at that man's tattoos. That is disgusting. He is pathetic." Clearly they didn't think I was worldly enough to speak their language, so as I walked by I told them, in Greek, "I understand you. I know what you're saying." They were even more horrified. And it *ruled*. They didn't say a fucking word after that.

All day long I kept trying to get Heather to go euro and show a little skin and that was silly. It had been my fantasy for a long time to take my wife to the Greek Islands and lie there carefree with her on the sand—so I wasn't going down without a fight. I'd pull at her bikini top, I'd untie it, and every once in a while, I'd just take one of her titties out. I had no interest in having her go full frontal for me; topless was all I was after, but it didn't matter. I understood her reasoning: She was a big TV actress and she didn't want her picture taken naked on a beach. But I refuse to follow that rule. If you are a public figure and you spend your free time walking around worrying about how you are perceived, your life will be reduced to a camera lens. And that ain't living.

My marriage to Heather taught me a lot—and one of the first lessons I learned involved compromise. We went down to Cabo San Lucas with some friends shortly after we were married and one day I went deep-sea fishing. I hooked this nine-and-a-half-foot marlin that fought me for two hours without breaking free. For those who don't know about marlins,* let me tell you what they do when you hook them in the mouth. Much like any person or animal you might stick with a hook, they do not dig it at *all*. They dive straight down as far as they can, which usually breaks the line, but if that doesn't do it, they'll also try to cut themselves free with their swords by turning their heads in a circular motion as they swim. But this fish didn't get away—I fought that whale forever and almost died doing it. I'd let him dive until he got tired and then start reeling him in, but when he'd get near the surface, he'd get pissed off and dive again. By then I'd be so tired I couldn't stop him, which meant at least twenty extra

---

* For more information, see Hemingway (*The Old Man and the Sea*, published 1952).

minutes of work on my end. Finally, after fucking forever, I get him close enough to the boat and the crew guys gaff him, bring him on the boat, and tool the fuck out of him with a baseball bat. I'm watching, shouting, "Dudes, that's my fish!" It was crazy—one guy is bashing him while the other holds the sword with gloves because the fish is thrashing around, pissed off and still able to cut the fuck out of somebody.

I sat there exhausted, with no feeling in my arms, strapped into this weird dentist chair with a huge rod stuck in a hole between my legs. And man, was I proud of that fish. I'd never caught anything *anywhere* near that big. The dudes on the boat knew it and they set me up: They arranged to have my fish sent to a taxidermist and then shipped to me. They chopped off the head and tail, put them on ice, and made a shitload of steaks out of the rest of it to give to the poor people in town.

I'm home a week or so later when that huge fifteen-foot wooden crate shows up. I'm so stoked to see my fish that I bust it open right there in the driveway in front of the UPS guy. I pull my prize out and head into the house, all victorious and shit, until Heather sees me. She stops me before I get to the door and says, "*What* are you doing? *Where* are you putting that?" That's when I remembered that I never told her that I had my marlin mounted and dreamed of hanging it above the bar. I look at her and I say, "Baby, this is my fish. I'm putting it above the bar. It's gonna be amazing!" She looks at me like I'm on crack and says, "I don't think so, dude." It was like my birthday party just got cancelled. I say, "But . . . baby? I *caught* it. I'm just going to hang it over the bar. I've got the perfect spot for it." I wanted it where everyone could see it as they sat down for a drink. Well, they'd see it way before then—everyone who walked through our front door would see it. My wife was not having it at all.

There I was, standing in the driveway, bummed, hugging my fish, and right then, I truly realized what it meant to be married. Stuff like hanging a marlin above the bar was no longer just up to me. Stuff was no longer mine—it was ours—and from then on I'd have to check in before I hung a nine-foot fish in our house.

Heather and I stayed in that house for a couple of years and my marlin lived in a lonely corner of the garage until one day our housekeeper took him. I'd love to see where the hell she hung him.

I had some expectations of married life and one of them that worked out perfectly was finding our dream house, the one Heather and I moved into next. I didn't see the house or Heather a lot because I was always on tour with Mötley, but it was our palace: a hilltop spread on a golf course. When I found it, Heather was out of town working, but I knew right away that it had to be ours because it had what our first house lacked: room for a studio, privacy, and the most amazing panoramic mountaintop view I'd ever seen. The house was just a frame on top of a hill when I first laid eyes on it, but I called her and told her we were going to buy it. I sent her photos and she hated it. I took her to the site when she got home and she hated it. Once it had windows and walls, she changed her tune—in fact, she still lives there.

Our house was on a golf course, so I got a membership to the club, because, believe it or not, I do play golf. It wasn't your average membership—you paid sixty grand one time only and there are only two hundred members allowed. The day I strolled down there with my check, I was told I was subject to board review, which was a drama and half, let me tell you. One of the foofy rich guy members got his hands on a tape of me playing live, bashing my drums and pulling my pants down, just cursing, going full-on sack and ass in the wind. Somehow they thought that I wouldn't be a good addition to the community. When I met with the board they told me that they'd reviewed footage of my performances and found me to be unacceptable. I told them they were crazy, that what I did for a living was entertain, and what they were looking at was not what was going to happen on their golf course. I said, "Every day I drive up to my beautiful three-million-dollar home, right here on your course, and usually I see some old man with his dick slung out peeing by a tree. What's the fucking difference? I'm disgusted by looking at that every day."

Eventually, they let me in and they didn't fuck with me after that. Well, I followed the rules, and as you all know rules are meant to be broken. At the time Nikki Sixx lived just below us, down the hill, directly across from our house on the other side of the course. I had a Harley at the time and one day I just thought, "Fuck it," I need to get over to Nikki's quick, so I took the shortcut, across the golf course, tearing up the grass. It felt great, burning rubber through the most perfect rolling green fairways I had ever seen. I finally felt like I got my sixty fucking grand's worth.

I used that golf membership to entertain my musician friends, whom the country club hated. Nikki never did golf because he's the biggest antisports guy *ever*. He never got tired of telling me what a big fag I was for playing golf. He didn't realize that what I liked the best was just getting the fuck outta the house and seeing trees, grass, birds, ponds, and sand, all the while drinking beer and driving the cart around like Mario Andretti.

Over those seven years, Heather and I learned to live with each other and compromise very well. At the time of this writing, I can honestly say that we're still very close friends—and in this business and in this world, that says a lot. I see her once in a while, we talk all the time—and that's amazing. I think that says how very, very cool she is, and I wish that every-body who has ever loved each other could follow our example. She's still so beautiful and she's what she's always been: a great big sweetheart.

We did get divorced in 1993 though. Both of our careers were at their height during our marriage. We talked about having kids a lot, which is something that I'd always wanted, but she wasn't really feeling that. I love kids, and when Nikki Sixx and his first wife, Brandi Brandt, had them, I wanted them more than ever. I'd be over at their house crawling around on the floor with the kids for hours.

When I truly saw that Heather and I weren't going to have children, I started to lose interest in the relationship. And all I can say is that as soon as that started happening, I didn't know what to do. I started wandering emotionally and after that, my eyes started window-shopping and my dick started to talk.

THAT'S RIGHT. AND I'M LIKE E. F. HUTTON: WHEN I TALK, PEOPLE LISTEN.

I started doing crazy shit, like letting temptation be my copilot.

I was monogamous and true for seven years and in that time I had forgotten all about the stripper and porn star telephone network. Here's how it goes down: When someone with any degree of fame fucks around with a stripper or porn star, the girl immediately—and I mean *immediately*—gets on the phone and brags to everyone she knows. When I slipped, I really went for it. I did it with a porn star, on location, at a shoot, on break, between scenes.

Like so many scenes from my life, it started innocently enough. I got a call from Ron Jeremy, who was shooting a feature in a house just up the street from where I was mixing the self-titled Mötley Crüe record at A&M Studios in 1993. When we're on break, I go up there to visit Ron and just watch—why the fuck wouldn't I? Wouldn't you?

HELL YEAH, I'M READY FOR MY CLOSEUP!

Believe it or not, I had never been to a porno shoot. There's fucking going on everywhere and after I'm there for about five minutes, I spy this hot blonde, and just out of curiosity, I ask Ron her name. He doesn't tell me, he just tells me to go to the bathroom and stay there. Two minutes later the hot blonde comes in, fucking rips my pants off without saying a word, and sucks the fuck out of my dick.

HELL YEAH, SHE DID! I LOVE HER. THE BLOOD RUSHED TO MY HEAD SO FAST THAT I BLEW CHUNKS! WHAT'S HER NAME AGAIN?

After I cum, she bails immediately, metal style, and there I am with my pants down feeling like a groupie, wondering what the fuck just happened. It was epic; she fucking *worked* me and left.

WHEW. I GOTTA LIE DOWN. YO, CAN I GET A HAM SANDWICH AND A CIGARETTE?

It was an all-pro blow job but, damn, that was the nail in the coffin of my marriage. Before I'd even zipped up my pants, the porn star telephone network had broadcast the news. I watched this happen with other band members, but I never thought it would happen to me.

I leave the porno shoot and go back to the studio to start working again. It took less than an hour for the network's news flash to reach my wife. When it did, she phoned the studio with an urgent message. "Hey baby," I say. "What's up? Is everything okay?" She's says, very matter-of-factly, "Were you just at a fucking porno shoot?" My first reaction is denial. "*Porno* shoot? What porno shoot?" I ask. Then say, "No, no way." Heather says, "That's interesting. The girl who does my makeup is best friends with the makeup artist who does all the porno chicks and she said you were up there at the shoot today. She said she saw you go in the bathroom with some blond chick. Did you fuck some porno girl?" Uh-oh, I'm fucked. I'm a really bad liar, but I try my best anyway. I say, "What are you *talking* about?" Heather saw right through that shit—anyone could have. She's all calm, cool, and collected, and she says, "I don't fucking believe you. You're a liar. This is fucked."

Click. Dial tone. Divorce.

7

STATE OF TOTAL DISREGARD

a.k.a.
YOU KNOW WHAT?
FUCK IT!

Fuck it, is right—I've always felt that way about life, about dares, about doing what I was told not to do. But after it was clear that Heather and I were getting divorced, my motto was *Fuck it* with a capital *F*—I didn't give a flying *fuck* about *shit*. That period of my life lasted, I'd say, from the day that blow job blew up my home life until we finally signed the papers in 1995.

> I HAVE FELT GUILTY FROM TIME TO TIME
> ABOUT URGING YOU TO HIT THAT PORNO
> SHOOT, TOMMY. MY BAD. YOU SHOULDN'T
> HAVE LISTENED TO ME. MAYBE YOU
> SHOULDN'T LISTEN TO ME MORE OFTEN. . . .
> AH, WHATEVER. YOU KNOW WHAT? FUCK IT.

I was mad at myself for ruining the best relationship I'd known up until then and I was mad at Heather for not wanting to take time off work for what I thought was the real reason two people get married—to make a family.

I didn't know what else to do, so I got really loose from the moment Heather hung up the phone on me. I knew I wasn't going home that night, so I figured I might as well go big. I call Ron Jeremy and tell him to bring the girl who blew me down to the studio with as many of her friends as she could pack into the car.

I was in the studio that night working on *Mötley Crüe*, the one album we did with John Corabi on vocals. We were mixing that night and Corabi, a few roadies, our producer Bob Rock, my friend and sound editor Scott Humphrey, and the studio staff were there. Four girls show up and one of them possesses one of my favorite traits in a woman: yes, my favorite, a *squirter*.

FUCKIN' A, CHIEF! WHERE'S MY RAINCOAT?

The girls come in and lie across the half-million-dollar SSL recording console in our studio and start ramming one another. They are already drunk and they're splashing their vodka-and-cranberrys all over this expensive piece of equipment while the studio engineers freak the fuck out. These guys are frantically wiping up the booze trying to save the equipment and their jobs without missing the show. They were watching a porno—and it wasn't on TV and when Ol' Faithful shot her stuff all the way across the room and into a bowl of fruit, coating the board and everything else in range with her rocket juice, none of us could believe it.*

---

* For further information on the phenomena of projectile female ejaculation, consult your local bookstore, SquirtingBeavers.com, or DVDs such as the *Rainwoman* series (1–17), *Squirting Illustrated* (1–8), *40+ and Squirting, Big Tit Squirt Queens,* or *She Squirts 'Till It Hurts Again.*

I knew that in the studio next door Nine Inch Nails was recording *The Downward Spiral*. I had met Trent Reznor before and I was friends with his bassist Danny Lohner. I knew it was Danny's birthday and here in front of me was the perfect present.

If you read the credits of *The Downward Spiral* you'll see a special thanks to Tommy Lee on "Big Man with a Gun" and here's why. The beginning of the track is the sound of one of those very same girls cumming. They reversed it and fucked with the tone of it, but if you listen closely, you'll hear her. I bring the girls across the hall into the Nine Inch Nails studio, lay them out on Trent's grand piano, and say, "Dudes, set up the mikes, get some grapes, roll the tape, and have a seat. You're not gonna believe this." The girls take grapes and stick them in the squirter's pussy only to suck them out and stick more in. Soon enough, here we go, I can tell it's squirt time again, so I turn to everyone and say, "Dudes, you'd better duck." This time Ol' Faithful hits the wall and everyone freaks. And that was just the appetizer course, because the girls keep playing with her and fifteen or twenty minutes later she's screaming again, which is the cue for the spew. *Woah, hey, woah,* here it comes—juice flies everywhere. I had been around the world many times. I'd looked high and low, and finally I'd found another squirter. She was the only other one I'd seen since my first girlfriend. It was a mindfuck of a day, and all I could think was, "You lose some, you win some. I lost a wife but I found another squirter."

A few days later I moved my shit out of the house I shared with Heather and into a beach house I rented for myself. It cost me seven grand a month and it was right on the sand in Malibu. It was where I needed to go to air my head out and start over. I was in a lot of pain, so *fuck it,* I lost myself in pleasure to forget about it and embarked on a completely illegal summer. Here's some evidence from the files: One night I was sitting around with about four buds—all of whom have already thanked me for not naming them here. We had been drinking, we were all fucked up,

DUDE, CALL A PORNO CHICK.
I LIKE THEM.

so *fuck it*, I call a porno chick.

When she arrives at my summerhouse of sin, she finds five *really* horny, *really* fucked up guys there. She sits and has a few drinks, then a few more, and then one or two more after that. My bed at the time was a huge canopy contraption that looked like an old carriage that Cinderella would ride to the ball in. It was perfect for our purposes. She walks into the bedroom and has us tie her up by her feet, so she's hanging from the epicenter of the love sled. She's dangling upside down and can be conveniently spun in a circle to better suck everyone's dick. She was weightless, free to just go 'round and 'round, take everyone's manhood, sample the all-you-can-eat cock buffet, and ride the penis-go-round until the carnival shuts down, and everyone on the ride gets off.

One of my shameless nameless bros declares, "I am the ringleader," and leads us into the fun house by wacking her bottom with my big fat leather paddle. She moans and she loves it. Then, all of a sudden, the circus pitches the big top—and here come the clowns to make her laugh as the ringleader becomes the lion tamer who uses a soft whip to increase her pleasure. She's begging to be spanked more and spanked harder—perfect for the freakshow.

After the final bows and the spotlights go out, the tent comes down and she bails. Fifteen minutes later the phone rings and it's her, calling from her car. She says, "Hey, Tommy, I just wanted to call you and your friends and tell you that I had the *best* fucking time *ever*. I fucking *love* you guys! Let me know when the next party is!" We couldn't wait to invite her back with a few of her friends for a three-ring extravaganza. I love the circus, always have.

8

STATE OF THE CRÜE

a.k.a.
WHEN WE STARTED THIS BAND, ALL WE NEEDED WAS A LAUGH; YEARS GONE BY, I'D SAY WE KICKED SOME ASS

When I was about thirteen or fourteen I was the chosen guinea pig among my friends to go into the store and steal candy. It turns out that I was really good at it—I stole pounds of it, I'd wear a big down jacket in the middle of summer and let my buddies fill every pocket, the hood, the insides, and even my underwear. When I could barely walk straight, I'd stroll out of there with candy falling down my ass. I didn't know it at the time, but it was great training for feeding my other family later in life.

In 1980, Mötley Crüe nailed down its lineup: Me, Nikki Sixx, Vince

Neil, and Mick Mars. Mick is older than we are, so he had no interest in living with the rest of us. He was smart—the rest of us were still in our late teens and we were disgusting, insane party maniacs. Mötley was no overnight success story and while we waited for the world to notice how much we kicked fucking ass, Nikki and Vince and I lived in a nasty-ass house in Hollyweird, right off Sunset Strip. We played shows in clubs, we never took out the garbage, we never cleaned up the empties, we had nasty sex, we never did dishes—and we only had one dish to do. We killed the armies of cockroaches climbing all over our walls with a lighter and a can of hairspray. We had no food because we had no money. And when we did have money, we sure as fuck didn't spend it on a meal when we could spend it on the essentials—more liquor and more hairspray.

We were part of the Sunset Strip scene that spawned bands like Quiet Riot, Ratt, Poison, and a bunch of other motherfuckers. But back when it was getting cooking at the dawn of the eighties, no one did it like we did. Our first album, *Too Fast for Love*, was something the other bands weren't doing. Everyone was stuck on the Knack and "My Sharona." Every band—all my friends—were cutting their hair off, wearing skinny ties, and jumping on that bandwagon. Cool song, but *fuck*. It was either that or they were into something very different, like Black Flag.

We were definitely the kids doing our own thing, going against the grain. Nikki was writing songs that were poppy and all I heard was ways to make them heavier and more rhythmic. And as much as we changed over the years, those two elements remained the same. We recorded our first album in ten days—at least that's how it felt to me. We were recording in the Valley (I think).* The album was recorded live, off the floor, with all of us in one room. It's a lot of people's favorite and I get why: It's raw, it's

---

* Hello again, readers. Yes, it's me, Anthony Bozza here, once again, reporting live from the footnotes. *Too Fast for Love* was actually recorded in three drunken days at Hit City West Studios on Olympic Boulevard in Los Angeles. It cost $6,000. The band was unsigned and the album was released on Leathür Records, their own label. They thought up the name at a Denny's. The cover featured a closeup photo of Vince's crotch and his hand making the devil horns sign. In sign language it means "I love you."

fast, and it's us in the early days. Sonically, it's my least favorite record because anyone who knows about recording can tell that it was done way too quickly. We didn't have any money so we didn't have a choice. In fact, to get free studio time I fucked a female engineer every night for a week or so after we finished recording. It wasn't easy, but it had to be done.

JUST CLOSE YOUR EYES, DUDE, I GOT THIS ONE. I'M A TEAM PLAYER TOO, YOU KNOW.

I took many for the team over the years, but she was the roughest.*

Our early shows were ridiculous: We had alcohol-burning funny cars,† fake blood, mannequin heads, and any other cheap horror props we could think of that would freak people out. We'd walk around all the time, in stiletto heels with makeup on looking like chicks, so we got in fights with people just about everywhere we went.‡ We used to set Nikki on fire while he played bass by rubbing pyro gel on his legs that Vince would light with a torched sword. It was fun practicing that routine in our

---

* Yes, Tommy did trade sexual favors for studio time after their two-hour allotment ran out. But the band wasn't trying to complete their first album, they were recording their first demo, which included Nikki Sixx's songs "Stick to Your Guns," "Toast of the Town," "Public Enemy #1," and a Raspberries cover, "Tonight."

† In August 1982, Mötley played a show sponsored by a car racing promoter at the Santa Monica Civic Center. Nitro-burning dragsters were onstage and revved up during the show, shooting flames from their tailpipes. Clearly, show insurance premiums are not what they used to be.

‡ Far too many adversaries to name, from undercover police to male and female fans, to bands sharing the bill, to bouncers at clubs like the Whisky A Go-Go, the Rainbow, and every other rock pit on Sunset Strip. One particularly dangerous situation developed at a charming venue called the Oil Patch in Alberta, Canada. The audience consisted entirely of oil riggers and lumberjacks boozing it up at their local watering hole. Considering that the standard male inhabitant of the area wore only jeans and flannel Pendleton shirts, Mötley wasn't exactly a hit, musically or otherwise.

apartment. We'd dress all in leather and rock like we owned the fuckin' joint—and we did. And afterwards, we'd invite the entire show back to our shitty little apartment just off the Strip. It's amazing that that shit shack didn't just fall down, because after not too long there wasn't much left. Our door was smashed in because the cops had kicked it in so many times. Even if the door did close or lock, you could still just get in through the front window. It was smashed by a fire extinguisher heaved through it by my old girlfriend (the squirter). I don't remember what I did, but she was craise.* We didn't have much besides a stereo, a couch, and some records on some crappy little entertainment center, but trust me, she trashed all of it that day. Our bedrooms weren't much better: The mirrored closet doors in the room I shared with Vince were toast. One of them fell on David Lee Roth's head one night, and I'm proud and amazed to say that when the door hit his dome, he didn't flinch, he didn't stop rambling about whatever the fuck he was talking about—and he didn't spill a speck of the cocaine he wasn't sharing with anyone.

In some ways, those were the days, because nothing mattered, none of us gave a fuck, and we thought we'd made it. In our little world, we had reached the top. Even so, we were still scum-ass poor most of the time, so my skills as a klepto came in handy. I usually made a run or two a week to keep all of us boys fed, and I always got the five-finger discount. I don't recommend it unless you are really desperate, but I will say that it's pretty easy to justify that kind of shopping when your attitude is "Dude, we gotta *eat*."

The liquor store catercorner to the Whisky A Go-Go, just down the

---

* craise: cray'se [sounds like "erase" minus the "e," plus a "c"] n., adj.: Slang for crazy. Origin: Tommy Lee. Connotes craziness. Can be used [addition to the O.E.D pending] to reference both positive and negative varieties of craziness, insanity, and all significant forms of otherness. Sample usage: "Dude, I was driving down Hollywood Boulevard today and I saw this guy at a bus stop with flaming yellow hair and pleated jeans hitched up to just below his tits. I thought to myself, 'That guy's pants are *craise!*'"

block from our house, was one of my regular targets. In 1982, I believe it was, that establishment provided us with a meal I'll never forget. It was Thanksgiving Day and we all decided that we needed to get ourselves some form of turkey, any shitty form of turkey, to get into the spirit. Our attitude was, "Hell, we deserve turkey, dude." So we slid into that liquor store and the dudes stuffed a few turkey potpies in another of my trusty down jackets. I was a white puffy Michelin Man in a black coat filled with turkey potpies. When we got back home, we turned to one another, all excited. We hugged and jumped up and down, just shouting, "I love you, bro! Happy Thanksgiving, bro!"

Before the money started rolling in and before we were picked up by Elektra Records,* we started to realize that there was an alternative: dating girls who would either bring us food or were rich enough to give us money for food on a regular basis. We never talked about it, but it became the unspoken rule. They were our sponsors between the day we first laid our songs on vinyl and the day we signed our name on the dotted line. It was bizarre sometimes, and maybe it was wrong, but I look at it this way: It wasn't illegal. To all those girls: Sorry where sorry is due. And a thank you, and you, and you, you, you, and you. You know who you are. I hope you do, because I do.

Motley's first two albums, *Too Fast for Love* and *Shout at the Devil*, came out before MTV even existed and it's weird to think that it used to not exist. Some people think hip-hop divides the generations more than anything, but if you ask me, it's MTV. Before MTV, you had to do more work to find your scene and learn about music. You had to interact, talk to people, and go to certain stores and certain clubs to get to the music you liked. Now you can stay inside and have it all beamed to you. Whatever.

I'll be the first to say that Mötley profited a fucking ton from MTV.

---

* May 1982. The band accepted Elektra Records's offer over that of Virgin Records (who were willing to pay $25,000 more), because Electra was located in Los Angeles.

We were one of the first bands on there and we were on there constantly because those fuckers didn't have too many other videos to show! Our image, our attitude, and our message was as antiauthority, proshock, and indulgent as you could get. It didn't hurt that we looked insane, that we were insane, and that all of us, separately and especially together, were trouble magnets. Naturally, MTV always had editing issues with us. They were always telling us what we had to cut out of our video to get it on the air. We learned that it was best to send our videos to them in the worst format, with as many R-rated elements as possible. That way, after the edits, it would still be kick-ass. Our music was a soundtrack of pleasure-seeking, adolescent rebellion, danger, and extremism that was as fucking rock-and-roll as you could get at that time. If you go back and hear it now, it still is. Times might have changed, but maniacs still crave a theme song—and Mötley hit that shit on the head. We definitely stood out in 1983, when *Shout at the Devil* broadcast us into households across America.* At the time, bands like Men at Work, Hall and Oates, or Michael Jackson were at the top of the charts and people were paying money to see movies like *Mr. Mom* and *Flashdance*. Next to that, we were like a freight train from hell that tore the ass out of pop culture.

As we settled into our style and became bigger over the course of the decade, with records like *Theatre of Pain* in 1985, *Girls, Girls, Girls* in 1987, and *Dr. Feelgood* in 1989, we watched our effect on music

---

* Some facts for you: *Shout at the Devil* was released in June 1983 and sold 200,000 copies in two weeks. It eventually reached number 17 on *Billboard's* Top 200 Albums Chart. It included a cover of the Beatles's "Helter Skelter" and had a black album cover with a pentagram that scared the crap out of many a parent and churchgoer, as did the band's new look: leather and war paint inspired by the films *Mad Max* and *Escape from New York*. The video for the single "Looks That Kill" cost $75,000 (the cost of catering on a high-budget video these days) and shocked MTV with images of fire, near naked caged women, and, well, Mötley Crüe. The album went on to sell more than three million copies.

and on younger bands coming up. We were always about the rebellion at the heart of America not only because we lived that way but also because rock-and-roll has always been salvation for horny, aggressive teenagers as much as it's always been nothing but a fucking racket to their parents.

We were a group made up of very different guys and if you ask me, that's why it worked. Each of us brought to the mix so many different influences. Nikki brought his love of punk and pop and melodic glam-rock songwriting style. Mick was a full-on blues monster, who would rather listen to classic guitar players like Jeff Beck and Jimi Hendrix than any new band I'd try to force-feed him. Vince, well, Vince liked Robin Zander, and since Cheap Trick is God, that was cool. He didn't bring much to the musical table, but like David Lee Roth, he didn't need to—he knew how to be a good front man. And me? I brought all kinds of shit: the funk, the big beats, the drum solos from hell, and a sense of musical arrangement that we needed. In the studio, I was usually the guy who figured out where all our parts should go and how we should take the pieces we worked out jamming and make them into songs. Being a drummer, I got turned on by the rhythm in all kinds of music, from George Clinton to Pantera. I was always the guy blasting some new tunes over the rehearsal PA system. I'd be shouting, "Dudes! You gotta hear this shit!" It didn't always go over well. Whatever.

I've got to take a moment here to say that Mötley's break came courtesy of the rock royal family, when we were picked up by Ozzy Osbourne as the opening act on his *Bark at the Moon* tour in 1983. That was a huge tour for him as a solo artist because the album kicked ass and rock-and-roll fans were going crazy for it that year. The tour was sold out everywhere and playing a sold-out gig at an arena was fucking heaven for a band at Mötley's stage in the game. Sharon and Ozzy could have picked any band to open that tour—plenty would have done it for free, including us (I'm just glad they didn't ask). They picked us and I'm forever indebted to them for seeing that Mötley wasn't fuckin' around. Sharon and Ozzy gave us the chance to rock shit every night and we earned ourselves a huge fan base in return.*

Theatre of Pain was what we made of all those days on the road and everything that happened to us after making *Shout at the Devil*. We'd seen friends die, seen girlfriends come and go, we'd broken shit, done everything we wanted, and had a huge success with that album too. But "Home Sweet Home" was the first song we recorded for *Theatre of Pain* and it says it all.† That tour was itself a Theatre of Pain. Nikki and I were at our all-time high in terms of drugs and alcohol: We'd shoot up cocaine and heroin onstage if we wanted to and we'd shoot Jack Daniel's or gin to come down after the show. It was ridiculous. Thank God we're alive.

The *Girls, Girls, Girls* record, in my opinion, brought together a huge chunk of all-American subculture: tattoos, Harley-Davidsons, strip clubs, the New York Dolls, plus a dose of English glam shit like T. Rex. It was everything we were into: We all rode Harleys and we had a riding club called the Dark Angels. We were all into strip clubs and that's what

---

* That tour yielded many examples of unequaled rock debauchery: Tommy and Ozzy urinating on a police car, Ozzy snorting ants and adorning Tommy's hotel room with his own feces as well as lapping up Nikki's urine; Ozzy and Vince stealing a car and using it to menace pedestrians before destroying it; Tommy, Nikki, and Jake E. Lee from Ozzy's band ending up in a knife fight in New Orleans; and Mick Mars getting arrested instead of Tommy after Mr. Lee graced the halls and surprised the guests of a Denver hotel with a naked 100-yard dash. The tour's final show involved Ozzy's band dousing Mötley with flour and custard, and Mötley responding by sending Vince onstage in a suit of armor to pelt Ozzy with a goblet full of flour during his set before the entire Crüe invaded the stage in monk's robes only to drop them and reveal themselves—completely buck-ass naked. Ozzy booked the calmer seventies hard-rockers Slade to open the next leg of his tour.

† The album was released in July 1985 and debuted at number 90 on *Billboard*'s Top 200 Albums Chart. It cost $200,000 to produce. A cover of Brownsville Station's "Smokin' in the Boys' Room" became the band's first Top Forty single, peaking at number 16 and remaining on the charts for fifteen weeks. The album eventually reached number 6. At the time, it won the highest position of any Mötley Crüe album to date, until the release of *Girls, Girls, Girls*.

the title track is about.* That album was Mötley and it was everything American that no one else on MTV talked about back then.†

Dr. Feelgood was when we really hit our stride. It rocked like fuck—it had melody and pop hooks you couldn't forget. All of us were clean and sober while we recorded, after I led the charge for each of us to enter rehab, and it shows. It even hit number one the week of my twenty-seventh birthday in October 1989.‡ Still, we never won a Grammy—and that year we should have. I remember sitting in the same row with Metallica at the ceremony that year. They were nominated for *And Justice for All* and we were for *Dr. Feelgood*. As they named the nominees, we all looked at one another because we knew those were the two fucking biggest, baddest hard rock albums of the year. We knew one of our bands was going to take it home. You've never seen a bunch of guys more fucking shocked to lose when the Best Hard Rock Album of the Year went to . . . Jethro Tull. Are you *fucking* kidding me? The lead singer plays flute, what the fuck is *that*? Another example of the tired old fuckers on the Grammy committee voting for their favorite fellow old fuckers. Thank God the Grammys have gotten a little bit better. Still, every year, there's always some big crime against music at that ceremony where the out-of-touch board members' choice wins over what was good and what people really loved. Whatever.

---

* Michael Peters, owner of the Pure Platinum chain of strip clubs began playing the song every hour on the hour in his establishments, and continues to do so to this day.

† The single "Girls, Girls, Girls" peaked at number 12 on Billboard's Top Forty in May 1987, and spent fifteen weeks on the charts. The album, released the same month, debuted at number 5 on Billboard's Top 200 Albums Chart and shipped platinum. It became the highest debut of an album since Stevie Wonder's *Hotter Than July* (number 4) in 1980 and was the highest debut for a hard rock album since Led Zeppelin's *Song Remains the Same* (number 3) in 1976. *Girls* peaked at number two, kept out of the top spot by Whitney Houston's *Whitney*. By September 1987, *Girls* had sold more than two million copies in the U.S. alone.

‡ Yes, indeed, Tommy's got that right. The album was released in September 1989 and featured the title track, which peaked at number 6. The album dominated radio, MTV, and the charts for more than a year.

After we lost, our band and Metallica looked at each other, shook our heads, got up, went straight to the bar together, and got drunk as fuck. We didn't need the Grammys to tell us we kicked ass.

In just a few years, Mötley went from nothing to a crew of guys who had everything. We are all extremists, so in a way it makes sense that our career, once we hit, went from zero to sixty that quickly. It doesn't mean that we were capable of dealing with any of it then. Before we got clean, we were drunk, we were crazy, we snorted mountains of cocaine, Nikki and I shot heroin and drank Jack Daniel's like the world was ending tomorrow, and none of us, for a while there, would have cared if we were the biggest band in the world or died the next day. If anything, that to me is Mötley: four guys who were the greatest fucking rock band and the biggest fucking train wreck at the same time. From moment to moment, it was either win it all or lose it all.

It was rad and it was intense, but I look back at it now and I'm like, "Jesus, that was so . . . then." The eighties were definitely incredible for us. It was raw dog, all the time.

HALLE-FUCKING-LUJAH!
CONDOMS?
HATE 'EM!

Please, chicks would come backstage or up to my room and fucking *boom*, their clothes were off and it was on.

FUCKIN' A, HOMIE!

Now there's a bit of negotiation involved, where they said, "Hey, you have a condom? Can we do this?"

THAT'S WACK!

Those days were so fucking insane that I don't remember a lot of them. I'm just glad that I left a mark and that my band made such a big-ass dent in the decade it made people copy us so much that we just had to laugh. If you check in with VH1 Classic for a minute, you'll see hours of what pissed me off as the eighties came to an end. We watched metal bands get more theatrical and Mötley-lite acts like Great White and Warrant enjoyed their one-hit wonder success by offering up a safer alternative to the real thing. That shit was wack and all of us in Mötley just sat there and watched it all go down—downhill, that is. We'd come out with a rad new album and video and then see other bands hire the same director, work with the same producer, throw on the same style of makeup, and shop where we bought our clothes. It was ridiculous.

We did it right and I dare anyone to say we didn't. We rocked harder and we looked better than anyone out there. And though some people tripped, I liked being as naked as I used to be on stage—no one else did that shit. Yes, I do like to be naked,

OF COURSE WE DO.

but part of it was strictly comfort: Do you have any idea how hot you get beating a drum kit for two hours? Trust me, you don't want clothes you don't need. It was all good, though, because when I was hidden back there behind my drum kit I got away with shit someone like a guitar player couldn't. It was easy to get hooked up with a bottle cap full of coke as often as I wanted, which was pretty often. My roadie could come up and jam a beer cap full of it up my face without anyone knowing shit about it. Not that I'd give a fuck if they did know back then.

Playing drums and rocking the fuck out of the place—that's as primal as it gets.

NO IT ISN'T.

You realize that you have the power to move the entire audience with every beat you play. It's scary and amazing at the same time. You are dictating the cadence, sending out the energy to the fans. It isn't a one-way street—that electricity goes through them and comes right back at you, amplified. It's the World Series and the Superbowl taking place on New Year's Eve and that night, you're fucking your favorite porn star. Still . . . that's not even close.

Let me take a minute or ten to talk about my drums. Once Mötley had some money, I was like Dr. Frankenstein creating his monster. I got into this insane tradition of retardedly large drum sets and bigger than Jesus solos. By 1987, I had a kit that I was strapped into that spun full 360s like a gyroscope at the front of the stage. Are you kidding me?

It all started innocently enough. I just wanted my minute in the spotlight during showtime to fuckin' rock so as we got bigger, I built bigger drum risers. It got to the point where I had nowhere left to go but up in the air. And of course I was told that I couldn't do that, so I went and did it. I don't like "no" and "don't"—those words have been as much of an inspiration and motivation to me as the sound of a drum. If you think about it, when you're told you can't do something, it's not true. There's always an option. Trust me.

The drum monster grew to the point where we had to fly. I met this cat, Chris Dieter, who was a former hydraulic specialist on a navy submarine and he told me, "I will make you fly and we'll make history." And we did.

That guy built me two rigs: the one that spun me upside down on the *Girls* tour and the one that flew me out above the crowd on the *Dr. Feelgood* tour. He was a master. That whole cage he built me for the *Girls* tour was welded to a fork-lift, somehow mounted on yolks from your neighborhood garbage truck, all connected with a ton of cables and pumped up into flight by some crazy hydraulic fluids. Before I met him I had a recurring dream about flying through the arena, above the crowd, playing drums. I told the band and our managers about it, and they just looked at me like, "Whatever, Tommy, party on." But I've got to give props to my bandmates because once I found the maniac who could build the machine I needed, they let me do my thing. It was like eighty grand to build that rig and they were like, "Cool. Fuck it, let's do it."

When I'd rotate on the *Girls* tour, I could only make five revolutions because there was only enough slack in the microphone cables to turn that many times before we had to rotate me backwards to unwind them. If we did it today we could do the whole thing wireless. Damn, if we did it today I could turn 360s until I puked.

Thing is, my monster became a problem. The fans left our shows just saying "What the *fuck!*"* And that means the next tour I had to give them even more. I couldn't let them leave saying that our last tour was better, you know?

After spinning circles on the *Girls* tour, it was hard to outdo myself. I figured all I could do was give the people way back there in the shitty Stevie Wonder seats a front row ticket. The only way to do that was fly the drums all the way out from the stage to the very back of the arena. So I did on the *Dr. Feelgood* tour. And it was rad. For a few minutes, the worst seat in the house was now a front row ticket. All those kids in the back had the best view, and I could see them every night freaking the fuck out. It made the whole thing worth it.

My real dream is to build a true roller coaster where my drums roll on a track to the back of the arena and do a loop in each direction. I want cameras mounted all over my kit so everybody can see on the big screen what I'm seeing and feel what I'm feeling. I want a seat at the back of it just like an old hot rod. I want to strap fans to it every night and take them for a ride. It can be done—I've checked on it. The companies that build roller coasters can hook it up. The only problem is insurance. And don't

---

* That would be "What the fuck?" in a good way. As in "What the fuck was that! Fuckin'-A! Mötley Crüe rules! Tommy fuckin' ripped! Did you hear that shit?"

get me started on that—paying money to cover your ass just in case something happens? That's tight. But in a lawsuit happyland, you're fucked if you don't take precautions.

When Mötley was preparing the *Generation Swine* tour in 1997, I was told that a roller coaster wasn't going to be part of the package, so I settled for making the drums disappear, magician style. I asked David Copperfield how he'd do it. Then I met the guys who are the real magicians in Copperfield's show—the engineers who blow shit up and create diversions so that you don't see them hiding that 747 right in front of your eyes. I'm not going to give away their secrets because stuff like magic and Santa Claus make the world go 'round for kids of all ages. But I will tell you that those cats fuck shit up. They make the big shit disappear into itself. They can take a truck and outfit it with hydraulic systems that make it fold up into a shoe box. It's crazy. You should have seen them grinning with ideas of how to make a drummer vanish into thin air. And we did it. We did it big.

I had it dialed. When it was time for my solo, I started out ripping it on the set I used throughout the show while Aborigine dancers with bones through their noses danced in dust with their titties bouncing. We got into this insane tribal drum thing that I fucking loved! As I went off, another drum kit was rolled out onstage. I went over and continued the solo on that kit. We had a full video production going, capturing the dancers and flashing pictures of atom bombs going off and roller coasters dropping as I played. When I moved to the new drum set, the video stopped and the magic began. As I was playing, a space man came out and watched me play. He walked around me a few times, and then raised a white curtain around my drum set. You could see me through the curtain, but what you didn't know is that we could also project images onto the curtain. We had prerecorded footage of me playing that we rolled while I was behind the curtain and the drums were lowered onto the floor. The spaceman came behind the curtain, and I changed into his outfit really fast. While I was changing, the audience watched what they thought was me playing the drums. When I was done, I came out from behind the curtain as Mr. Spaceman and started watching the videotape of me playing drums. I loved that part. Then we'd start playing one of my favorite songs, Josh Wink's "Higher State of Consciousness," which is one of the most fucked-up dance tracks I've ever heard. I'd start raising my arms up and the drums would start elevating, higher and higher. When they were at their peak, while the projected image of me wailed away, I raised my spaceman gun and shot myself. The gun exploded, the drums exploded, and the curtain dropped, revealing an empty drum set, hovering up by the lighting rigs. That's when I'd turn around and peel off my space helmet. *Abracadabra!* It's me! Looking out at a sea of confused faces every night was epic. For a second there, I was David Copperfield and I realized how much magic is just one big illusion.

Oh, fuck, I wasn't supposed to tell you how we did that. Sorry. While we're at it, there is no Santa Claus, there is no magic, and there is no fucking Easter Bunny. The Tooth Fairy was your goddamned mom, storks don't deliver babies, Pop Rocks and Coke won't kill you, there is no Middle Earth, Mikey never liked Life cereal, you can't get pregnant from kissing, you won't go blind from jerking off, and when Jack and Jill tumbled down that hill, they was definitely fuckin'.*

* * *

* If any of these revelations prove difficult to comprehend or erode your emotional and spiritual well-being, I suggest reaching out to a trained and/or licensed member of the mental health community. Obtain a list of in-network referrals from your insurance provider, your employer's Human Resources department, or let your fingers do the walking through your local Yellow Pages until the letter "t," where upon further page-flipping they will find "therapist." Afflicted readers with a religious orientation should, in addition, seek out a duly elected official of their chosen order. In the rare and serious instance that spontaneous breakdown should occur, I suggest you dial the number of the nearest poison control center or call 1-800-Suicide, a convenient, toll-free, national suicide prevention hotline. If uncontainable problems persist, I, Anthony Bozza, will provide free consultation on a case-to-case basis. In extraordinary circumstances, Tommy Lee, subject to availability, reserves the right to stage an intervention the extent of which will be determined with the cooperation of ailing readers' loved ones.

Mötley was always about intensity and indulgence, and we were always a band living on the edge. I'm fearless, but there were more than a few situations that I got into in my Mötley days that scared the fuck out of me. Here's one of many. We had a pilot I nicknamed Dick Danger and a private jet service I nicknamed Dangerous Airways during the *Shout at the Devil* tour (I think).* Dick Danger nearly destroyed us several times. Ol' Dick was flying a tiny, tiny plane—a twin-engine prop plane, which is the kind of plane that goes down all the time if you check the obituaries. Anyway, Dick was this older guy, in his fifties at least, with white hair and a suitcase full of Hawaiian shirts.

I liked to keep an eye on Ol' Dick, not because I thought I'd be able to do anything if some shit went wrong, more because he was like a trippy math problem: I needed to know what made this motherfucker tick. So I'm sitting up there in the cockpit next to Dick Danger one day, and I'm definitely toasted and I'm like, "Dude, could I fly this? Is it hard to do?"

---

* Gold star, Tommy. That was indeed the *Shout at the Devil* tour.

Dick's all, "Take the wheel. Go ahead." Our manager at the time heard this and completely freaked. "Do NOT let Tommy fly," he said. "No, no, NO." I look back at him and of course I take the wheel. I guess I thought it would be like a car or a video game, so I'm not even fully realizing that I have my entire band's future at risk. I'm just thinking, "Fuck . . . I'm flying!" I'm glad Ol' Dick didn't tell me how to do a barrel roll—because you know I would have.

There we are: me, piloting this two-engine tin can, while next to me, Ol' Dick has his hands free. I watch as he reaches into that Hawaiian shirt pocket, pulls out a vial, and pours himself a huge cap of cocaine. Woah . . . he does blow? That's fucked up. Pass the cap, dude. I thought it was amazing to sit up there in the cockpit while the pilot did gaggers and I flew the plane. (I've grown up a bit since then.)

Eventually, we had to complain to the company we chartered our planes from because we realized that it wasn't just Ol' Dick—all their pilots were on drugs all the time. Our managers stood for a lot but they wouldn't stand for that: We were enough of a problem, they didn't want to deal with coked-out captains. Think about it, when you're cruising in a plane with a coked-up pilot, you really start to freak when he gets on the speaker system and tells you to brace yourself for turbulence. You're sitting there, thinking, "Fuck. I don't want to be Lynyrd Skynyrd right now."

On one of our tours we had a security guard named Vinny who beat up a fan. The kid got lippy with him and since Vinny was a crazy New York fucker, he lost his mind all of a sudden and started pounding away. This kid was probably sixteen and his blood flew everywhere. We were like, "Dude! What the fuck? You can't do that." I've got a picture of Vinny sitting on the curb afterwards. He's covered with blood, he's finally realized what he's just done, and he's bumming out, because he almost beat that kid to death.

Recently, I had a security guy who should have been with Mötley back in the day. He'd pop out his glass eye with a knife. That was a little much, especially when he would flick it into girls' drinks. The guy had no peripheral vision on one side. He did the rest of the job well, but I figured that anyone could sneak up on him. I always made sure to stand on the good side—his left—where I'd be safe.* Who is hiring these people? I should have found myself a blind bus driver while I was at it. Back in the Mötley days we would have been into that. We probably would have gotten him really great sonar and a navigation system that talked to him. He would have fit right in.

We did ridiculous things in Mötley, many that worked and some that really didn't. One of those bunk ideas, the kind you realize you should have thought through a little better, was a photo shoot we did on the top of a glacier when John Corabi was in the band. When Corabi came in the band, Mötley was a different monster. It was 1994, and bands like Nine Inch Nails and Nirvana had changed rock-and-roll. When the rest of us felt that Vince wasn't taking the music or his duties as a singer seriously, we parted ways and Corabi stepped in to replace him. Corabi's singing style was different—grittier, harsher, and more where the rest of us wanted to be at the time. Poor guy, he had enough to deal with stepping into Vince's shoes, he didn't need to be dragged onto a glacier outside Vancouver, Canada. But he was, and it was an act of sheer dumbassedness. We just jumped in a helicopter in our street clothes. Idiots! I was wearing jeans, a leather jacket, a T-shirt, and sneakers. I had a hat, because the night before, Phil, the singer from Pantera, had shaved my head, so I knew I'd be cold as fuck. My hat put me leagues ahead of the other guys. None of us had gloves and there we are, freezing to the bone at the top of this chunk of ice with hundred-foot crevaces all around us. Corabi didn't even have a jacket. He had to be sitting there thinking, "What is wrong with these people? Why am I up here?" Corabi and I did have some fun making the one album and tour that we did in 1994–95. But we should ask him about that. Lucky for you, my readers, John stopped by one day while I was writing this book. He posted up at my bar, grabbed himself a beer, and reminded me of all the nasty good times we

---

* "Eyeball" replaced Tommy's tour-tested, well-trusted security guard, Hawk on the *Methods of Mayhem* tour in 2000.

had. John tells a pretty good story, so without further ado, ladies and gentlemen, I'm going to let him tell you all about it, in his own words.

JOHN CORABI

Tommy and I got into a lot of trouble on that tour. We were the only two in the band who were single, drinking, and partying at the time, so we had our own bus while Nikki and Mick, the sober, mellow cats kept to themselves. Man, where should I start? One night this chick came up to me backstage, so I took her to the bus and fucked her. We're just about done when all of a sudden our security guard comes back in the lounge of the bus and tells me that she's got to go — NOW. Her husband was at the door of the bus and was pissed. I come out of the lounge tucking my dick in my pants and I see this guy through the windshield and he's steaming. His lady gets her clothes on and as soon as she steps out of the bus, without a word, her husband decks her, just like that. All I could think was, "Welcome to the world of Mötley Crüe."

Here's how much of a stud Tommy is: We're in Salt Lake City and I bring these two girls on the bus, hoping to get something going. One of them sees Nikki and she's off to the other bus, chasing him around. Her friend is still with me, and she says, as soon as we're alone, "I'm going to fuck you." I say, "Okay. Do you want a drink?" I hop off the bus to get a mixer and I see Tommy go up in there. I'm gone from the bus for maybe three minutes and by the time I get back in there, no one is around, but I hear something going down in the back room. I walk back there and the chick is standing on the couch holding on to the roof of the bus while Tommy is behind her just bangin' her. He was going so hard that the chick ripped a lighted panel out of the ceiling in the lounge. Mormon chicks are fucking insane.

I THINK EVERY STATE SHOULD BE DRY.

One time we were rolling down the highway while in the other bus, Nikki is sitting going over figures with the business manager. Our bus is full of girls and the music, the lava lamps, and the disco-light system we have are bumpin'— it's a full-on party in the middle of the day. Nikki looks up from his meeting as we pass them, and he sees all of these girls hanging out of the windows. The look on his face is priceless: He gets on our bus the next day and tells us he fucking hates us.

> Change "while" to "whilst"? "Whilst"? This isn't Shakespeare, Sherlock. Don't you at least need to be a knight to use a word like that? Should we change all the "comes" to "cometh" whilst we're at it? Save that shit for Sir Elton John's and Sir Paul McCartney's autobiographies, Squire.

I won't say what city we were in because I don't want to get anyone in trouble, but at one stop some cops from the bomb squad paid us a visit because they heard that Tommy likes explosives. They just hand him a brown bag full of these things that are bigger than M80s—they're like a half stick of dynamite each. It didn't take Tommy long to get into those. We're in Chicago and I'm fucking the shit out of this chick when I hear the biggest fucking *boom*, and then another one, and then another one. The next day, I'm hanging out with some of our crew outside, checking out the divots those bombs took out of the street. Right then, Tommy's in our bus about half a block away when *boom!*, he drops another one. The bus driver, who is one of the guys standing next to me, suddenly screams and falls to the ground because a piece of the street has just blown a huge hole in his arm. Poor fucker.

Tommy was definitely crazy for fireworks—he blew like $2,000 bucks on them in Virginia Beach. Our back lounge was like a fort—every cabinet stuffed with mortar rockets, Roman candles, firecrackers. We had it all.

The biggest bomb he dropped on that tour wasn't even an explosive. We get to Hiroshima, Japan, and T-Bone gets a genius idea that he keeps to himself. He talks to the sound guy and changes the intro music. As we come onstage—and I couldn't fucking believe this—the Gap Band's "You Dropped a Bomb on Me" is pumping through the PA. I turn around and he's just sitting back there behind the drums laughing his ass off. I'm standing in front of eight thousand Japanese fans thinking, "This is not going to be a good night." Somehow though, it was.

After the show, I ended up hanging out at some club with this American model who was living over there and after I liquored her up, we're leaving when I see on the club's board that the Vince Neil Band is playing the following week. I say something about it and she says to me, "Oh, I'm going to see that show." So I tell her to say hi to Vince for me and that Vince and I go way back. A week later I get a call from her and she's pissed. "You're an asshole," she says. "I went up to Vince Neil and told him 'John Corabi says hi.' He said to me, 'Who?' I said, 'John Corabi, the singer for Mötley Crüe. He says hello.' " When she said that to Vince, he said, "Fuck you, I'm the singer for Mötley Crüe!" He flipped a table over, threw a bottle at her, cut his hand open, and went completely insane.

* * *

Thanks John, you're a good man and a very talented musician. Thank you for the music, for being my accomplice, and for remembering the details that I forgot. And good luck.

That tour was called *Anywhere There's Electricity* and it happened in 1994. It was the last tour I did with Mötley in my full-on debaucherous single-guy mode, after I ended the year of complete sobriety that followed our recording *Dr. Feelgood* in 1988. In 1995, I met Pamela Anderson, the woman who became my wife and with whom I share two beautiful sons. But that's a story that deserves its own chapter, if not its own book.

Mötley was a powerful force from beginning to end and I can't explain how rad it is to hear from fans that our music was the soundtrack to some of the highest points of their lives. We had the power to move people, and onstage you could feel it—on our best nights, it felt like we might lose control of the energy we were sending out. And sometimes we did.

We have been charged several times by the authorities for inciting a riot, two of which in particular happened in Charlotte, North Carolina, and in Las Vegas at the Aladdin Hotel.

In Charlotte, in 1997, during the show, we noticed that this one black security guard was punching a girl in the face in the front row. Nikki decided to stop the show and call that motherfucker out. He said, "Anybody who hits a girl is a nigger." Uh-oh, here we go. It was on. The guard jumped up onstage and went after Nikki. Vince and Mick bailed, but I hopped over the drums and got my boy's back because shit was about to get ugly. Nikki had his bass by the neck like a baseball bat, looking like he wanted to hit a homerun with the guy's melon. I jump in and start throwing my drink at the security guy to let him know that Nikki wasn't alone and that he'd better chill out. By that time, our security had grabbed the guy and calmed him down. They got him offstage and off the premises real quick. A couple of days later we were served with a lawsuit. We spent a lot of money to make it go away.

The Las Vegas incident happened in 1999 during Mötley's *Greatest Hits* tour. That ruckus was as loud and as gaudy as Vegas can be, and let me tell you, what happens in Vegas doesn't always stay in Vegas. We were told before the show that we would be the last band to ever play the original Aladdin Hotel before it was torn down and remodeled. That's why we agreed to play. Being the nice guys that we are, we figured we and our fans should lend a hand in the remodeling. Nikki gets on the mike and, of course, announces that the building we're all standing in will be torn down. "We're the last band that will ever play here," he says. "So I want you all to help tear this motherfucker up." And they did. Our fans went crazy—they ripped seats out of the floor and pay phones off the wall, basically destroying the fucking place. The next day, we found out that the Aladdin was remodeling everything BUT the arena we'd just played in. Oh damn. You should have seen the shopping list of destruction that showed up at our office: clean-up charges, union expenses, phones, walls, seats, and personal injuries out the ass. If Mötley did a residence at the Aladdin Hotel, Celine Dion style, starting now . . . maybe we'd break even in 2010.

The *Greatest Hits* tour was the last I'd do with Mötley Crüe and that night in Vegas was the end of the line for me. The tour was booked while I was in jail that summer for violating my probation and pleading no contest to spousal abuse (to avoid a serious gun rap). To be honest, I didn't want to do the tour, but I felt like I couldn't let my brothers down. "Fuck it," I thought, "one last rip playing the greatest hits would be good for me." You have no idea how bad and how hard I wanted to hit those drums after being locked up.

Speaking of hitting, that's why I left the tour early. After the Aladdin demolition derby, we were shuttled to the airport to go home for a day or two. We're sitting in the airport because we're flying a commercial airline home. Ashley from our management office came up and gave me my tickets. Vince starts yelling at her, saying, "Why are you kissing Tommy's ass? Why are his tickets ready before mine?" He is going off on Ashley, who works for us, and I tell him to relax. I say, "Who gives a shit whose tickets are ready first? We're all getting on the same plane, dude." Vince is not having it and he tells me to fuck off. Uh-oh. I say, "Do NOT tell me to fuck off, dude." And what does he say to that? "Fuck off. What are you gonna do, hit me?" I said, "No, I'm not gonna hit you. You just need to fucking calm down."

Blam! He cracked me right in the face, right there in front of the ticket counter at the gate while the passengers waiting to board freaked out. That was it, I was done, I couldn't deal with him or this situation anymore. I tackled him, put him in a headlock, jacked my fist back, and thought, "This is worth going back to jail for." Before I could send Vince off to the land of emergency rooms and white coats, my security guy Hawk—thank God—grabbed me by the neck and the shirt and while he's carrying me onto the plane, I'm watching Vince standing there, all puffed up, screaming at the top of his lungs. "Police!" he shouts, with his wife/chick du jour he flew in for the night/whatever standing there next to him. "I've been assaulted!" he says over and over. "I've been assaulted! Police!" The last thing I saw before he fell out of view was him standing there with no one coming to his rescue—not even an airport rent-a-cop.

Everyone knew damn well that since I was on probation, if I got into any kind of trouble at all on that tour, I was going back to the Gray Bar Motel. Vince and I had had our run-ins before when our egos clashed. I had known him since high school and I had never approved of how he treated people. The more money and fame we got, the worse he was to anyone and everyone. He yelled at everybody and I never dug that, but trying to send me back to jail was it for me. Right there in the terminal that day, it was clear to me that Vince did not give a flying fuck about me. I sat down in my seat and was steaming when Nikki came on the plane. He took one look at me and he knew the tour was over, that was it, my ass was goin' home—and staying there. Nikki tried to play referee, coaxing me to bite the bullet and finish the dates, but this wasn't one I was willing to take for the team. "I quit," I said. "I don't need this shit anymore."

I got home and the phone started ringing off the hook as my band members and management tried to reach out to me to talk me into finishing up the last twelve dates on our tour. I didn't answer the phone and when I did, I just said, over and over, "There's no way. I'm done."

I wasn't done—at some point I realized I'd feel better about the situation if I finished what I had started. I thought about the fans who had bought tickets to see Mötley play their greatest hits and I wasn't going to let one asshole ruin it for all those people. So I decided I'd do it—with a fucking laundry list of conditions. I demanded my own bus, my own dressing room, and that management and security made sure that Vince and I did not come in contact at any time before or after the show. Still, it sucked being onstage with him. I was doing everything that I said I would never do: I was faking it because even though I didn't want to be there, the show must go on. The fans had no clue, but I felt like a fucking whore up there every night and I counted down the shows until it was over.

I don't know why I was surprised. There had been beef between Vince and me for years. We recorded Dr. Feelgood, our most successful album and tour, completely sober—and it wasn't easy to be straight for that year. At every hotel we checked into, our travel agents and tour managers made sure that all the liquor was removed from the minibars, and in our dressing rooms, where Nikki and I used to have a bottle of Jack Daniel's each, there was no booze to be found. Hell, Nikki and I would chug an entire bottle of Jack onstage just a few years ago. Mötley world had become a ghost town with no liquor stores. In Hawaii, we scheduled a few days off before the final two nights of the tour and we did it right: We rented Ferraris, hot rods, and Harleys, cruised around, and hung out on the beach. That night Vince and I went in search of tits and ended up at a strip club, which is probably the hardest place to be sober. There we are with all these fine-ass girls parading around us like stallions to every strip club's theme song, "Girls, Girls, Girls."

GO T-BONE.
TELL THEM YOU WROTE THAT ONE, DUDE!
FINE, I WILL!
HE WROTE THAT FUCKING SONG.
IT RULES! HE WROTE IT FOR ME!

When the waitress came around with a rack of irresistible test-tube shots, Vince and I looked at each other and said, "Fuck it." Between the chicks and our dicks, there was no way we weren't drinking. It was on.

THANK GOD! IT WAS A LONG YEAR, PEOPLE.

It was fucking awesome, but the whole time while we were whooping it up, I kept thinking about the other guys in the band who were back at the hotel, sober. What was I going to tell them?

The next day, me, Mr. Honest Guy had to confess.

DUMB-ASS!

The whole band is in the dressing room and I'm sitting there hung the fuck over. I say, "I've got something to tell you guys. I'm sorry I let you guys down, but last night I got fucked up at a titty bar." Vince is standing right there and he says along with the other guys, "That's okay, dude. You fucked up, but that's cool." I'm waiting there, ashamed, bumming, looking at Vince. That's tight. I look right at him and say, "Thanks, bro, right on." Dick. He never said a word about it, that fucker. I put myself out there to be straight with the brotherhood and he sat there and watched me do it. I'm convinced that he was drinking here and there behind closed doors throughout the tour. The craziest thing was when I looked at him at that moment he looked at me like I was on crack. He looked violated, like, "Why are you looking at me? I didn't do shit last night." Yeah, you did, dude. But whatever.

After that I was officially out of Mötley Crüe and since then people have not stopped asking me to sum up what it was like. I always tell them this: I have been everywhere and I've seen nothing. I've seen so many hotels and arenas that they're all just one big room to me now. I saw a few road signs too, and a couple of menus. There wasn't much time for sightseeing. I've made up for it since, but it's crazy to think about how many times I went around the world with Mötley and how little I saw of it. Most of the landscapes I remember are framed by a van, limo, or plane window. And no matter where I was, the exact same deli tray was waiting backstage. Yuck.

One thing I don't miss about being in Mötley Crüe is seeing Vince's bloated, disrespectful, fucking ass every day, and it's too bad that after knowing each other for so long, we haven't found a way to get along. Who knows? Maybe someday we will—and I hope we do. I am happy that since the old days ended, I lose less clothes than I used to. From the beginning to the very end of my touring days with the band, I can't tell you how many times I woke up to find that the chick I had brought back to my room and the clothes I was wearing the night before were gone. Usually I didn't have a lot of clothes on to begin with, so losing even one item sometimes meant full nudity. It became a little strategy game: trying to get laid without losing my pants. Those girls would take anything—my shirt, my pants, my shoes, my underwear if I was wearing any. I tried to stay aware enough to hear them when they left my room or I'd try to remember to leave my clothes where I'd be able to find them when I made my escape. But it was always a losing battle. Let me tell you, it's pretty fucked to wake up naked with no pants in sight. It's much better to wake up in the morning to find that the Japanese fan you brought home has folded all your clothes, cleaned your room, didn't take anything, and is completely gone. They're so respectful! Arigato!

What I *did* see every night and that always blew me away was Mick Mars's playing. He is one of the most underrated guitar players of the era. His riffs on the Mötley records are amazing. His tone sounds like two or three guys playing at the same time. He took blues guitar and gave it a facelift and plugged it through more Marshall stacks than God on distortion. And nobody gave him props. Maybe it was because he was the quiet guy. Maybe it was because he refused to do interviews, stayed as far in the background as he could and loved the dark. He wasn't the most popular Mötley member, but he didn't give a fuck because he doesn't like people—and I think they could tell. He is the fucking loner vampire of all time, the recluse of all reclusives—that cat does not like people at all, any people, anywhere, any time, any of them, ever. I can relate to that and generally I think people suck. But if you take that feeling too far, you'll end up at home, alone, every day, never seeing anyone. In my mind, whenever I hear myself saying that people suck, I always add that *most* people suck—but not everyone.

I'm a lot like Mick in one way: I'm definitely an agoraphobic.* If you rolled with me for a day to the mall, the supermarket, or a rock show, you'd see why I like meeting people, but *it* tends to get weird real quick.

---

* ag·o·ra·pho·bi·a [Greek agor, marketplace; see ger- in Indo-European Roots + -pho-bia]: an abnormal fear of open or public places. Ago·ra·phobic, adj., n. (*The American Heritage Dictionary of the English Language, Fourth Edition*; Copyright 2000 by Houghton Mifflin Company.)

Funny thing about my agoraphobia is that I live in the town of Agoura. How fucked up is that?

But Mick's agoraphobia is different: He's got hate mixed in there, a kind of redneckish, unfriendly, pick-up-truck-with-a-gun-rack vibe. He grew up in Indiana so I guess it's in the blood. He would never in his life walk up to someone and say, "Hey, dude, what's happening?" He was cool with those of us in the band and our inner circle, but whenever anyone outside our little army spoke to him his reaction was, "What the fuck do you want?" I fucking love that about him. That is what makes Mick one of the most unique, amazing people I know. I wouldn't change a thing about him.

As much as there are times when I wish I could get Mick to be a little less Mick and come out and participate in the world, I will never be mad at him for being the way he is. He just wants to be home and if he's not home, he just wants to be inside playing video games or his guitar until it's dark. I used to stop by his room when we were touring and invite him out to the pool, trying to lure him out there by telling him about all the girls lying around with us, and he'd look at me like I was crazy and say, "What? Dude, I don't go out unless it's fucking dark." He'd lie around in a white robe, with black socks and black sunglasses on, with all the shades drawn, watching *Three Stooges* reruns over and over and over. He hated it when I would open the curtains and let some light in. "What are you doing? I hate light. I hate everybody. I hate everything." It was gnarly. I'd say, "All righty then! See you, bro!" When Mick did have to go out in daylight, he always wore a black hat pulled way down and the biggest, darkest pair of sunglasses he could find. He'd keep those glasses on all night sometimes.

Everyone always asks about it and once it almost happened. For my forty-first birthday I jammed with Sammy Hagar, Jerry Cantrell, and Chad Smith from the Chili Peppers down in Cabo San Lucas, Mexico, where Sammy has his club, Cabo Wabo. Sammy called me to come down and celebrate my birthday with him. We're both Libras, we get along, and we've always wanted to jam together and never had the chance. It coincided with the end of writing this book, so I was like, "Fuck yeah!" I grabbed Anthony and we bailed to Cabo the day we handed this book in.* We were ready for a long-awaited celebration after working for four months.

Sammy does this birthday bash for himself every year. It's two weeks long, he gives away all the tickets for free, first come, first serve. It's crazy—people fly in from all over the place. He's got so many friends who come down to celebrate and play with his band that Sammy's party turns into a freestyle jam, and if you're not there for the music, you've got no business being there. There's no money to make, no interviews to do, we just rock shit, party, drink tequila, soak up the sun, and dread the day that we have to go home.

When we got there, Sammy informed me that he had intended a whole other kind of birthday present. He had talked to the other guys in the Crüe because his plan was to surprise me with a cake and a reunion. I just looked at him and tripped. I couldn't believe he would go that far to freak me out. I just sat there going, "Woah." Then I thought, "Woah, hey, that would be kinda cool." Well, it didn't happen. Let's just say that ninety-five percent of the Crüe was down, the other five percent wanted a contract and payment up front.

This story doesn't fit too well. This is the chapter about Mötley, right? This story is about a Mötley reunion that almost happened. Where should we put it? It stays. It definitely stays, Limey.

---

* Tommy is correct on the date, which was October 2, 2003. And let it be known that the trip was more fun than humans should be allowed to have. For the record: "big ups" to Tequila Sheila (hope that shoulder healed nicely), Stalker Steve, Date Rape Dan, and the mustached father of two who drunkenly slid naked down the slide at the pool in broad daylight because someone (it might have been me) asked him to. Go ye in peace and prosper wherever ye may be. Let it be known that those nicknames have not been changed and bear no resemblance whatsoever to the actual names of the individuals referenced therein.

From 1980 to 1999 Mötley Crüe was epic. It was half my life. We've already published the autobiography of the band and it's still not summed up. How can I condense that much time into words or anything that will make sense to anyone else? Well . . . I'm going to try. Thank you, Nikki, Mick, and yes, even you, Vince, for all of it—*it* being everything you could ever possibly imagine: all your dreams and goals achieved with three other guys who came, saw, and kicked the world's ass. Thank you for something that every guy wants: a brotherhood, a gang, a home away from home, the biggest block party ever, and all the rad shit that comes with being a rock star! It was us against the world, we made the rules, we broke the rules, and loved every fucking minute of it. Thanks for the music, the money, MTV, the cars, the mansions, the fame, the fortune, the tits, the ass, the drugs, the drama, the crabs, the roaches, the poverty, the pillage, the hairspray, the drum kits from hell, the parties from heaven, the stack of multiplatinum albums, the fans, the road crew who did the impossible, the history, the pyro, the porno, the private jets, the fights, the love, the blood, and if I went on, the scroll would hit the floor and the credits would roll forever. All I can say is what we said every December: Have a Mötley Christmas and a Happy Crüe year.

9

STATE OF LAWLESSNESS

a.k.a.
THE CODE OF THE ROAD

I could never fucking relate to the dudes who were married and doing all kinds of fucked up shit on the road. They didn't seem to think so, but it fucks with your mind, and it sure as hell fucks with your relationship. What the fuck is the point of getting married if you plan on fucking around? I'm not naming names, but I've seen guys do crazy shit I really couldn't believe. Their wives would be coming up the elevator while band security took hookers out of their rooms and tossed them down the stairwell. That's not just wrong, it's fucking *insane*.

Worst of all, I always got stuck talking to my bandmates' wives while their husbands were off fucking groupies, or "girlfriends," who lived in whatever city we were in. Now that shit *sucks*. When you're in a band, you're in a family, so my friends' wives were my friends and they'd always feel comfortable asking me what their man was up to on the road. What the hell was I supposed to say? I'd hear myself mumbling some transparent lie like, "Um, hey, sweetie, you should probably talk to him about that because I don't really know what the fuck he does." I just couldn't understand how a guy could have his wife join him on tour while he fucked everything with a pulse backstage, even while she was around. Those situations are such a mindfuck because your morals are at stake on the one hand and your professional relationships are at stake on the other. Aside from the music, a successful band is a fucking business that keeps its members paid and no one wants to fuck up their livelihood. But it is a tall order to tell a woman who deserves respect and who is either completely in the dark or holding on to some vision of reality that is so not what is really going on. These women would always be so psyched to be on the road for a few days watching their husbands rock shit. They're at the side of the stage, all happy, never knowing that band security strategically parked them there early so their husbands can get in a quickie in the dressing room before the show. I'd watch it all go down but I'd never say shit.

Sometimes I didn't have to say shit. Some guys' wives had a fire burning in their eyes that said, "I *know* that motherfucker. I know he's lying, and I *know* you're lying." Girls have radar, they know. I'm a shitty liar, I didn't stand a chance.

Touring is fucking lawless, so you've got to show up with your own set of rules. When I first started touring, I was seventeen, so I learned as I went, and it wasn't always easy. When your life is lived out of a suitcase, and some days you're too wasted to even open it before you're off again, shit gets weird. Every night after our show, we'd party all night in whatever town we were in—and when we were really in tour mode I didn't even know what town it was—then show up in a new town the next morning, rock the fuck out of it, fuck the fuck out of it, and move on again. The only constants are a tour bus, a private plane, the show, and the after-party, as well as the after-the-after-party party, the before-traveling-again party, the pre-preshow-party party, and, of course, the preshow party. It's like traveling in a human aquarium where you can see out but no one can get in and touch you unless you want them to. It's a circus with every vice on tap, and you're the ringleader. Believe me, you get worshiped in all kinds of weird ways that change you, no matter who you are.

I'm not big on rules and regulations, but the one rule I have for myself is that I am monogamous when I am in a relationship. That's it—everything else is up for grabs. I'm one of the horniest, most sexually interested people I know. But if you're really in love, it isn't hard to be monogamous. My rule has its downside: It fucking sucks on the road when all I've got is long-distance love because the phone is *wack*. I don't like talking on it *ever*, and trying to maintain an intimate relationship for weeks or months at a time using a telephone, when the only body I want to be next to is so far away, is fucking torture. Plus there are so many beautiful women who want to play that temptation is everywhere. It's a test of character and of a relationship every single night. All I can say is, watching is good. Watching doesn't count . . . does it? I used to believe that head didn't count. Then I thought about turning the tables, and when I pictured someone else eating my girl's pussy, I changed my mind. Yes, head counts. Head *really counts.*

There's an old saying that's been said in many ways: What happens on the road stays on the road. Las Vegas stole that shit from us, please believe. But I guess Mötley owed the city—well, at least the Aladdin Hotel. We pushed that rule to the limit too. One of my bandmates took the pursuit of pussy to a whole new level. I am going to omit the names here to protect the innocent. Fuck the innocent, I'm just protecting myself, because this next story has lawsuit stamped all over it—and I sure as fuck don't need another one of those. There was one guy in the band who was married but couldn't seem to get enough of matrimony. This guy had more than what I'd call a mistress—in fact, he had more than one of them. He'd set these girls up with apartments, jewelry, clothes—all of it. And then, he'd drop the Big Lie™. A girl would come rushing into our dressing room backstage and show off her new engagement ring to the rest of the band. We'd be totally silent, like, "Oh . . . right on." It always ended up bad, of course, because he was already married! Duh! It was just a matter of time before the girls would rush into our dressing room again, asking us all what happened and wondering why he broke it off. Well, let me see, hmm, I don't know . . . uh, maybe . . . let me see . . . maybe because . . . he's *married?* How could she not know that? It wasn't hard to find out. And what the hell was that guy *thinking* anyway? What can I say, we were young and it's only human to make mistakes. You never know, maybe he was thinking of moving to Utah and converting to Mormonism.*

---

* Mormonism is a religion based on Mormon, an ancient prophet believed to have compiled a sacred history of the Americas, which was "translated" by Joseph Smith in 1830 and called the Book of Mormon. The religion once allowed men to marry multiple women though it no longer does. For a detailed exposé on the history of Mormonism, consult your local library. For a sick, satirical analysis of the same, see the animated series *South Park* episode "All About Mormons."

10

STATE OF MATRIMONY: THE SEQUEL

a.k.a.
PAMELA

It's time for me to admit something: I have a terrible memory. I'm not sure if I've always had a terrible memory—because I just can't remember—but I do know that I have a bad one now. Whether it is just my nature or my lifestyle—or both—here I am, and a lot of days I don't recall the fine print. So I'm dialing in Pamela for some assistance in this chapter. Do you guys know Pamela? My ex-wife Pamela Anderson? You've definitely seen her—she was on *Baywatch* and *V.I.P.*, and she's been on the cover of *Playboy* quite a few times. She's hot, dude, and she's going to interrupt me when things get blurry.

Pamela and I met on New Year's Eve, 1994. I was chilling, just having a good time with my friends at this club called Sanctuary that she partly owned. I was not at all in meeting-you mode. I was single and recently divorced from Heather Locklear, so I wanted nothing to do with getting involved with a new girl at all. Then here comes a shot of Goldschläger, that crazy cinnamon schnapps with the gold flakes in it. The people who make that shit should sponsor both of us and keep our freezers packed for life. The shot was from Pamela. I was like, "*Whoa*, right on!" I asked the waitress if Pamela was at the club and she pointed out where she was sitting across the room, drinking it up with a bunch of her girlfriends—and no dudes at the table. I grab my bottle of Cristal, slam the shot, and go over and sit right next to her. I don't say hello. I don't say a word. I just lick the side of her face like a fucking big dog. She's like, "Oh my *God!*" and her friends start freaking out, just shaking their heads and saying to her, "No, no, no, no, NO!" They are not happy at all when I bite an E in two and put half in her mouth.

Pamela: Tommy thought that he was the only one I sent the shot to. I had sent Goldschläger to everybody in the whole club, not just him. He didn't know this either, but as he was flying across the room with the bottle of Cristal in his hand, there were two or three guys behind him heading my way, trying to do the same thing and thank me personally. Tommy just got there first. I don't remember anymore who the other guys were, but they weren't nearly as cute as Tommy, so it was fine with me that he won the race.

I had not tried Ecstasy before, and he did not give me any that night. All of Tommy's crazy friends were doing it though.

Whatever, Pamela. You swallowed some—you know you did. But that's cool.

Pamela: Tommy sat down and licked my face, so I licked my girlfriend next to me, then she licked our friend next to her, and we went around in a circle like that for a while. Then Tommy slammed his shot and threw the glass at the bar, breaking all kinds of glasses and bottles. He said, "What can I say? I am Greek and I'm happy! And when we're happy, we break shit!" And then he shouted, "Opa!" That's when I looked at my girlfriend who just started shaking her head and saying, "N-O, NO." But I didn't care. I was looking at him, thinking, "Hm, this is interesting." I was also thinking, "I am one of the club owners and I am going to have to pay for all that."

I hung with her all night. At around two in the morning she's ready to bail and I'm not having that at all. I walk her to the car and plant a kiss on her. She's like, "I think I'd better go." I'm like, "Oh my God, *no*. No *way*. *Please* don't go." She was flying to Cancún to work the next day. I wasn't having that either.

Pamela: I was *not* going to Cancún the next day. He's confused, again. He followed me to Cancún a month later. He really needs to start taking that Ginkgo biloba I gave him. I didn't stay around at the club too much longer. I took off because I had to be up early in the morning. I didn't stay around until two in the morning either, like he thinks I did. And Tommy is forgetting something else: He hadn't just broken up with Heather Locklear and he wasn't single. He was going out with someone named Bobbie Brown at the time—and she was at the club with him that night, circling our table the entire time.

Pamela's friends, by the way, were not having me—at *all*. That whole night they were just trying to make whatever was happening between us stop. Her best friend, Melanie, hated me from the beginning and kept hating me for a long time. She is one of those controlling personalities and it was obvious to me right away. Pamela told me later that that night Melanie kept shaking her head and telling her, "Pamela, he is fucking *trouble*. You are not going *anywhere* with him." I didn't give a fuck. I asked Pamela for her number. And after I got it, I started calling it right away. It wasn't even an hour later and I was like, "Hey, what are you doing?" She's packing, getting ready to bounce to Cancún, and I'm like, "Without me?" She just kept saying, "I have to work. I can't hang out with you, I have to work. Do *not* come to Cancún."

Pamela: Like I said, he's confused. I had heard about Tommy when I used to hang out at a place called Bar 61. One of the owners there knew him and told me that he really wanted to meet me, even though he was still married to Heather Locklear at the time. I knew he was in Mötley Crüe, but I didn't know much about the band. I just knew that Tommy was a dark-haired guy, that he was married, and that he wanted to meet me, so I thought, "Eeew." The night I met him he told me he wasn't married anymore, but that "eeew" idea of him was still in my mind.

After I left the club that night, I went back to the Hotel Nikko. I was staying there with my girlfriend because my condo was getting redone. I had told Tommy that I was there under my own name and the whole ride back my girlfriend Melanie just kept saying, "No, no, NO. He's trouble." Tommy did start calling immediately—he's got that right. He called and called, leaving about twenty messages, just drunk dialing. One of them was him singing his version of the Oscar Mayer theme song: "My baloney has a first name, it's L-A-R-G-E. My baloney has a second name, it's P-E-N-I-S. I like to use it every day, and if you ask me why, I'll saaay, "Cuz my Large Penis has a way with P-U-S-S-Y today!"

HAND ME THE MIKE, BRO! YOU KNOW I CAN SING!

Actually that was the message that got me interested. I call him back as Melanie sits there shaking her head and I tell him, "I'll spend twenty-four hours with you and that's it. Then I never want to see you again." Tommy said, "Okay, fine. I'll pick you up tomorrow." He promised to make me chicken cacciatore or some other famous dish of his that he cooks up in a Crock-Pot. Melanie and I have been best friends for twenty-five years and that night is the only time we've ever fought. I still had a few

It's ON!!

drinks in me, so when she told me I was crazy for even talking to him, we got into a full-on screaming argument.

I woke up the next day and thought, "Oh, shit, what did I do?" The phone started ringing soon afterwards, and it was Tommy calling over and over. He was saying things like, "Where are you? I'm gonna find you. I'm coming over there to pick you up." He was being psychotic, and it was a little scary. I tell my girlfriend to tell him that I'm not there. She takes the next call and tells Tommy that I'm getting my nails done. He says, "Where?" Melanie is caught off guard, so she says I'm at the salon in the hotel. He hangs up and calls back a minute later. "Put her on," he says. "There's no salon in the hotel." We bolt right away because he's coming to get me for his twenty-four hours. I heard later that he'd made a few pit stops—one of them was at a sex shop called the Pleasure Chest, where he bought chains and stuff. I'm sure they went to good use, but he didn't use them on me, not the next time we saw each other at least.

BUT WE DID USE THEM ALL RIGHT.
YOU KNOW WE DID. AFTER YOU BLEW US OFF,
WE HEADED BACK TO THE BEACH HOUSE OF
SIN AND CALLED A PORN STAR.
CHECK THE STORY A FEW CHAPTERS BACK.
ACTUALLY, LET'S READ IT AGAIN.
IT IS ONE OF MY FAVORITE
MISTY WATER-COLORED MEMORIES,
ONE OF THOSE TIMES T-BONE AND
I REALLY SAW EYE-TO-EYE.

A month passed before I spoke to Tommy again. I don't know how he got my home number but he did.

What are you talking about, baby? You gave me your home number the first night I met you. Maybe *you* need some ginkgo biloba. Whatever.

Pamela: I had a system—when someone important like my manager would call me, he'd call, hang up, and call again right away. A month later, that's what Tommy did, so I picked up the phone and he said, "Hey, what's going on? What are you doing?" I was literally walking out the door to go to Cancún to work. I say, "No. I've gotta go, I'm going to Cancún right now, I've gotta work." And he says, "You're going to Cancún without me?" I freaked out and said, "Don't you dare come. I don't want you there." And as I'm hanging up the phone, I hear him say, "Okay. I'm coming."

To me, that meant get your ass to Cancún *immediately*. I hang up, turn to my buddy Bobby, who's hanging with me, and tell him to go home, pack a bag, and call our friend Doug because the three of us are going to Mexico—*now*. I keep calling Pamela all the way down there—in the car, in the airport, on the plane. I'm calling about every twenty minutes. I keep leaving messages saying things like, "I'm on my way," "I'm on the plane now," "I'm here," "Where are you?" We check into a hotel and I call every hotel in Cancún until I find hers. I've left so many messages that she is either too scared to answer her phone or pretty fucking confident that I'm so insane that I will find her no matter where she is. I do find her hotel, of course, and I leave a message and start waiting.

Pamela: I told security at the hotel that if they saw anyone with tattoos hanging around, not to let him in. I didn't sign in under my real name, and I tried to make myself hard to find. Tommy kept leaving messages on my home phone, saying things like, "I'm

It's
ON!!

on the plane," "I'm having a shot of whiskey," "I'm at my layover
in Miami," "Hey, I'm here!" I was convinced that he was really
crazy.

I'm out of my mind and I really don't know what to do. My buds
and I are chillin' poolside, eating, swimming, and getting stupid. Every
twenty minutes I go back to my room, hoping to see that little red
light blinking on the phone. I think about going to her hotel, but I don't
want to *totally* be Mr. Stalker Guy. But *fuck*, I want to see her. I *have* to
see her.

I run back and forth to my room like a jackass for a few hours until, finally, the red light is blinking. I'm like, "Yes! That's *awesome!*" It's
Pamela, she's in her room, and she says that I should call her back. *Yes!*

Pamela: I had brought a few friends with me, and on the last night I
was in Cancún we went out with a client and the guys were so
boring that I was falling asleep at the dinner table. I tell my girlfriends we should meet Tommy and his friends for a drink because nothing could happen—we were leaving the next day. We
ditched those guys, went back to the hotel, and I left Tommy a
message. Within five minutes he called back.

After I get her message, I don't call her back right away. I just chill for
two hours. I take a bath, I read for a while. I call my mom, I meditate, and
do some yoga. I pull a horseshoe out of my ass. And if you believe that
crap, I've got some swampland in Florida to sell ya.

I call her back *so fuckin' quick*. I don't need a pen, paper, nothing. Her number is so important that for once, my short-term memory
works. Waiting for her to answer, I'm pacing back and forth so crazy
that I rip the phone right off the nightstand. She answers and I just
say, "Dude, I'm here." She pauses for a long minute and then she says,
"You are fucking out of your mind." I go, "I know. Are you done working yet?"

She was there with three of her girlfriends and she told them to get ready because they were all going out for just *one* drink with Tommy. It would be fine, what could it hurt? We met at the Ritz-Carlton and I was wearing a tank top, of course, so they kicked us out.

Pamela: Tommy shows up with his friends and all of them look the same — white tank tops, tattoos, jeans, and wallet chains. I wasn't sure which one he was. None of them had jackets so we had to leave the Ritz-Carlton. We went somewhere really classy after that.

We ended up somewhere ridiculous like Señor Frogs or something stupid like that. That one drink turns into many drinks, and we move on to this massive club called La Boom, which is a loud as fuck dance club. We ran into someone with some E and all I remember about that night is Pamela and I staring into each other's eyes for hours, only taking breaks to blink and drink. I *had* to marry her. *Right now*, in Mexico, as soon as fucking possible. I'm definitely my father's son — he knew he wanted to marry my mom the first time he laid eyes on her.

Pamela: We go to La Boom and I'm wearing Lucite heels and a miniskirt so small that, really, it's more like a belt. My girlfriends are dancing on the tables and there's a bikini contest going on. It ended up that those girls became our wedding party — the winner of the contest was my maid of honor because we needed people. We stayed for another four days. That first night at La Boom, we were drinking champagne and I didn't know it, but one of Tommy's friends was breaking capsules of Ecstasy into my drinks. I had never done any drugs before so I didn't know what was happening. I was always against drugs and really, really strict, like Ms. Put You in Rehab if it seemed like someone had a problem at all.

Tommy and I locked eyes, and it was one of those really romantic things that felt like love at first sight. It might have been the chemicals but when he looked at me and said, "I've never felt like this before. I want to marry you," I said, "I've never felt like this before either. I want to marry you."

I turn to my friend Bobby and ask him to give me the ring off his pinky. I put it on her and ask her if she'll marry me. She says yes, and four days later we did it. But first, we went back to her hotel and it was fucking insane. She was in the penthouse suite and the elevator went right into the room. It had a swimming pool in there and a huge sound system. It was fucking *sick!* That suite had everything you would ever need. That night we made love, and I couldn't believe I was fucking Pamela Anderson. Neither could my friends.

Pamela: We stayed together for four days and we didn't have sex until we were married, even though Tommy thinks we did. I had the penthouse suite, with a pool and everything. We'd party all day and go to La Boom at night, just back and forth, back and forth. We had the wildest time. I just thought we were madly in love — I had no idea that there were chemicals keeping me awake. I was taking baths all day long because my skin had never tingled so much. I was rubbing myself, I was rubbing him. We should have been two piles of dust we were rubbing each other so much. I could feel my nerve endings and every bump on my skin — I just thought that I was really in love. I definitely thought we had to get married. It was so intense that there was no way we could have sex right away. It took us a few days to even get there. We were too busy sucking every single hair and freckle on each other's bodies. I'm glad we waited until marriage — until it was proper in the eyes of the Lord.

WHATEVER, PAMELA.
I HAVE A BETTER MEMORY THAN EITHER
OF YOU TWO. TRUST ME,
THERE WAS SEX BEFORE MARRIAGE.
I WAS IN THERE, FRIENDS.
I CAN STILL SEE IT.
I COULD DRAW YOU A MAP IF YOU PAID ME.
THAT'S A JOURNEY I WON'T FORGET.
I TOO, WAS FUCKING PAMELA ANDERSON.

I'm with you on that, my man. We were totally in. The next morning after that first night, I watched Pamela go into the room connected to her suite where her girlfriends were staying and show them how big you are, using her hands like she'd just caught a huge trout. (She had.)

That morning her girlfriends were like "Woah, *hey!*" They were all the people who didn't want us to be together. Whatever. When all our friends were together having breakfast, Pamela and I told everyone we were getting married. They freaked.

Pamela: I remember being in the bathroom that day, and asking my girl-friends, "He's cute, right?" They were like, "Yeah, he's really cute." I said, "For real? Okay, I'm going to marry him."

There were things to take care of before our nuptials. We had to get blood tests—and we did, at like two in the morning in some scary, shady Mexican hospital.

Pamela: It was really shady. We walked up there, and I'm wearing huge heels and a miniskirt. I don't know why we thought we had to get

It's ON!!

blood tests. You don't even have to get blood tests in America to get a marriage license anymore.

Then we had to find a priest. It was now the weekend and also some Mexican holiday so all of the priests were busy. We called everywhere and finally found one. He came to the hotel, met with us, did the paperwork, and set a time. Pamela wanted to get married on the beach in bathing suits with cocktails. It was crazy. Neither one of us called our parents or any of our friends—we just did it. Everyone found out about it through the tabloids. Who knows how they got the pictures—we never saw anyone taking them. Sneaky bastards.

Pamela: We searched everywhere because priests don't work on Sundays in Mexico—I don't know why. We looked in phone books, we called the front desk. Tommy actually cried at one point because we couldn't find a priest and he wanted to do it so badly.

What? No I didn't. Are you just puffin' your chest up, baby? Isn't it already puffed up enough?

Pamela: We finally found a priest and we got married in lounge chairs, on the beach, drinking chi chis. We didn't realize that people recognized us until we had the ceremony. A crowd totally formed around us—a spring break kind of crowd. After we were married, Tommy picked me up and carried me into the water, and all those people followed us into the ocean and swam around us.

It was an amazing ceremony, right there on the beach in the late afternoon, just before sunset. I remember when the priest said, "You can now kiss the bride." I picked her up and carried her straight into the waves. We kissed, swam, and played in the water forever. Our friends were up on the sand, standing there waiting, like, "Are you guys done yet?"

Pamela: Afterwards, I called Melanie and she started crying. She was horrified that I got married without her. I called my mom and she threw the phone. She didn't come out of the house for two weeks. She lost twenty pounds. I called my brother, who was like, "Oh, cool." Then he called back and yelled at me, and said, "So, what's your last name going to be? I bet you haven't even thought about it."

Hey, Ms. Not Always Right, you didn't talk to your brother until we got home. Don't you remember sitting on the floor at my beach house while he yelled at you and you cried? It was gnarly. You called your parents from Cancún and I called mine. My parents said they were happy as long as I was happy. They were just bummed that they weren't there to see the ceremony.

While we're flying back home, Pamela is asking me where I live and what I like for breakfast. It was so bizarre—we clearly don't know each other at all. She asks me if we're going back to her place or to mine. I say, "Back to my place. I live on the beach in Malibu, right on the sand."

Pamela: I remember being on the plane and asking Tommy what our last name was going to be and he said Lee. I remember asking him if that was his last name—I'd always thought it wasn't. Then I asked him what he liked for breakfast and where he lived, because I had no idea. We didn't know anything about each other. I think it was the wildest, greatest thing I ever did.

When we land, there is a paparazzi feeding frenzy waiting for us in the airport. They follow us back to my house and camp out, and it is the beginning of all that fucking bullshit. We have to hire twenty-four-hour security guards to keep the photographers off the hills and the beach. I had to deal with that shit in my other marriage, but this was much, much worse. We are being stalked like you would not believe—and it's never let up to this day.

It's ON!!

Just before I met Pamela, I had found the place where I wanted to live and love. I put the place in escrow. I knew when I saw it that it would be my castle—and now I had found my queen. It was a house with no neighbors, on the top of a hill in Malibu. When I walked in, I noticed that every room was different—it wasn't your normal setup at all. Some rooms were round, some were angular, it had an elevator, there were different levels in the main rooms, and there was a lot of land ripe for whatever type of landscaping I could dream up. I've always loved designing my environment, whether it's my bedroom, my house, or just dimming the lighting in my hotel room by putting towels over the tops of lamps. This place had the potential I had been waiting for. You'd never guess it by looking at me, but I'm a closet horticulturalist. I love trees (don't tell anybody). When I saw the bald yard behind the house, all I could think about was going to a nursery and creating something you'd see in a postcard or at some four-star resort. I'd traveled constantly for so long that I wanted my home to feel like I was on vacation. And I knew what I wanted. I'd seen some of the most exotic places in the world on vacations over the years and had taken notes and shot pictures of the plants, trees, and architecture that I loved. I couldn't wait to show Pamela our future Love Palace.

Pamela: That house must be built over an Indian burial ground because it's got a good vibe, but everything we ever tried to do to it went wrong. There's just a lot of crazy stuff and a lot of energy there: We buried both the boys' placentas in the yard and I think it's some kind of spiritual land where someone was not properly buried or something before we lived there.

Woah, *hey!* Slow down, Ms. Jumping Ahead! That's how you feel now, but I don't remember you being spooked when we planned to start our life and family there.

Pamela: When Tommy took me up there for the first time, I was so excited. The place had the elevator and a few other things we kept, but it did not have one tree on the property. We would stand there and get so happy as every little bush or tree was planted. It was fun to buy a place and rebuild it together. We got way too excited about everything—way more than normal people do.

After we moved in, the two of us started redoing everything. All the walls were white, and when we walked through the house with our interior designer, I took a can of spray paint and wrote, "White walls are for hospitals" on them. The original doors were verde green—some Mexican or Mediterranean color of the month. It's like teal—and I *hate* teal.

ME TOO, BRO. IT'S A PARTY FOUL. MAKES ME AND THE BOYS WANT TO ROLL UP AND HIDE IN YOUR BELLY.

We redesigned our house from the ground up and we renamed it the Love Palace—because we made it that way. If you've seen *MTV Cribs*—and I know for a fact that those fuckers released my episode on DVD without breaking me off any extra change—you already know how fat this pad is. We did it right. We've got a movie room made of purple velvet where the couch is sunk in the floor and the subwoofers are under your ass. We tore out the original bedroom because it was all his-and-hers (What the fuck is that?) and made it one big Love Space. It has an open shower that you can see from anywhere in the room,

OH YEAH. PERFECT! GLAD YOU HEARD ME CALLIN' FOR THAT ONE.

a terrace, a fireplace, a mirror above the bed, and another one that slides across the window, triggered by remote control, by the massive round bathtub. We've got heart-shaped front doors made of glass and iron, a pillow room with a fireplace out of *I Dream of Jeannie*, and a thirty-foot swing in the round living room that hangs over my grand piano. Basically, we made it into a huge adult playground.

Everything was perfect in my mind. I was building my dream house with my dream girl—and I'd made sure she was that. There's one way to separate the beautiful women from the truly beautiful women and that is by their toes. If a girl's toes aren't lovely little piggies, she is completely off my radar no matter what she looks like. She can be Miss America, but if I look down and her feet are busted, it's *off.* Let me give you an example of the worst kind of toe jam: Picture clear plastic, high-ass, come-fuck-me stripper pumps with a set of crooked toes hangin' ten over the front. For God's sake, ladies, do what you have to do, because there has to be a solution. Is the shoe too big? I haven't worn pumps, but it seems to me that if they fit right, them thangs wouldn't slide out there on their own like that. When they do, it's like a fender bender: Everyone slows down to check it out then speeds up and moves on real quick, knowing that no one is hurt but the shit is mangled and in desperate need of a toe truck.* Pamela, my ex-wife, the mother of my kids, one of the most gorgeous women I have ever laid eyes on, has the *most* amazing toes. When we were together I had to keep myself from eating them right off her feet every fucking day. Dude, it was hard. Her toes are perfect. *Fuck,* her whole set of feet is rad. But I knew that before I met her. I'd seen nude pictures of her before we met and the first thing I did was clock her toes.

In the first few years of our marriage, Pamela and I had way too much

---

* Never fear, there are solutions. No-Slips are rubber inserts that adhere to the sole of an open-toed sandal or pump to form a clingy surface between foot and shoe. In field-testing conducted by experts at the Tommy Lee Finishing School for Female Feet, introduction of No-Slips has been found to greatly reduce toe-hang. In extreme instances, Lee's team of experts recommend the insertion of Toe-Beds, an orthopedic insole, into all closed-toe shoes to aid the prevention of painful corns, calluses, and unsightly toe-squish. Consult your local shoe salesman, pharmacist, or orthopedist for more information.

fun—more fun than humans are allowed to have. That very first year, for my thirtieth birthday, she threw me the raddest birthday party in the history of partying.

Pamela: It was your thirty-third birthday. Hello? Ground control to Major Tommy? You were thirty-two and I was twenty-seven when we got married.

Pamela had a huge village built and called it Tommyland. That little pleasure carnival was the closest I've ever been to seeing the circus that marches through my head actually walking around in real life. There were tents with tons of pillows on the floor, midgets wandering around on stilts, a cage of tigers—one of my favorite animals—and contortionists from Cirque du Soleil performing for us. There was a Ferris wheel, a merry-go-round, and one of those crazy swing rides that has no other purpose but to make you sick and dizzy.

The little people (which is what they like to be called) and dudes on stilts greeted everyone as they arrived. The little guys blew horns, rang bells, rolled out a red carpet, and shouted, "Welcome to Tommyland!" in their little Munchkin voices as we all walked between rows of torches into my kingdom. I thought, "Finally, we're here. I've made it to the Land of Oz!" There were sword swallowers, flame eaters, and most of our friends were in costumes. I had this insane moment in the tiger cage. I sat there with them, just stroking their fur, tripping out on how huge their paws are, how insane their muscles are, and freaked, knowing full well that if they wanted to, they could end my time here real quick. It was the trippiest Fellini movie you've ever seen; a living, breathing one, starring me and my friends.

Pamela: It took me an hour to think it up. I was in the bathtub and I had a yellow legal pad next to me and came up with the idea just like that. It took me a month to put it all together, but the idea only took an hour. It's crazy, I can still pick out a hundred Christmas gifts for Tommy before I can figure out what to buy anyone else. When you are really in sync with someone, it never goes away. It's great, but it makes it really hard to be with someone else. You just don't have the same interests and don't understand each other the same way.

The best man at my wedding, Bobby Hewitt, the drummer from Orgy, and his twin brother, Fabio, came dressed up as naughty nurses and that fucking killed me. They did it *way* too well and they were the backup singers in a fucked-up lounge band that Pamela found. The lounge set closed the night and it totally freaked me out. Those dudes played old Sinatra songs, horrible disco ballads, and except for the dancing nurses, they were all dressed in these white polyester suits looking like some crazy combination of Elvis, John Travolta in *Saturday Night Fever*, and Mel Tormé. I was scared.

There was a full-on rock show before that though. A band named Crown played and when I got my chocolate cake, I was so fucking into it that I went right up onstage and fed the entire band, midsong. It was *my* party, dude, I could do whatever I wanted, and the band *had* to have some cake. That cake, by the way, was delivered to me on the shoulders of a dude dressed up as Mighty Mouse—one of my childhood heroes.

After Crown's set—which was fucking *awesome*—we had a jam session and after that we made a huge drum circle. Pamela had my drum kit up there and just about every other kind of percussion instrument you can imagine. It was retarded—and so was I. By that time I was so wasted, so happy, and so far gone that when I went onstage to thank my wife, I fell over the monitors. I was *That Guy*, Mr. Shitty, the one who falls over in slow motion and has no idea he's even falling.

But when I first got onstage to jam, Pamela led me over to the piano. I tripped out because it was beautiful: It had iron legs, gold leaf all over it, and an intricate, hand-painted design of crosses and pearls. I'm sitting there, taking it in when Pamela tells me it's my birthday present. She had taken my old white baby grand and had it redone—I didn't even recognize it. I was so happy and so fucking in love with her. I kept telling her so and I kept thanking her but those words couldn't express what I was feeling: No one had ever done anything so amazing for me. It was the greatest spectacle I had ever seen—and I would have thought so even if it hadn't been my party. But it was, and to think she'd done it all for me was paralyzing. It crippled me with love.

There was so much going on and I was so into every bit of it that I'm glad Pamela hired a film crew because I sure as fuck wasn't able to take it all in. She didn't go for video either; she made it a film. Watching it back now on 35mm is fucking amazing. It made that night as epic as it really was—it captured all the colors and all the moments I missed. The crew and editors were complete pros. They used slow-motion filter effects in the film and added Radiohead's "Planet Telex"—I fucking *love* that song—for the introduction as we all marched into Tommyland.

Did I tell you guys how Pamela dressed me? I was all done up in a royal purple cape with a white fur collar. I had a crown, because, after all, *I* am the king of Tommyland, and she painted my face in black-and-white makeup. I looked like Marc Bolan from T. Rex starring in *The Crow*. She was dressed in black with the biggest top hat you've ever seen. She was the ringleader.

The crowning touch was Pamela's choice of transportation home. Picture this: You're at a huge party in a field, with carnival madness all around. You're totally faded and then you see lights and hear sirens coming across the grass. You're not sure what's happening—it could be the cops, it could be the Fire Department coming to rescue someone. But it's not, it's a fleet of ambulances she hired to make sure everyone got home safely. By that time, we definitely needed stretchers, a few needed body bags, and we all welcomed the caring hands of professionals.

Pamela spent a shitload of money on that party and I'm happy to say that it really did surprise me. Nine out of ten times the person you're throwing a surprise party for finds out, but Pamela had it on lock and I knew nothing. I still don't know how she did it and to be honest with you,

It's ON!!

that scares me. The whole time Pamela planned the party, she was so devious and secretive that I was convinced that she was cheating on me.

I WAS GETTING READY TO HURT SOMEONE, YO. I KEPT ASKING TOMMY TO JUST GET ME IN A ROOM WITH THAT GUY FOR A FULL-ON PANTS DOWN CAGE MATCH. TRUST ME, HE'D GO HOME LOOKING LIKE JOHNNY BOBBITT.

It was *the Party*, people. Pamela absolutely killed it. We've never done anything less. From chartering yachts and houseboats so that we could be naked on the water for weeks at a time to riding up to the front door on a white horse in full knight in shining armor, to getting married four times over, renewing our vows in space suits, we were always on a mission to blow each other away.

Pamela: We kept getting married because it was fun. Tommy would say he wanted to get married again during that first year we were together: He'd get the priest and I'd get the outfits. Since we used to call our house Mission Control, the first time we did it I got silver space suits. I went to a costume place and ended up fighting with the lady in the shop who told me that there was no way I should have only silver space suits because space people are also green and blue. I wanted all silver, so I had to take one Statue of Liberty costume for Melanie, my maid of honor, so that we'd all be silver. We had big bowl helmets on and Tommy wore a cape. It was great—our priest could even moonwalk! We did another wedding that was nondenominational and New Age, that my makeup artist's mother did. One time we got married on Christmas Eve, and that was amazing. Tommy was dressed in full armor and rode up to the house on a horse. He flipped up his visor and read to me from a scroll, saying he wanted to be my knight in shining armor. Then he took me for a ride. We were just crazy when we got married. We went to a friend's house and signed his guest book in blood because it felt like forever. We'd go to parties, and I'd swing on people's swings for hours and you couldn't get me down. And that's how it was — we were totally out of control. The happiest time of my life was when I was married to Tommy, especially in the beginning. Everyone who falls in love and gets married knows what I'm talking about. We felt like it was us against the world. You feel like nothing can hurt you, nothing can go wrong, you want to have babies and multiply. I've never been with anyone else but Tommy who made me feel like I just wanted to eat him. That's the difference — when you want to devour each other it's beyond romantic. It's some caveman shit. I'd always said I'd never get married until someone knocked me on the head and dragged me back to his cave by my hair. That's pretty much what happened.

Pamela and I were so in love, we couldn't wait to have kids, so after a year of honeymooning, we got right to it. I can't even explain what making love is like when you want to make a baby. That said, it's nothing like making love once you know that your child is inside your wife. You're making love, hoping that you're not bashing his head in with your penis. It's the next level of love, dude. I can't . . . Hold on, I have to sit down and dissect this a bit. The craziest thing is that Pamela's body felt at least ten degrees hotter than normal. I wanted to snuggle, but I couldn't even get next to her in bed because it was like hugging the water heater. Her body was so hot, I wondered if I could cook breakfast in bed on her stomach. We had our first son, Brandon, in June, and I felt bad for her. It was summer, it was hot as fuck, and there was no way she was getting cool; she was a walking incubator. Her body didn't stop changing after the boys were delivered either—the whole lactating thing was amazing. Pamela's breasts have never been what you'd call small, but when she was breast-feeding, they were *giant* and leaking milk everywhere. One day, after our first son was born, Pamela's mom is over helping out, making some food in the kitchen. The girls are cooking, standing over by the stove, and while her mom is busy stirring something, Pamela turns around, lifts up her shirt, whips out one of those bad boys, and squirts milk at me. It flies ten feet through the air and I'm catching it in my mouth, loving it because it tastes so sweet. It was the cutest, nastiest thing ever—we were both enjoying our two newest toys, the milk cannons. And her mom had no idea. Uh . . . until now.

While Pamela was pregnant we looked forever through books of names, not really knowing yet if it was a boy or a girl. If we were going to have a girl I wanted to name her China because I love that name. We agreed on Brandon if it was a boy—and he was: Brandon Thomas Lee. A little more than a year later when we did it all over again, we named our second son Dylan Jagger Lee. (And if one more person asks me if we named the two of them after the dudes in *Beverly Hills 90210*, I'm gonna fuckin' sock 'em!)

Pamela delivered both our boys at home, in the bathtub. She did not take any drugs throughout her pregnancy, not even aspirin. Her delivery was the same—totally natural. Read that again. Do you understand what I'm talking about? I have more respect for her than words can say. Pamela wanted to experience childbirth the way women did before the days of epidurals. Women were made to give birth naturally—that is what they do.

We did our research and decided that giving birth at home was the best. Here's why: When babies are born in a hospital, there's bright lights and surgical steel everywhere, and they're weighed on a scale right away and given vaccinations. The doctor will usually do circumcisions right away too. That's their first memory to retain somewhere in the brain. Immediately the nurses wrap the baby in a blanket and no matter how soft it is, to a newborn it's like sandpaper after living and growing in water. Babies have never even seen light. Pamela and I watched tapes of hospital-style delivery and then watched midwives doing natural childbirth—and it was just beautiful. It made the whole hospital trip look like a scam. Why should so many decisions be made for them the minute they're born, like cutting the skin off their dicks?

When each of our boys was born, there were lit candles everywhere and soft music playing—it was Andrea Bocelli and Orbital—and Pamela was in a tub of water at the perfect temperature. It is best to deliver a baby in water because skin has ten percent more elasticity in water, which makes the birth more comfortable. And since newborns have been living in water for nine months, it's a more natural transition.

Pamela and I are very private people—and by then, we were stalked day and night. The last thing we wanted was thirty or so people watching her give birth, even if they were our friends and family. There was no way we were going to share our most intimate, intense, and beautiful experience as a couple with anyone else.

While Pam was giving birth to Brandon, I was worried about everything. I was constantly running out to the balcony off our bedroom to smoke like a chimney in winter. It's so crazy being a dad-to-be. You are helpless as your wife does the impossible, delivering this package that is both of you into the world. Watching that is incredible and scary at the same time.

I'll admit it now—I was afraid that I was going to pass out. You might think you know all about it, but nothing can prepare you for the moment a slimy head pops out of your wife's baby canal and looks around like some alien midget man that just landed on planet Earth. And believe me, that's just the beginning, but I'm going to spare us all the rest of my play-by-play.

Pamela and I laid in bed with Brandon, gazing at him, touching him, adoring him, and welcoming him into the world. I felt inspired and while they rested, I ran downstairs to the piano and wrote a song about him. The piano is the first place I go when I want to express myself. It's not a one-way conversation: I'm not playing the piano, we're playing each other. I'm feeding those keys my feelings and when the hammers strike the strings, they resonate back to me, echoing my emotions like a mirror.

Heavy songwriters always talk about those times when a song comes through them so effortlessly that it feels like it wrote itself. I'd had moments like that, but the day my first son was born, I really knew what they were talking about. I called the song "Brandon," and when I was done writing it, I realized again what I'd already known: The best songs come from extreme pain or extreme happiness. Everything else in between is watered down and you can tell. Think about some of the greatest songs you know, whether it's Eric Clapton's "Tears in Heaven," or Eminem's "Kim." You know when it's real. I'm proud to say that one of those came through me that day. I don't feel right taking credit for it, and I don't expect everyone to understand because it's almost impossible to explain, but it's one of those experiences that makes humans feel that there is a higher power out there. It's something that happens, and I felt like a vehicle, or like someone else was delivering a message with my voice. Sitting alone at the piano in my living room as my wife and newborn son slept upstairs, I watched my fingers play by themselves—it's something that doesn't happen very often.

It was so personal that I couldn't expect anyone else but Pamela to really understand it. Some people hated it when I played it in concert with Mötley. It was something new for us—fans had seen me get off the drums and play piano before, but they'd never heard me or anyone else in the band sing about something as personal as the birth of a child. I couldn't fucking believe that people dumped on me for writing it in the first place. To me that was insane. I wasn't writing a love ballad, I was writing a song about the most amazing thing that's ever happened in my life. I was writing a song about my son. What, are the dudes in Mötley never supposed to write songs about anything but drugs, chicks, and played-out rock-and-roll bullshit until we die? Guess so. Thanks superfans, that's tight! You guys really love us.

If you are a musician, a writer, a painter, a poet, or creative in any way, you put your life experiences into your art. Some of our fans dug the song—they told me so—and typically they were parents too.

After I had written the song, I knew what sound would make it complete. Months before, when I went with Pamela to the doctor and heard our son's heart beating for the first time, I recorded the sound with my portable DAT player. I'm in the doctor's office, hearing my boy's heartbeat, tripping because it sounded so cool. I ask the doctor, "Um, do you have a line out on that Ultrasound machine?" He did. Awesome! Brandon's heart sounded like nothing I'd heard before—his tiny heart thumping inside Pam was something I had to capture. There was a cadence, an echo and a resonance to the sound of his heart coming through that machine. I knew I had to have it and I knew I'd use it because no mike, no studio, and no filter could duplicate it. His heartbeat became the intro and tempo to "Brandon." I couldn't think of a better place for it to be immortalized.

11

STATE OF UPBRINGING

a.k.a.
THE MONKEYS

The first year my sons were alive, like every infant, they were complete blobs. They ate, they shat, they pissed, they cried, they screamed, they threw up all the time, and their heads rolled around on their necks like Linda Blair in *The Exorcist*. Most of the time, I could barely get close to them. Pamela is one of the most efficient, anal people I know, so she had the situation on lock before Dad could get in to lend a hand. I did change diapers and feed them though, and let me tell you, baby poop is as gnarly as they say it is—even when it's your own child. A few times, not even a diaper could hold in all the poop. That's when you just pick them up and run to the nearest sink or bathtub, as the crap runs down their legs.

In those early years, you spend most of your time trying to figure out who they most look and act like—and so does everyone else. People would constantly point out how each of them was like Pamela or me in ways I just did not understand. It's a weird time, because they're changing month to month. The bone structure changes and so do their personalities: When my boys were born, both of them had light hair and I thought they would be blond like their mother. Slowly their hair got darker and turned brown to the point that it's more like mine.

By the time they were a year and a half, they were little people—little people we had to chase. Once they learned to walk, they were like blind guys driving a Ferrari: an accident waiting to happen. They'd blast off full-speed ahead with no idea of how to drive or where they were going. We had child-proofed the house already by installing locks on the cabinets they could reach, but we weren't done. The tile in the kitchen had to be replaced by carpet after a few faceplants left dents in their hoods.

Brandon's first word was "pickle." He'd say it over and over, just "pihkl, pihkl, pihkl." I don't know where he got that because he wasn't eating them then—there ain't no Gerber strained pickles for babies. Dylan's made more sense, it was "da-da." Both of the boys learned the word "pool" right away. They loved the water and I loved swimming with them. They'd splash around and giggle and then freak out for a second when I'd dunk them. It was amazing to see that much joy and surprise in their expressions. To this day, I can't keep them out of the pool. I've had to invent a rule, the raisin check: The little guys show me their hands and when their fingers are more wrinkled than an elephant's ass, I say, "All right dudes, out of the pool."

My two boys are so close in age that it didn't take long for them to become a two-man army. I really noticed it when they were four and five. They started getting into sports—karate, T-ball, basketball, soccer—and it brought them together. It also fired up the old sibling rivalry, which is, to this day, a constant struggle for superiority. I should just buy an official WWF referee uniform because not a day goes by that I'm not breaking up a smackdown in the kitchen. It doesn't matter that they know what comes next: a time-out. I put each fighter in his own corner, where he can't speak, can't move, and can't do anything but think about why he's there. They get a minute for each year they've been alive. Every once in a while I give myself a time-out when I'm dying for some peace and quiet. It's the only way sometimes to guarantee sanity—and forty minutes with nothing to do.

My boys each excel in different areas. Dylan is the more physical one: He is amazing at sports and goes at it like a pro. His coaches have all mentioned that he's got something special and when I hear that, I fast-forward the movie in my head and watch him play at either Dodger Stadium, the Staples Center, or in the Olympics some day.

Brandon is verbal; he's a great storyteller, even when he's lying. He'll admit it too, if you ask him. He'll come out with all kinds of things, like one time when we were sitting at the dinner table and he said, "They're filling people's heads with nonsense in school. Nonsense about brushing your teeth." Where the hell does he get this stuff? Across the table, his little brother started brushing his teeth with a lambchop. We love him, we call him Random Brandon. At times like that, I see him becoming either a comedian, a writer, or a lawyer—they're great storytellers and liars too.

Pamela: Brandon is so philosophical. When he was two, I caught him shouting up at the sky, "Is anyone up there?" I asked him what he was doing. He said, "I'm just talking to God, Mom." One time when we were riding our bikes I told him to make sure he stayed on the right side of the yellow line. "Blast me," he said. "Blast me til my skin comes off and I'm just a skeleton, Mom." That was weird. He's been talking since he was one. He's a poet who is random but always right on. He'll say, "Mom, the cat is downstairs in the garage," when there's no way he could know that. He's really connected and intuitive, and able to communicate what he thinks very clearly. I always listen carefully to what he has to say about the world around him. One day I was on the phone with my ex-boyfriend Bob, and I wasn't saying anything negative at all, but when I hung up he turned to me and said, "Why are you wasting your time, Mom?" He was right. I always take what Brandon says to heart. He's like a little messenger who will say things like that—and then goes off to play again.

Our boys, like all little kids, are into everything they can get their hands on, like a pair of monkeys—so that's what I call them: the Monkeys. Those two little maniacs pounce on me at seven in the morning and keep me running until they fall asleep at night. They make me love life — and I already do love life. They're nuts, and they have more energy than children should be allowed to have.

Right now they're still at that age where everything is a wonderful adventure. I love watching them trip out, whether it's about the new fish in our fish tank or riding dirt bikes. It's amazing, and their enthusiasm sends mine into overdrive. Here's what I'm talking about: Brandon's favorite drink is cherry Kool-Aid, so for his birthday I filled the bathtub with it and set him down to soak it up. He was in heaven, just filling his mouth with his favorite drink and marinating in that flavored bathwater. He couldn't wait to tell everyone at school that his dad gave him a bath in Kool-Aid. I'm thinking, "Great, that's a parent-teacher conference waiting to happen." After ten minutes, he started to turn red, which cracked me up, but I scooped him out and washed him off before it got too bad. A dyed-red kid is not good.

I have a koi pond and a Japanese garden in the back of my house, which is usually where I like to take my time-outs. One day, Brandon decided that he and his brother should get in there and swim with the fish. I put their masks and snorkels on them, and we all jumped in. The fish freaked out and, of course, both Monkeys chased them around, trying to catch them, ride them, hug them, or whatever. Between their speed and the natural slime on their scales, there was no way the boys were going to catch any koi. It was funny watching them try. It became a tradition until I got eleven more fish, some of which are forty years old and about three feet long—nearly the size of my boys. Once they saw those Japanese whales, they stayed away from the pond for a while.

I hope that when they're older they'll tell people how their dad was just like them when they were little. I want them to say that their dad was just a big kid who gave them all kinds of insane experiences and did the craziest shit with them. I also want to do something involved with their world before they get much older, like do a voiceover or create music for a cartoon, or get one of my songs in a video game that they play. Getting inside their little kid world that way would be amazing. I've got to do that now because before I know it, they're going to be sixteen and asking me for the keys to my car. They'll be coming home with sixteen-year-old hotties asking me if the girls can stay the night. I'll have to just tell them to be safe. Jesus, they're going to be wanting to have parties in my hot tub! I know when I tell them they can't because they're too young, they're going to just look at me and say, "Are you kidding me, Dad?" I still have a few years to work out an answer and I'm gonna fucking need them. (I just hope that the Mötley Crüe autobiography, the videotape of their mother and I having sex, and this book are all out of print by then.)

Taking the Monkeys to the toy store is tough enough. I sound like a man much older than my years when I say the toys they got today, that shit is *crazy*. PlayStation 2, Xbox, all kinds of remote-control jeeps and cars, quad racers, and little gas-powered buggies. I had a red wagon full of rocks that I collected in the yard, and I thought *that* was rad. Being a little kid right now is insane, and I wish there were some way for me to communicate that to them — especially when they get bored. They've got it all here and they're already over it. It's all a matter of what you're used to as your point of reference. Some days I think I'm way more into their stuff than they are. I'll set them up with a new video game and in a matter of minutes I hear two voices in stereo: "Dad. *Dad!* We're bored." I can never believe it and say, "Dudes, entertain yourselves. You guys don't have anything to play with? Let Dad write a song for a minute." But you know that deep down I'm really pumped that they'd rather hang out with Dad than go off and play by themselves.

I am concerned though, and I talk to their mom about this all the time, that our boys have *too much shit*. You need to be careful, because if they're all overstimulated this young, they might not ever use their imaginations. We need to stop buying them a million fucking toys! Let's give them some pens and let them draw. Let's give them whatever instruments they like and listen to them create. It's crazy with these toys, dude. I mean, I had a *fire truck — one* fire truck. And I took *care* of that motherfucker! My kids have eighty fire trucks and they're not afraid to break them. I'll watch them just bash the thing into red plastic rubble and ask them, "What are you guys doing? You broke it." They'll turn to me and say, "It's okay, Dad. We can go to the store and you'll get us another one." Great.

Before it gets any worse, I've been doing my best to give the Monkeys a sense of reality. I'm trying to introduce the concepts of money, earning, and spending into the program now. These days when they break their shit and want something new, Dad and the boys go to the piggy bank to see how phat they're rollin'. And they're not living off handouts either. I told them that any change they find lying around the house is theirs, but that's not it. When their mom or I curse in their presence, we owe them a quarter. Since you've gotten this far in my book, you can probably guess that the boys have made plenty of bucks off Dad already. I'm getting better, but shit, I just can't fuckin' stop godammned cursing, you know? So the boys are learning about earning. In addition to their little trust fund built on Dad's foul language they also get Tooth Fairy cash. When we go shopping now, they can buy whatever they want—if they can afford it. Brandon was pretty dumbfounded when he was confronted with how much the stuff he likes costs. Since they don't know, they'll just point at something in the store and I'll say, "Well dudes, that costs forty-two bucks. Let's see what you've got." They'll count it out and have like forty-one bucks and three cents. So I'll say that I'll loan them a dollar if they do their chores. Of course the toys they really want are like sixty bucks and they'll just start pointing. "Dad, Dad, look at that. *Dad.* I want that. Hey Dad, Dad! Dad? We don't have sixty bucks, but *you* do." I stay strong; I don't give in.

I hope our boys are starting to understand how the world works a little bit. If they're not, at least they're learning that toys don't just magically appear. And best of all, this whole process is cutting down on the amount of toys around here, which, trust me, is getting close to ridiculous.

I'm so glad that Pamela and I agree that we will do everything we possibly can to keep them out of the public eye. We do not take the boys to events where there is going to be some dumb-ass red carpet bullshit and when we're with them, we avoid photographers as best we can. Of course that makes all the leeches who wait in cars with lenses long enough to shoot professional sports or African wildlife even more hungry for pictures of all of us together outside my kids' karate dojo. We're like some endangered Siberian white tiger to them—a rare fucking big-game trophy that the paparazzi poachers could turn into a fucking gold mine. Hey, let's send my writer, Anthony, to talk to one of those guys and find out what the hell is wrong with them.

Anthony: Hi, folks, Anthony here, reporting live from the gas station across the street from the Lee boys' dojo. I'm standing in front of a Toyota Corolla with tinted windows and no license plates. I can see that the driver's side front window is cracked and a long lens is sticking out like a periscope on a submarine. Let's move in for a closer look.

"Hey, man, how are you doin'? What's up?"

"Nothing. I'm just out here enjoying the weather and the beach."

"Oh, really? The beach is behind you. Are you getting gas? C'mon, man, who are you stalking today? I'm just wondering because I'm doing a story on what makes paparazzi tick."

"I'm not paparazzi and I'm not stalking anyone. I have a right to be here. I can take pictures of whomever I want. What is that, a tape recorder?"

"Yes, it is. So you *are* here taking pictures then. How much does a picture of Pamela and Tommy and their kids go for these days?"

"Please leave me alone. I'm just doing my job."

"So you *are* working then. It's Saturday, bro. You should take a day off once in a while."

Ladies and gentlemen, from where I'm standing I can see

that this man has all the paparazzi essentials: lots of camera equipment, a cell phone, and empty coffee cups. I see what appears to be a sleeping bag in the backseat too.

"Sorry to pry, sir, but for the sake of curiosity, may I ask what you get out of your occupation? Is it satisfying? Seems to me that if this is your ride, you can't be cleaning up like I hear some of you do."

"This is my work car. I have another car. I do fine, buddy. Why don't you take a walk."

"Why don't you take a ride and let those two be alone with their kids. Actually, wait here, I'm going to get my camera. I want some pictures of you. Would you like to meet Tommy? I can get him over here."

"I've met Tommy before. He's old school, he's got a bad temper. I'm not interested in Tommy. I want pictures of Pamela. She doesn't care about this shit. She knows the deal."

"Cool, man. Sit tight then. Can I get your name?"

"Just call me John."

"Okay, *John*. I'll be right back."

I'm sorry ladies and gentlemen, but before I could snap a few party pics of John and me at the beach, he sped off, circled the block, then disappeared—for now. This is Anthony Bozza, live from the parking lot. Back to you, Tommy.

Thanks, Anthony. We protect the Monkeys as much as we can, but they're getting old enough to start realizing what Mom and Dad do. I mean, when they talk to their friends and hear what a lot of the other parents do most of the day, they've got to realize that something is up. And if they're being bad by staying up too late watching TV, they might see Mom on *Celebrities Uncensored*—it's definitely sinking in no matter what we do. I heard Brandon tell his schoolmate the other day, "My dad's a rock star and he works *really* hard." As usual, I don't know where Random Brandon got that one—I didn't tell him anything. I'm assuming that

David LaChappelle.1999

Dr. Bangenstein in the lab: Tommy at his kit. Reader, witness a true union of master and muse akin to King Kong and Fay Wray, Dali and dreamscapes, and Fellini and freakishness.

Tommy making music through the years: on stage during the *Never a Dull Moment Tour* and right at home, in the studio.

Postcards from Tommyland: The entrance to the carnival that was Tommy's 33rd birthday; donning the crown and makeup (with male nurses) later that night; chilling naked—his second favorite thing in the world to do; on the set of the "Hold Me Down" video; strutting the red carpet with P. Diddy; flying the bird; and at home in the pool.

my being gone on tour a lot means, to him, that I work really hard. He doesn't quite know yet that my work is fun. But it's not as much fun as being home with my sons. I had so much fun in the summer of 2003 for just that reason. I didn't tour for once—I just played with those guys in the pool, barbecued, and enjoyed my home life with them to the fullest. And those moments are better than any tour or any concert I've ever played, please believe.

It'll be cool one day to sit down and show them their dad's legacy. They've seen a few videos and things once in a while, but they have no clue. Dylan has a Mötley shirt that he wears. But he doesn't even know who Mötley Crüe is, the same way he doesn't know who Korn is—he's got a little shirt of theirs too. He just likes the way those shirts look so he throws 'em on. I love that. Yeah, it'll be cool to sit the Monkeys down and show them what their dad has done. Then again, maybe it's not such a good idea.

I LOVE YOU GUYS,
YOUR DAD

12

STATE OF INVASION*

a.k.a.
STOP THIS RIDE,
I WANNA GET OFF!

> This chapter runs way too long. I'd make it two chapters if I were you.
>
> Well, Pippin, you're not me. Why don't you go make some tea and munch a crumpet?

Disclaimer:† All of the following events may or may not have occurred. All similarities to purportedly true events as reported by the celebrity/tabloid "press" should be considered opportunities to interpret fictional works. Said "press" can, after all, create so-called history with a few thousand dollars and a picture. Let it be known that the author, Tommy Lee, insists that what follows, to the best

---

* This chapter will be closed-captioned due to overly (sur)realistic content.

† So recorded and duly noted by Tommy's witness in this regard, A. "F." Bozza, erstwhile, so-named and elected Notary (Non-Re) Public(an) of the Living, Breathing Estate of Tommy Lee. My credentials are available by request (serious buyers only) at anthonybozza.net.

of his knowledge, must be regarded as a nightmare, as such is his only experience of these events, and should be treated thusly and equally as a fixture of nonreality. Any coincidence herewith that any persons, living or
dead, believed to exist, is strictly accidental, in every sense of the word.

Let me tell you how fuckin' craise it is being followed around everywhere
you go. I thought I'd gotten used to the paparazzi when I was married to
Heather, but I had no idea. The level of attention Pamela got in the mid-
nineties was insane. She was more than a *Baywatch* TV star and a *Playboy*
icon—she was an international sex symbol. The invasion of our privacy
was constant. I'm not complaining about what comes with fame, like
those bitchy little fucking Seattle boys who hate success.* I can never understand that attitude. Everyone in entertainment chooses this path. And
none of them should be surprised when they find a huge target on their
back. (See the back cover of this book, dudes—you painted the target and
I'll wear it.) It's part of the deal.

But you gotta know where to draw the line. Pamela and I are both
public figures, but we were also a couple. And when you're in love and
someone disrespects your girl and stalks your family, none of that fame
matters. You do what any man would do: You become the man of the
house, you defend your loved ones, and you hold down the fort. That's
how I was raised. Despite what the tabloids say, I don't feel like I've ever
lost my temper just to lose it—there's always been a legitimate reason for
my actions.

Before we had Brandon, Pamela had a miscarriage,† which is trau-
matic for a couple waiting for months to have their first child. After
you grieve, you have to accept that something was wrong and that
it wasn't meant to be. For the woman, it's much worse: The emotional

---

* See Grunge, 1991–1994, specifically Vedder, Eddie. See also, Cobain, Kurt, for a
more talented, anterior reference.

† 1995, the first year of their marriage.

pain is combined with physical pain. The day it happened, Pamela went to the hospital and when we were ready to leave, we went out the back door and found a crowd of paparazzi waiting up on a roof across the street. It was the worst photo op either of us could imagine—but it was their dream come true. Anyone could see that we weren't leaving the hospital happy. I'm still not sure why anyone would want a photo of me walking her to the car, with one thing in mind: getting her home so she could rest.

We took off down the 405 freeway and, of course, we were followed. A little family of French paparazzi—a man, a woman, and their dog— chase us, speeding in front of us and on Pamela's side, snapping pictures. It was so fucked and I was in such a bad mood that I start running them off the road in my truck. Eventually I did so, driving them over to the shoulder of the highway and cutting in front of them, *Starsky and Hutch* style. They try to back up, so I back up, fully trapping them. They're right next to us and Pamela loses it—she opens her door and starts bashing it into the side of their car. I've had it too. I get out of the truck, jump on their hood, and smash a hole in their windshield with my boot. Before my foot went through the glass, I saw how scared they were and I remember thinking, "What the fuck am I doing? I'm on the 405 destroying some fucker's car." The dog is going crazy in the back and they didn't speak English very well, but they understood what I told them. "If you follow us after this point," I said, "I will fuck you all up." They didn't come after us—in fact, I bet they probably quit the business.*

Pamela: It was a horrible day. All we wanted to do was go up to our house and be where we couldn't wait to live. The contractors weren't done working on it, but we didn't care, we just wanted to sit there, with our dogs, and think about what we'd just been through. I couldn't believe we were being followed and I just lost it. Tommy

---

* If in fact they did exist. Said events may or may not, to the best of everyone's knowledge, have happened and said French photo hounds may never have been anything more than *un mirage malheureux*.

was moving over to run them off the road and when we got close to them, I started smashing their car with my door while we were still driving. We were so fed up. I was screaming at them, "I had a miscarriage because of you! Fuck you!" It was like a bad B movie—these screaming French people in their car and Tommy on their hood, kicking their windshield in. I only told him to stop when I saw a dog in their car. The dog was the only one I was concerned about, being Ms. PETA and all.

We definitely weren't going home after that episode—we figured more photographers were waiting for us there. We decided to go to the Ritz-Carlton in Marina del Rey to hole up for a few days. We get there safely, charter a yacht the next day, and start to relax. Then one evening, a few days after the miscarriage, we're heading back into the hotel, my arms are full of our stuff, and as we make our way to the elevator, I drop my cigarettes. Pamela bends over to get them, and right behind her is this guy who had come out of the bar or restaurant ahead of his wife and kids. He was clearly wasted, and he says to Pamela, "Nice ass!" I look at this family man and I can't fucking believe it. I say, "What did you say?" He says, "You heard me." I say, "I'm just checking that I heard you correctly. What the fuck is wrong with you?" And he says, "Fuck you." That was it. I say, "Fuck you?" I had, among other things, my Motorola cell phone in my hand. The year was 1995 and back then, phones still came as big as walkie-talkies and so tough that you could drop them from your roof and they'd still work. It was time for this motherfucker to go night-night. So I wound up and cell-phone-whipped his ass, watching the birdies circle his head as he dropped like an amateur on the receiving end of a punch from Iron Mike Tyson. While the guy's kids watched the concierge scraped him off the marble floor, his wife asked me what had happened. I said, "He's a fucking asshole. He told my wife she's got a nice ass when she bent over."

Pamela: That guy was disgusting. He was some purple-nosed drunk businessman type. His wife should have smacked him before Tommy did.

After that, we went to our room and bolted the fucking door. It wasn't long at all before the police came. I told them what happened, about what we had just been through at the hospital, and how this drunk fuck was in the wrong place at the wrong time. They weren't going to take me in and they said the guy wasn't going to press charges, so I thought everything was cool. A month later, here comes the lawsuit—and there goes some money.*

You might not agree with me after what I just told you, but I don't have a bad temper at all. I'd say that I actually let too much shit slide. After that incident, I was pretty shaken up about what I did, so I asked my dad what he thought about it. He thought I'd done the right thing and said that any man on the planet would agree. He said he would have whupped his ass too—and that's all I needed to hear. I've walked away from many situations like that one: I'm not a fighter, I'm a lover. But right then, on that day, I just thought, "Fuck this disrespectful piece of shit."

The paparazzi problem got worse—they creeped around our house like pedophiles at a grade school waiting for recess. One day, just after our son Brandon was born, I was in the driveway when I noticed a pine tree across the street swaying—and there wasn't any wind. I go over there and some motherfucker is up in the tree with a camera, waiting to snap the first picture of Pamela and our son. I look up at him and say, "Dude, what

---

* The cash debit to which Tommy refers does not directly reflect or otherwise indicate that any dollar amount was ever paid by him to the aforementioned lewd lush. He is referring to a more universal truth: a good sock-up—however warranted—does not come cheap. Whether or not that rude dad profited monetarily from his inexcusable behavior, in actuality, is irrelevant. To clarify: In such situations, whether or not a settlement for damages incurred is reached, in or out of court, a defendant such as our man Tom always loses. Once one is embroiled in the legal system via a suit filed by an aggro lawsuit-happy ass, one is obliged to fork over mad cash for lawyers, court costs, and many other expenses, just to play the game. "I'm sued" is a popular American pastime known to drain defendants' bank accounts faster than a cotillion of crack heads—and that's where Tom ended up. Lawsuits like these are a lose-lose situation that so many famous folk contend with each and every day as a corrosive side effect of public success—even if they win their case. And in this case, Tommy was not only insulted, he had to pay an army of legal eagles kindly for that insult.

the fuck are you doing up there?" He says, "Bro, listen to me. If you can just get Pamela to come out here with your son, I'll take the picture and split the money with you. She'll never know." What is wrong with people? What kind of a guy did he think I was? I thought about grabbing my chainsaw and putting an end to this guy's future as a stalkerazzi, but I was too fucking disgusted and stunned.

Change "stalkerazzi" to "pinerazzi"? Yuk, yuk. That's pretty funny, Paddington. Do you moonlight as a stand-up comedian? I can call the talent booker at The Tonight Show with Jay Leno if you need a hookup.

I just went inside and locked the door. I didn't even tell Pamela—that situation was just way too stupid. That day I realized how crazy people can get. I started to look at the pictures of us in the tabloids in a different way after that. I'd check the angles to figure out where these guys were posting up.

Pamela: You can still see one of our best run-ins on one of those *Celebrities Uncensored* shows—they rerun the footage a lot. Tommy and I were just married* and were lying in bed. We didn't have trees in the yard yet, and we didn't have the pool, so everything back there was still so open that photographers could just shoot right into our bedroom window. Sure enough, they were out there. Tommy went out on the deck with his sawed-off shotgun and pointed it at them and told them he'd shoot them all if they didn't fuck off. I remember the show that used the footage was *American Journal* and when it aired, they said on the program that as our wedding present they wouldn't sue us.

People thought we were crazy, but what would the average person do? Probably the same thing. It was terrible: We were just try-

---

* The year was 1995.

ing to figure out how to live our
lives in the middle of a siege. The
worst is that we got sued constantly. And the only reason
everyone sues is because we
live in Hollyweird.* Everyone
is a coward out to make
money any way they can in
this town.

> What is _American Journal?_ I've never heard of it.
>
> What? Heathcliff, I thought it would be one of your favorite TV shows. _American Journal_ is the most lowbrow, scandalous, tabloid shit show on stun. It's a TV show version of _Hello!_ I thought a bird like you would know all about that shit.

The plot of land on one side of our
house is state-owned conservation
land. I thought that was fucking awesome when
I bought the place because it meant no one could build a house there.
What I didn't realize is that anyone can legally be on state-owned land.†
Great. That meant the Papanazis could build a shantytown out of tripods,
coffee cups, and old doughnuts if they wanted to. Pamela's dad, Barry,
went for a walk one day just after Brandon was born ‡ and noticed three
guys with cameras rustling around in the brush, just on the other side of
the wall around our house. He came inside and told me about it, so we
went to check it out. Sure enough, they were there, hiding behind some
bushes with duffel bags full of photo equipment—tripods, lenses, cameras, all of it. We snuck up on them and surprised the fuck out of them. I
grabbed a tripod and held it up like a baseball bat. One of the guys pulled
out a can of mace and a cell phone. I say to them, "I'm taking all of your
shit. You're on private property." I'm wearing a hooded sweatshirt, so I

---

* That would be Hollywood, L.A., Los Angeles, the City of (Lost) Angels.

† True indeed, as stated in the Constitution of the State of California. California, our
31st state, was admitted to the union in 1850, and in 1931 adopted a new state bird, the
Valley Quail (*Lophortyx californica*), known for its distinctive, sloping black plume and
creamy white, golden-brown spotted eggs.

‡ June 5, 1996.

pull up my hoodie to protect my eyes and I tell that fucker, "You've got one shot. You'd better hit me with that mace because if you don't, I'm taking you out." Barry and I snatch their duffel bags and throw them over the wall, back onto my property, as the three of them back away. They were trippin' and ran the fuck out of there.

Once Barry and I hopped back over the wall, we grabbed the bags and dumped them in the fountain at the front of our house. I was glad that I wasn't the only one who was that pissed off: Barry had seen enough of this bullshit on his routine patrols of the perimeter. It felt good to know that I had a partner, another father, and someone else besides me who was tired as fuck of seeing his daughter stalked.

By then I was on a first-name basis with everyone in the Malibu Sheriff's Department, so when they rolled up in their black-and-white, I thought it would be a friendly visit. I wasn't worried about the mace-wielder calling the cops—I thought it would be all good. Well, this time it wasn't. Great. They ask me to return the photographers' shit, and they aren't happy at all when I pull it out of the fountain. A month later, of course, here comes the lawsuit—and there goes more money.*

One day when Barry and I traded shifts and I was on day patrol, I was in the backyard when the sun reflecting off of a distant camera lens hit me right in the eye. I tracked that fucker to a hill behind the house, and like any good security guard, I went to check it out. I hopped in my car and left the compound by the back exit where the distant cameraman wouldn't

---

* To reiterate, Tommy is not referring to a dollar amount paid to the plaintiff in this suit. Even if he were so inclined, any such settlement is typically accompanied by a clause restricting the defendant from revealing such information under penalty of further litigation. Furthermore, even if he were free to do so, Tommy would never disclose such information for fear of rewarding such a deplorable profession with any degree of lasting recognition/acknowledgment. Suffice it to say that the lawsuits endured by the hunted, filed by the nameless photographically inclined stalker/hunters, had by this time (which by no means signaled the end of such hardship) caused undue financial drain by way of their lawyers' and the court's fees. To paint a more accurate picture, the hunted often dish out amounts well in excess of the gross yearly income earned by the average American.

see me. I drove to where I knew his car would have to be and there it was, a nifty sports car pulled off on the side of the road. My house isn't exactly in a populated area: Unless it was broken down, it had no business being there. I didn't want to be hasty, so I went down to the equestrian center just down the road from the auto in question. I asked everyone in sight if that sporty ride belonged to anyone on the premises. No one claimed it. (I'm glad I asked though, because every time I go in there, everyone who works there tells me how considerate they thought that was.) *

Anyway, I headed back to the perpetrator's car and then the craziest thing happened. I turned away for a minute to admire the beautiful foliage all around me when suddenly I heard the crunch of safety glass being smashed. I don't know how it got there, but when I turned around to look at that guy's car again, his windshield was gone and a huge boulder was sitting in his passenger seat. "Woah, hey, that's craise!" I thought to myself. Fuck I still don't know what went down. There must be bad-ass gnomes with an attitude in them thar hills. Mean-ass gnome, I owe ya—you did what I never would have done. As I drove home, I smiled, thinking of that Papasnotty meeting his new pet rock for the first time and enjoying the wind in his hair and the bugs in his teeth as he cruised home in his brand new magically improvised convertible. I was even happier when, a month later, for once, there was no lawsuit—and Mr. Wallet stayed closed. Can't sue what you don't see, people—but I figured he'd try anyway. It's a good thing because I still don't know how it happened. Do you believe in unexplainable phenomena? I do.†

The whole Nonstoparazzi situation had hit an all-time high that was more ridiculous than the worst joke I had ever heard. I never minded that

---

* Indeed, they do, as do most of Tommy's neighbors. But for the infrequent occasions when he forgets to close the windows in his studio before rocking the fuck out at 3 A.M., he is a very considerate member of his community. And when the odd slip-up occurs, the man is quick with an apology.

† They are much like a dream: over as soon as you talk about it—with the dreamer left as the only eyewitness.

the public wanted to know about our lives—I just had a problem with the way these hacks with cameras were going about informing them. Pamela and I were trying to start a family amid something that was so unreal. It got so bad that I started to daydream that there was a way for us to give it back to them. I dreamed that there was a totally legal way for people who were hounded day and night to get back at those who made a living out of making us miserable. It didn't have to be negative—it could be something fun for everyone! I imagined a sport called Scum Chucking where those who suffered from the Poopernazi problem could—legally—collar the most obnoxious Lenserazzi and use them to redecorate the pavement. In my mind, I ran with it—I saw it as an Olympic sport that took place right on the Hollywood Walk of Fame. Whoever's chosen bottom-feeding parasite left the biggest divot won. There were bonus points for scattered zoom lenses and double bonus points for creating human yard sales. It was a good dream—and one I knew would be popular among the famous residents of Malibu and Hollywood. I figured in the world arena, the U.S. team would be hard to beat.

After a month of being under siege and nurturing our newborn son, Pamela and I needed a night out on the town. We made all the arrangements and headed to the Viper Room* to see some music and cut loose. We had a blast, hung with some friends, and for the first time in a while it seemed like we might get home without any bullshit.

When we left, we were swarmed like a porn star at a gang bang. There were a ton of photographers, but one dickhead took the cake. He was right up in our faces with a video camera, blinding us with a bright light, saying stupid shit to provoke us. "It's two in the morning!" he said. "Why aren't you home with your child?" Pamela had a freakin' conniption fit. "Fuck you, you motherfucker," she yelled. I grabbed the guy by the camera and chucked him to get that light off us. His wrist was in the

---

* Part-owned by Johnny Depp, that place was rippin' in the 90s. With an intimate performance space upstairs, a small, nautical cabin of a bar downstairs, and VIP rooms to hide in, the spot was a playpen for those that the E! Channel call "hot."

video camera strap, so he went flying the Friendlee Skies.* I think I still hold the record for distance and points: The guy whizzed down the street and when he landed, his camera and his pelvis were busted, even though I only meant to take out the camera. His fellow Snooperazzi blasted both of us with mace as we shoved our way to the car, while EMTs scraped him up off the sidewalk. A month later, of course, here comes the lawsuit—and there goes *the most money ever!* †

Pamela: The Viper Room was the worst. It was such a setup—they were totally waiting for us. I'm shouting, "Fuck you, you motherfucking, cocksucking motherfucker!" I got maced. After we got in the car, I jumped back out and started pushing people. That guy was right in our faces, with that light right on us. Tommy pushed him and he just flew down this steep hill. Any man would have done the same thing in twenty different ways. We'd had enough. It was the first time we'd been out together since our son was born. And every day we saw them: They were hanging from our trees, hiding in the bushes, chasing us down the highway. It never stops—just recently I wanted to choke this guy who followed me to the supermarket with the kids. I don't want anyone taking pictures of the kids. One time a guy jumped out of the bushes at my mom, who dropped the groceries and almost had a heart attack—really! What pisses me off the most is that all these guys are such pussies. One time on the *Baywatch* set, a guy was taking pictures of me and I went up to him to ask him to stop. I was in my red bathing suit, hardly threatening,

---

* It's best if everyone, once again, takes a moment to read the disclaimer at the start of this chapter. You'll feel better if you do, and so will everyone else both loosely and closely connected to this project(ile).

† Yet again, my apologies, but the specific dollar amount must remain secret by the order of the court. However, the general ratio/broad strokes that Tommy is painting here are by all means suggestive of the truth, thereabouts—if any of this is actually true.

and he is standing there, this full-grown man. He starts shaking, pulls out a can of pepper spray, and says, "Back off, Pamela! Just back up!" He acted like I was going to attack him. They're way out of control. They'll say things to piss you off so that you'll look all upset in the picture. Once, when Tommy was in jail, I got off a plane and this one paparazzo said, "Tommy's out of jail, Pamela, and he's waiting around the corner to knock your block off." It's hard for the kids—those guys will go on school property to take pictures of them. I wish we had rules like they do in Paris, where photographers can't take a picture of you in the street unless you're at an event. It's crazy because when you see someone with a camera, you don't know if they're a stalker or a stalkerazzi. All that shit calmed down for a little while after Princess Diana died, but now it's just as bad as it's ever been. My son Brandon said it best after those guys chased us around the supermarket parking lot today:* "Don't worry, Mom, they're all going to hell anyway."

When Pamela and I were first married I took a lot of things into my own hands. I tried to be Mr. Security Guy—the one thing I never wanted to be. I always thought walking around with a bodyguard was wack, ostentatious, and just way too rock star. Looking back, it would have been a fuck of a lot cheaper than all those lawsuits. Not to mention the other shit stains on my record: that peeperazzi outside the Viper Room earned me probation, which came into play later when I violated it.

All of this undue stress wasn't exactly what I'd call healthy for our marriage. We are both intense people and we were so deeply in love that we wanted to start a family right away, in the midst of two very busy careers: I was still going on tour, she was still going to work. We felt invincible;

---

* February 2004.

there was no way we were going to slow down. And that's when all hell broke loose. The fact that we're still friends is amazing, because I don't know another couple who's been through more fucking bullshit in the first two years of their marriage. Name one, I dare you.*

While we were having our house gutted and rebuilt during the first year of our marriage, we lived in Pamela's condo, while the band and I used the construction hell that would become our home as a recording studio.† The whole place was open and fucked up and unlivable—and perfect for our purposes. We had the instruments set up in what would be the living room and the control room was in the garage. I had a safe in that garage too, hidden behind a carpeted wall. Pamela and I had locked up all our valuables in it: mementos, watches, jewelry, cameras, guns, knives, ammo, money, pictures, videos—everything. That year, Pamela and I went to London for Christmas and when we came back, the remodeling was behind schedule and nowhere close to being done, so the band and I resumed recording there. One day I went to the garage to get something out of the safe—and the whole thing was missing. I'm sitting there, kind of laughing, thinking, "Dude, where's the safe?" We already know I sometimes have a bad memory, so I thought I had forgotten that it had been relocated. I had to ask my road crew guys if they'd moved the safe. I even called the pool guy thinking that he had to move it to install pipes for the hot tub. Nope.

It was such an inside job: It required keys to the house and a gang of guys to move that thing. My recording gear was in there blocking the wall that hid the safe! That included a huge Neve recording console that weighs hundreds of pounds, as well as a few racks of outboard gear, each of them about six feet tall, awkward, full of wires, and heavy. There's no

---

* That is a tall order. Taylor and Burton? Sid and Nancy? Kurt and Courtney? Reader, it's your call, I'm not sure if the same rules apply. All I can say is that only the strong survive.

† The year was 1995 and John Corabi was the lead singer. The resulting album was called *Mötley Crüe*.

way one guy could do it alone and there's no way any random burglar would think to move any of it—not to mention find the hidden room that held the safe—unless he knew there was a payoff.

After I called everyone who knew it was there, my heart stopped for a second when I realized that it had been stolen. That meant, in one theft, we'd lost a big wad of cash and all our jewelry, guns, and irreplaceable memories. We did not expect to see one of those memories being sold on TV a few weeks later. We were having dinner, watching the news in the kitchen, when we see footage of clerks stocking the shelves at Tower Records with copies of a videotape of Pamela and me fucking. We were horrified. We were under enough stress already: home reconstruction, my recording a new album, her nonstop career, the birth of our son. We did not need this. I just dropped the remote and we sat there speechless. We knew that the tape was in the safe, but we never thought that the thieves were after anything but the guns and money. We got on the phone to our lawyers immediately. It was crazy, probably the craziest time in my life—and my life hasn't been normal, as you can tell by now. It was the straw that broke these camels' backs. I don't know how any human being could have fucking dealt with it.

There were a ton of workers in and out of the house who knew about the safe—a bunch of them helped us move it. Now that thing wasn't easy to move—it was as big as a fridge and weighed five hundred pounds when it was empty. It was made for holding guns, and it was full of them. There was no way it was going anywhere without a crane, a flatbed, and a crew of guys. A lot of the guys were gun freaks and I remember they were drooling when I showed them my collection. When I found out later that one of the workers used to be in the porno business, it all made sense to me how this could have happened once he found what else was in the safe.

We got our lawyers on the case and they put together a lawsuit that got bigger as more and more outlets sold and broadcast the stolen tape of Pamela and me having sex. The guy responsible for distributing it is named Seth Wasarsky, who had a company called Internet Entertainment Group. He basically went into hiding when all this started, then out of the blue one day, he called me on my cell phone while I was on tour with Mötley. I have no idea how he got that number, but he did. "Hi, Tommy, this is Seth Wasarsky," he said. "I'd like to offer you two hundred and fifty thousand dollars to settle this lawsuit." I said, "Dude, you can suck my big fat fucking cock. Don't ever call me again." What, was I supposed to split that with Pamela for our trouble? He was offering us beer money. Seth is on the run now, and no one can find him. His company was in Seattle, and now it's gone. It's crazy that we could never find this guy. There had to be a paper trail linking his old company to whatever new one he was using to cash the checks. Whatever. I guess he's hanging out with Osama Bin Laden, jerking off to web porn in some cave. Unfortunately, our Constitution also protects scummy little Internet businessmen.*

The lawsuit we put together to try to stop this tape bullshit was fucking huge. The tape could be seen in every hotel in the world, so we hit just about all of the pay movie channels and the hotel chains that were showing the video without a release, which is fucking illegal. But we got nowhere with it and it's unfathomable. The tape was ruled newsworthy because Pamela and I are public figures. How the fuck could that be newsworthy? Last time I checked, *60 Minutes* never launched an investigation to determine if Ben tapped J. Lo's ass proper like a real man should have.† I couldn't believe this was happening to us. All I could think about was how I'd explain it to our kids one day. And I'm still working on that one.

Pamela: It was great sitting through depositions, where old men with crusty white shit in the corners of their mouths would hold up

---

* Indeed, democracy has its pitfalls.

† If such an inquiry were to be made in the name of journalistic integrity, I hereby suggest that, for comparison's sake, said ass be tapped by an objective third party such as, but not limited to, myself. I would also like to suggest that *60 Minutes* correspondent Andy Rooney, that harbinger of reason, take this query as fodder for his next weaving monologue.

pictures of me naked in *Playboy* and ask why I'd even care that the tape was out there. Tommy was a rock star, so what did he care? Why did we even have the tape in our safe? They said the public had a right to know what was on that tape because it was newsworthy—as newsworthy as informing the public about information the government had on Russian spies or nuclear weapons. Those were the cases they brought up—we were public figures, we had sex, and everyone had a right to see it. I couldn't handle it. It got to a point where I could not go to another deposition with those sweaty old guys asking me about my sex life. They'd ask me whether I'd had sex in public before, whether I'd done it sideways. They were probably beating off to it all in the bathroom. They were asking me about my life, suggesting that I was insane, while they probably head up pedophilia rings. It was driving Tommy and me crazy, and it was ruining our relationship. I was home, pregnant with our second son, and on TV I'm watching a Pamela look-alike in a *Barb Wire* outfit signing our porno tape like she's me. It was on the evening news and they didn't even say that she was a look-alike.

We took our case to appellate court and to federal court, but it was a useless battle. After the first judge deemed it newsworthy, the others seemed to fall in line. I'll feel bad for the rest of my life for all the unpaid work our lawyer, Ed Masry, did for us. He took the case on contingency, and it went on for years. It's not like Ed was hurting for cash—he was a part of the legal team who won the Erin Brockovich* case, and that

---

* If you haven't seen the blockbuster of the same name starring Julia Roberts, Erin Brockovich exists and works for Masry and Vititoe as a Director of Research. She was a file clerk whose investigation led to the largest direct action lawsuit of its kind, resulting in $333 million paid by Pacific Gas and Electric to 600 residents of Hinkley, California, who had been exposed to the toxic compound Chromium 6 through the groundwater. Her efforts also paved the way to an Oscar for Julia Roberts.

homeboy rides around in a Rolls-Royce—but he did keep on it and never saw a dime. If we had won against any of those big corporations that broadcast the footage, Ed and everyone else would have cashed in. But we didn't. I'm still sick to my stomach that people believe that Pamela and I released the tape on purpose for profit. *The Wall Street Journal* named the tape the most profitable porno release of all time, estimating that it grossed close to $77 million. Considering that there weren't any production costs or actors' fees to take care of, that number was pure profit—for the fuckers that fucked us. That's tight. I wish I could say we had the last laugh and financed our kids' future off someone trying to rob us, but the truth is, I can't.

Our lives were crazy already: Pamela was working seven days a week on *Baywatch* and the movie *Barb Wire* while I recorded with a new version of Mötley.* When we had time together, we sat home and watched the insane bullshit around us unfold every time we turned on the TV. The stress of all that attention started to wear on our relationship. After Dylan was born, it got worse. The lawsuits, the porno tape, our schedules, learning to parent, and learning to be married to each other was insane—it was a fucking accident waiting to happen. But I didn't even see it coming, because trouble doesn't wear a bell, it just shows up, and you either have the tools to deal with it or you don't. And I didn't have them back then.

After children are born every marriage changes. You are no longer just lovers living for each other. You've got other responsibilities and we had done everything so fast—and had so much bullshit happening to us—that we could not fucking deal. We were both kids ourselves who were learning as we went along and didn't know what the fuck we were doing. When everything got overwhelming for us, Pamela focused on the children and let our relationship slide. She let us slip apart because her life became about being a mom. Of course I felt that the kids were num-

---

* The album that would become *Generation Swine*, released in 1997. John Corabi began the writing and recording of the album but was replaced by original singer Vince Neil midway through the proceedings.

ber one, but in my mind we had to find a way for everyone to be number one. I don't know, I guess something has to suffer when you add two new spices to the soup. But I didn't want that to happen.

Pamela: I know Tommy started to feel helpless and it drove him crazy. It was too much for anybody. All that pressure made our problems escalate: I think we could have handled it better and it could have been avoided if we had been more mature, but we just weren't. Instead of being on the same team, we started blaming each other. I withdrew and got really into the kids. And Tommy would be like "What about me?" And I'd say, "What do you mean, what about you?" It started getting weird. He wanted me to wear a pager on the back of my *Baywatch* bathing suit. I had to be on call for him.

Babe, we both had pagers. I was on call for you too. Isn't that why we got them?

Pamela: Then it got to the point where he'd come to the set and punch out all the cabinets in my trailer and do doughnuts in his Testarossa. He got wild. He'd be on every set I was ever on if I had to kiss someone. He'd sit there and threaten people, and just stare them all down. When I was on break, he'd scare everyone away. He'd be like, "This is *my* time, this is *my* wife." I was way over-worked—*Baywatch* during the week, *Barb Wire* on the week-ends. When I'd get home, I'd be exhausted, but to Tommy that was his time. I couldn't eat or sleep, and I was like ninety pounds. I didn't have time for anything. Thank God I got preg-nant. It made everything stop.

Yo! P, hold up. We're missing some information here. We were fight-ing a lot then, so it's not like I just showed up at *Baywatch* one day to re-arrange your trailer. We were having an argument that day—clearly you don't remember what it was about, and neither do I. I do know that I wasn't going to take out my frustration on you, so the cabinets had to take one for the Lees. Looking back now, I did the right thing—I had a head start on all those lessons I learned in my anger management classes a little later: 1) I did something physical to get it out of my system, and 2) I walked away. Well, not exactly. I drove away—same thing. And for the record, I didn't do a doughnut in the parking lot. I did a burnout—because I wanted to get the fuck out of there as fast as I could.

We had back-to-back kids, in just two years, and I didn't have the tools to deal with the changes, as I'm sure many new fathers don't. Kids don't come with a manual, and there's no tried-and-true how-to book on raising a family. I started feeling needy and wondering what happened to me in Pamela's priorities. I kept thinking, "Where is the love?" (Sorry to get off the subject for a minute, but I love that Black Eyed Peas song "Where Is the Love?" It was my favorite song of 2003—what a great message. I just had to say that.) I started to feel like a fucking baby-sitter to her and nothing else. I just didn't know how to deal with my own insecurities when I went from being the most important thing in my girl's life to number 3 on her *Billboard* chart. In my heart I know we could have worked it out if we hadn't been fighting the world at the same time. But timing wasn't on our side, so we started to get into little pissy arguments.

I'll say it straight up: Pamela and I are passionate people by ourselves. Put us together, and it's off the block. We make each other crazy and when it's good it's so fucking good. But when it's bad, it's all bad. I have a tattoo on my arm of two switches and one says "reset." I push it when I wish everything could be done over. That thing got a workout during this period, but nothing changed. These weren't problems that a button could fix.

Everything snapped one night just after Dylan was born. I was making dinner, we had just cracked a bottle of wine and were splitting the first glass together. It was one of those moments that started innocently enough and got more intense than I would ever have imagined: No one was drunk, no one was already pissed off about anything—it just exploded. Neither of us really know what started it. I think I was looking for a pan and one of us said something that rubbed the other one the wrong way. I threw the pan back in the cabinet, and I remember her saying that she was going to call her mom to come over because I was scaring her. I didn't want her mom over anymore—she was at our house a lot as it was. I asked her a bunch of times not to call her, but Pamela did anyway. With Dylan in one arm, she picked up the phone to call her mom. I went over and pressed the receiver button down as she tried to dial, and asked her please not to call. She picked up the phone again, and I hung it up again and asked her please not to call. She did it again, and then again, and each time I hung it up. And then, *blam!* she turned and clocked me in the jaw. I was stunned. I grabbed her by the shoulders and said, "What the fuck is wrong with you? What are you doing?" I didn't know what to do—and I couldn't believe this was happening. Both of our boys were crying, watching Mom and Dad fight. Pamela still had Dylan in her arms and she led Brandon with her into the playroom off the kitchen. As she did, I kicked her in the bum, and I'm so sorry I ever did that. I am—I still regret it to this day. I just want all of you readers to know that I'm not in denial about what I did. I take full responsibility, and I also want to be clear about this: I was not wearing steel-toe boots and kicking her like some drunk guy in a bar brawl. I was wearing my UGG slippers and it was an emotional reaction of mine to the punch I just took in the chops. At this point, I'm losing my mind. I just want the boys to stop crying and I want all of this to stop. I go into the playroom and ask Pamela if I can take Brandon outside for a walk. I needed one too. She didn't want me to and she corralled the kids around her, as if I were going to hurt them. Now I was running on nothing but emotions—and that is bad, at any time. Neither of us were thinking straight—we went back and forth verbally, and no one was letting up. All I wanted to do was separate everyone—the boys and us. We all needed time apart to cool down, to just breathe and remember how much we loved one another. Emotion ruled over reason and I grabbed Brandon to take him outside with me. She fought me, pulling him away from me, so I pushed her away. Dylan was still in her arms and unfortunately he bumped his head on the chalkboard next to where she was sitting. I'm so sorry, Dylan, I never meant for that to happen—and I regret it every single day. And as it was stated in the police report, Pamela broke a nail. They even have pictures of it.

We separated and I carried Brandon outside to the fountain at the front of our house. He liked to go down there to listen to the frogs, so that's what we did. While I was outside, Pamela called the cops. After our walk, Brandon and I were sitting in the playroom when I heard a man's voice asking me to stand up and turn around. It was a cop, already in the house, and I hadn't even heard them come in. Pamela had already told them her side of the story on the phone, so I was arrested without question. While I was sitting in the cop car, handcuffed, I asked the sheriff why he wouldn't listen to what I had to say. His answer was, "In California, it's whoever gets to the phone first. If you would have called, this whole thing would have been reversed." That was February 24, 1998, just five days after our third-year anniversary.

The next day, I was labeled a wife beater by the media. That's tight. At some point in her story to the 5-0, Pamela mentioned that there were guns in the house, which violated my probation. Guess I should have read the small print on those court papers. Fuck! My whole collection, the one I replaced after the first one was stolen, was confiscated and that's when this situation and whatever I was going to be booked for was bumped up a notch. I had everything under the sun, from .38 Specials to fully automatic Uzis and Mack 10s, shotguns, riot guns, .44 Magnums, Berettas, Glocks, and FNC assault rifles. Those were my toys, and most of them were illegal. When Pamela led the cops up to the gun safe, I knew I was fucked.

I was in jail for two nights. I called my good friend and producer Scott Humphrey twenty-three times in thirty minutes that day. He had gone out to do some quick errand and couldn't believe it when he came back and saw that many messages on the answering machine, each one of them saying, "This is a collect call from the L.A. County Jail."

On my third day in jail, a piece of paper was handed to me. I sat there and read it, and at first I thought it said I needed to post $100,000 for bail. When I looked at the number again, I thought it was an optical illusion. It wasn't—I had to post one million dollars for bail. I fucking lost it. I felt like I was being treated like one of the Menendez brothers, like someone who had committed a hideous murder. Needless to say, my lawyers posted bail and got me out of there. Pamela had taken the kids and left our home. When I got back there, I tried to relax, but the media logjam outside and all around our property was worse than it had ever been. I tried to ignore it and sort shit out, but after two days, I was ready to jump off the fucking roof and really give them something to photograph. I called in Scott to help me out. He said he would take me in, but he sure as fuck wasn't going to have the media circus pitching tents outside his house. I thought I'd be able to get over there without being followed, but that wasn't happening. As soon as I left my driveway a convoy of five cars, a couple of vans, and a fucking helicopter tailed me. I was on the phone with Scott as I was driving, saying, "Um . . . dude? We have a problem, there's a fucking helicopter, a few news vans, and a shitload of paparazzi behind me." God bless Scott. He and my engineer Frank came up with a plan: We met at the top of Runyon canyon at night when it was pitch-black. He told me to go to a certain street and look for the blinking flash-light. I get there, I see the flashlight, and there's Scott in the bushes holding two mountain bikes. He's shouting at me to jump out of the truck, into the bushes, and to leave my keys in the ignition. I'm shouting, "What the fuck?" as I dive into the shrubs on the side of the road. Scott hands me a flashlight, tells me to get on the bike and follow him. We took off in the dark, down a steep hill, leaving my truck and a line of photographers scratching their heads in the dust. Scott had planned our escape route, all along the fire roads in the canyon that he rode all the time. He had never gone for a spin in the dark though, so there we are, flying down dirt paths with two little beams lighting the way, getting a little bit lost and at one point just tearing through brush. We get to the end of a road that Scott thought would be open and we find ourselves staring down a twelve-foot gate. We throw the bikes over it, onto someone's property, and climb over. As we ride away all the security lights go on in the house and some big fucking dogs start barking. We're sitting there, freaking, trying to peel out and going nowhere because the driveway we're trespassing on is gravel. That's tight. We finally made it to the pavement, thinking we were lost, way out of our way, and totally fucked. Then we looked down the road and realized we were just a few hundred feet from Scott's house.

Scott was the best—the next day he ordered a shitload of tall ficus trees and had them planted on his back balcony so no one could shoot pictures of me from the hills around it when I wanted to go outside and get some air. He saved my ass in so many ways. When we got back to his place, he turned to me and said, "You're at the house of music, man. I've got a room for you." He set me up with more than a room: There was a studio downstairs and all the instruments I could play. He knew that I needed a place to figure out what the fuck was happening to my life and _oh shit!!_ get out a lot of emotions. And he realized the practical side of getting out of jail: You are going to fucking have diar-rhea until you get used to eating regular food again. He had stocked the place with all the basics I'd need to get myself back to normal.

Downstairs in Scott's studio Rob Zombie was recording *Hellbilly Deluxe* and one day while I was there, he and Scott realized that I was upstairs, sitting around, thinking way too much.

They came up to my room and asked me if I wanted to play some drums on the album and I don't think I've ever been more ready to answer a question: There has never, ever been a time when I wanted to beat the fuck out of some drums that badly in my entire life. I wanted to fucking hit shit—hard. It was epic; that invitation was the therapy any good, honest doctor would have prescribed: "Tommy, as your

Do people know what this is? He might not be English, Lord Byron, but Rob Zombie has a fuck lot of fans here in the U.S.A. He's a rock star, an artist, and he just wrote and directed his first movie, House of 1,000 Corpses. I've played drums on most of Rob's solo albums. The question in my mind is, Why don't YOU know what "this" is? Shall I send you some MP3s?

physician, I advise that you find some drums to destroy as soon as possible. Continue the medication every day until you feel better." I had a lot to get out, so I ended up playing drums on four or five tracks of that album. I'm grateful for it: Scott, Rob, thanks dudes. Fuck! I needed that.

I lived with Scott for a few months and started to work on the music that became my solo project, *Methods of Mayhem*. Scott gave me a computer rig for my bedroom and I had my home studio computer brought over as well after Pamela and the kids moved back into our house. I worked every day and it was the only thing that kept me going as everything else in my life got worse. I was already on summary probation, which is the lightest variety, for flying too many assholes first class on friendly skies. After my arrest and Pamela's accusation of spousal abuse, I was in deep shit. On May 21, 1998, I was sentenced to three years in jail. In the end, I served four months and was let out early for good behavior with probation. That was the time that changed my life. It's not anything I can sum up without losing the plot right here.

Between the time I was arrested and went to court, and then went to jail, Pamela and I were still talking, still fighting, still at each other, and still so crazy about each other that we could not leave each other alone. We were trying to work things out, and let me tell you it was minute-to-minute. It was a fucking box of dynamite in a gas station and I was sitting on it lighting a cigarette. It felt like everyone in the world was part of our breakup, which didn't help. I didn't want to go public with all the bullshit, but she did. She really did. She went for the full-on media blitz and made me look like shit in every available media outlet.

I've always tried to take the high road when I get into fucked-up shit with people. I try to never judge anybody and if I'm gonna do it, I never do it in public. So I didn't say anything about Pamela even on those days when I felt like going the fuck off on her. To me, being Silent Guy was the right thing to do, but it sucked because when you say nothing people automatically assume you're guilty. Fuck 'em. Let 'em talk. They don't know shit about me.

After I did my jail time, which you'll learn about in a moment, my readers, it looked like things stood a chance of being normal again with Pamela and me—and there was nothing that I wanted more. I tried my best to work things out with her when I was behind bars. It wasn't easy. She started dating her old boyfriend, that surfer, Kelly Slater, and if you don't think that hurt, you don't know shit. We did start getting along again though, and it seemed like we were on our way to getting back together. We would spend time together with the kids, as a family, hang out, and it felt like we were finally enjoying each other again. But it didn't last forever. I went on tour with Mötley in support of our *Greatest Hits* album in 1999, and when we were separated, the lines of communication got twisted again. Both of us were still angry: We were going through our ups and downs—and they weren't in bed.

YOU GOT THAT RIGHT.

On one of our good nights, which happened to be New Year's Eve, Pamela came over and we hopped in the hot tub and I made the mistake of cracking a bottle of champagne to celebrate what felt like a new beginning. I was on probation and consuming alcohol violated the fuck out of it—if I were to be tested or if someone testified that I had consumed booze at all, I was heading back to jail. That night, celebrating with Pamela felt right to both of us. I didn't realize for a second that the champagne we shared was a full clip of hollow-point bullets served to her on a platter. Bad move.

On May 26, 2000, Pamela pulled the hammer back in court and shot those hollow points at will. While I was on tour with Methods of Mayhem, I was informed that she'd told the district attorney I'd violated my probation by consuming alcohol. I was fucked. And I went back to jail for four days. I got out on May 30. I don't remember dates too well, but let me tell you, those who have been to jail remember the day they get out.

Around the same time, this shitty situation went from worse to worst. Pamela had been hanging around with a mutual acquaintance of ours named Bob, and before I knew it I started getting emails from hell from her, which of course I fired right fucking back. That was great. What was better was the wack-ass courtesy call I got from Bob, all stuttering, saying, "Uh . . . hey, bro? Uh . . . I need to tell you something, dude. Um . . . Pamela and I hung out in New York . . . and . . . uh . . . dude, one thing lead to another." I said, "What are you talking about, dude?" He stumbled on, like a drunk guy walking home, saying things like, "Dude, I know we're buds and all, dude. . . . Ah, dude, I don't know what to do, dude." I'm on the phone, listening to this fucking idiot fumbling, knowing I know the deal, thinking, "Of course. Pamela made him call. Because she could never fucking do it." When my patience ran out and I couldn't take it anymore I said, "Thanks for the courtesy call, asshole." Click. Later. Whatever.

Shit, Bob! I thought we were boys! I reminisced back to 1999, when ol' Bob* came by while I was working on my *Methods of Mayhem* album. He rapped or whatever you want to call what he does on one of my tracks. Thank God he didn't do any of that country shit he's doing now on my record. I thought about how I'd met him: I'd invited Fred Durst over to be on the record and he showed up with Bob. I didn't give a fuck—hell, I didn't even really know who he was. Those guys were early and partied with their posse down in the studio while I had dinner with Carmen Electra, my girlfriend at the time. After Bob made many trips to the bathroom, and I was done eating, it was time to throw down. I'd only planned on recording Fred that night, but Bob was hell-bent on getting on the mike. What the fuck did I care? We worked for hours and at the end of the night, when I went to save all the work we'd done, I hit the wrong key and deleted all those files—Fred and Bob were gone. Karma? Fate? I don't know. For better or for worse, we eventually rerecorded them. Anyway,

---

* Bob Ritchie, a.k.a. Kid Rock, whose third album of the same name sold far less than any of his other efforts. That's because it's a wack blend of pseudo-country and rock delivered by a performer who sounds better shouting than singing, but that, of course, is just this cowriter's opinion.

that was the first night I met Bob and I had met him only one other time after that, just chilling in his hotel room after some show or other. We had made music, we had partied, we were friends—and I thought this cat was my bud. After that phone call, all I could think was, "Why you gotta raise up on my ex, dude? There are so many other hot ladies on tap."

Whatever. The two of them started hanging out. Bob has custody of his son, so I'm almost positive that he got in Pamela's ear about getting full custody of our kids—at least that's what she told me recently. That's when it became a war, because I love my boys too much not to be a major part of their lives every step of the way. Within six months, the full court custody battle began.

I hated having to put our boys through the weirdness of us separating. Divorce is difficult for anyone at any age, but I'm very glad that my boys were young enough that they might just forget the details of the time that Pamela and I were butting heads. We were like two fucking rams. It was just terrible to be so mad at someone you love so much. But I think back to when I was around six and I can remember things about that time—generally, it's good shit, like my dad taking me fishing in Minnesota. The things that remain in your soul or your subconscious or whatever are snapshots that you feel more than see. It's the same way the smell of gardenias takes me all the way back to my mom's garden when I was a little kid.

I only hope that the tough times between Pamela and me—all the custody shit, all the divorce rage that went back and forth between us—did not register in our boys' memories. Because that time and the way we treated each other was not and is not their mom and dad. We were getting things out that they'll only understand much later, when they're older. On the divorce, on the lawyers, it was such a ridiculous amount of money we spent. We dropped six figures on all that fighting, and if we had been adults, we would have figured out some way to communicate, work out a plan, and put that money in the boys' trust funds instead of funding new wings on our lawyers' Beverly Hills estates. If we had had the tools to talk to each other, we could have avoided the legal system and the whole fucking endless train of paperwork—damn we killed a ton of trees. Pamela and I threw rocks at each other's glass houses, in transcripts hacked out by court stenographers, in arguments acted out by lawyers before a judge, in motions filed with the court—all the money we wasted went into everyone else's pockets. The boys got none of it. Looking back, I wish we'd just piled it up and lit it on fire. At least the Monkeys could have roasted some marshmallows on it.

13

STATE OF TRANSITION

a.k.a.
INCARCERATION +
CONTEMPLATION +
INITIATION =
SALVATION!

I went to jail in 1998. Here's the deal. After my arrest the night Pamela and I fought, I was hauled in. After Pamela led the po-po to my gun safe, I was looking at a stack of charges: spousal abuse, illegal possession of weapons, violation of my probation from piloting the uninvited, and a few others that spelled "fucked." After all was said and done in the courts, I pled no contest to the spousal accusation to avoid the much heavier sentence I would have gotten for weapons possession. The judge gave me four months in L.A. County Jail.

Jail was hell for me. I remember sitting there and talking to my manager at the time, and telling him how much I was freaking out. I was writing on the walls, counting the days. He was like, "Okay, stop counting the days. Just count the weeks. And every seventh day you're there, that's the day you can fucking lose your mind and freak out about being cooped up." He was right. I had four months to kill in there—an entire summer. And summer is the season I live for.

I couldn't see daylight at all in my cell. There were just walls all around me. My view was a tiny little window wide enough for my face, through which I could see down the hall. No bars, nothing, just a solid steel door. They'd open it twice a day to bring in food. They were casual about giving me my tray of mystery meat, but it wasn't that way with my cell's former resident. Before me, one of the Menendez brothers—I'm not sure which one—was in there. They painted a white line on the floor that he had to stand behind whenever they opened the door. Creepy. In my cell there was a little toilet, if you can call it that, and a bed. I don't know what time anything happened, but I'd guess it was about seven or eight in the morning when they'd wake us up by turning the lights on, bright as *fuck*. Or they'd bang on the door. Every two days they'd take me out for a shower. And once a week, every Thursday, they'd take me out to a cage on the roof. L.A. County Jail was like this high-rise with nothing around it—no trees, no people, no nothing. You could see a piece of sky and a bit of sun. They'd always take me up there toward the end of the day so that I'd see sunset, or a slice of it. It was like an escape-proof pigeon coop and I'd sit there with tears rolling down my face, staring at a sliver of sun.

I thought about a lot of shit in jail, but when I was in that cage, I couldn't think about anything else but freedom, about how much of it I've had all my life and how much freedom anyone who isn't in jail takes for granted. Other than that, nature to me was reduced to cockroaches and flies. I'd get all excited when I saw them in my cell. I'd talk to them, I'd get down on the floor and watch them walk around. They were my friends. There were three that lived with me and I named them, Manny, Moe, and Jack—they were the roaches who lived in my trash. Those guys only came out when the lights went off at night. They must have done some bad shit because they acted like they were never getting out of that place. I just know they're still there. What up, dudes? I kinda miss you guys.

It's strange to look at it now, and I guess this is some kind of natural reaction to a difficult experience, but I see moments in jail as if they are scenes from a movie that I'm not even in. There I was, up on a roof in a cage. I was left up there alone for fifteen minutes each week. I can't tell you how much I looked forward to Thursday. But some Thursdays I passed on my cage time because I just couldn't handle it. I cried every time I was up there, thinking about everywhere else I wanted to be. Those weeks that I didn't go topside, I exchanged my fifteen minutes of fresh air for a book. I just wanted to read and find a positive message, which I needed. Those weeks, Buddhism helped me more than going outside and dreaming about being free.

On my first day or two in there, I was initiated into one of the rituals that kept me going during my time in there. The brothers down the hall were beating on the metal bars, laying out a beat. I was so pumped to hear that, I'd jump up on my bunk and start playing the sheet of steel over my window. Drums! Thank God! Soon enough the whole block was rocking with beats. We did it all the time and you should have heard it. I wish I'd been allowed a tape recorder. You can't re-create the sound of pent-up inmates — it is tribal, it is raw, it is so many voices and so many stories being released, all of them bouncing off the same walls that hold them all in. I looked forward to that every day. It was monkey see monkey do: It didn't matter who started the rhythm, we'd all join in. And we'd fucking go off.

I looked forward to the weekends more than anything — that was my chance to get out of my cell and see the friends who came to visit me. I don't think I can ever thank them enough for sacrificing the time it took them to visit. They'd have to wait for hours in line, get searched, and deal with the hassle that comes with the corrections system, all to see me for just fifteen minutes. When you're locked up, you find out quick who cares and who doesn't. Seeing those friends was a lifeline, but it wasn't easy on me, and I could tell it wasn't easy on them. I'd be sitting there in my blue suit with my hands and my ankles shackled, feeling like I'd murdered somebody. I didn't expect special treatment, but I hadn't raped, killed, or done anything that most of the other inmates had done. I know everyone gets treated equally in jail and that being confined is a psychological process designed to break you down. But when my friends would visit, they couldn't believe what they saw: I was chained to the seat like a mass murderer.

There are two people who meant a lot to me when they came to see me. The first is Gerald Wil Rafferty, Ph.D., the man who has since become my life coach and spiritual leader. A friend told him to come see me while I was in jail. He changed my life and was there for me anytime I needed him. I was losing it in there: I didn't know what to think and I didn't know what to do. And when I met this stranger for the first time, I watched him walk up to the glass and wondered if he could really help me or if he was another one of those top-dollar, designer Hollywood gurus. He wasn't. Gerald has such an incredible calming and wise presence that precedes him. Even through bulletproof glass, I could tell that he knew something I didn't know and that he had knowledge I needed. He walked in holding meditational beads. He didn't say anything, he just pressed his other hand on the glass. I put mine up to meet his, and I felt that this man had been sent to me. Right then I knew that everything was going to be okay. We both cried after that, looking at each other through the window. I wondered why he was crying, because I was the one in hell, and he didn't even know me. Now I understand. He's been nothing but a guiding light to me since that day. Thanks, Gerald, you know how much you mean to me.

Gerald set his answering machine to accept all collect calls, so I could call anytime and just talk. There were times when I couldn't take it anymore, when I left messages about how I wanted to take my pants off, wrap them around my neck, and hang myself from the light fixture in my cell because I couldn't stand being in jail another day. I could call him and talk about anything at any time: I could just call and cry or spill any random thought that came into my mind. He became my sanctuary.

Sometimes I just called to hear his voice on the answering machine—sometimes that was all I needed.

The second person I want to thank is my best girl friend, Diane. I don't have the ability to put into words how she made my time in jail as pleasant as it could possibly be. I had a phone in my cell and could call her collect any time of the day and most of the time she was there to talk to me. I've always been able to relate better to women than to men and Diane was there for me; she was my angel. I would call her and she knew by the sound of my voice what I needed, whether it was music, a shoulder to cry on, or a best friend. Some days, she would just put the phone down for an hour and let me listen to music over the phone. I'd be on my cot, with the receiver to my ear, crying and listening to Sarah McLachlan. Let me tell you, when you call collect from a county facility, the charges are double and not once did Diane ever mention the cost. She is the only girl friend—and I mean a true girl friend—whom I've had in my life. She came to see me all the time and she was there for me all the time. My wife didn't come, none of my exes came, but Diane did, and I'll never forget that until the day I die. She's heard it all and she knows it all—and she helped me make sense of my life when everything became nonsense. I'm at a loss, trying to put this down right now, because I don't think the English language can capture how much I feel for her for being there for me—those words just don't exist. All I can say is that from the bottom of my heart, D, you kept me alive, and I'm forever in your debt. I love you. And if you weren't my best friend—and married to the man I introduced you to, who is also one of my best friends (and one of the best fucking DJs in the world)* —I'd marry you in a heartbeat.

I'd like to take a minute to thank everyone else who came to see

---

* That would be Mix Master Mike, born Michael Schwartz, a founding member of the world-renowned DJ collective Invizibl Skratch Picklz. Mike joined the Beastie Boys as DJ in 1998, following the release of *Hello Nasty*. Mike is an amazing turntablist—there are passengers and there are drivers. I suggest you don your seatbelts when he is in the house because Mike, when in full effect, is in the driver's seat, my friends.

me in jail: my mom and dad, my sister, Athena, Nikki Sixx, Mick Mars. And last but not least, Bob Suhusky, I'm telling you now, you're a good man. Thanks for looking after my house, even though a bunch of fuck-heads broke into it—that wasn't your fault, bro. While we're on the subject, I'm convinced that those nasty Pilferazzis are to blame. It wasn't hard to find out that I was living somewhere else for a while. Who-ever did it smashed the glass front doors of my house and instead of stealing the hundreds of thousands of dollars worth of studio equipment, all they took was my 35mm camera. They were clearly looking for pics from my Going to Jail party. Whatever. For the record, Bob is the one who set my answering machine to accept collect calls, so he's partly re-sponsible for *Methods of Mayhem*. Without Bob, all those lyrics and melodies would never have made it out of the concrete walls of my cell. Thanks to my friend Bob Procop as well. I'll always remember his visit. He strolled up and slapped porno mags against the glass. I thought I'd hit the jackpot.

WORD MUTHAFUCKA!
IT WAS THE FIRST PUSSY WE'D SEEN IN
MONTHS! I WAS TIRED OF GETTING CHOKED,
I THOUGHT I WAS FINALLY FREE!! YAY!

It was less than a minute before the wardens confiscated his porno, but it didn't matter. I kept those images in my head for the rest of my stay. You rock, Mr. Procop.

In jail, any "famous" person is separated—they call you a K-10, a keep-away—from the general population. But I began to feel so disconnected in solitary confinement that I started to think it would be better to be put in with the other inmates than be alone every day. When I was up in the cage I'd look across the roof to where the other convicts were playing basketball and lifting weights, and I wanted to be over there. I just wanted to talk to someone—*anyone*. I asked the guards if I could do that and they shot that idea down real quick. They told me that Robert Downey Jr. asked for the same privilege until the wardens caved and let him go out there. They said it was all of five minutes before motherfuckers were all up in his face. The guards told me he mouthed off and got his ass beat real bad. I said, "That's cool, I dig the cage."

In jail, all you do is eat, shit, work out, read, think, and sleep. I filled some trash bags with water and used those for weights, until they took them away. I did push-ups, I did handstands against the wall. I did anything I could think of to make one more day go by. My lunch came with an apple that had a sticker on it, so I took those stickers and made them into a huge flower on the cell wall. That kept me sane until I was allowed pencils and paper—that was a good day. I drew this amazing sketch of me under a tree, in the middle of nowhere, looking around at my life. I sat and made that picture in one day: It was a portrait of where I wanted to be. I love to draw, I love to put my feelings into symbols, but I've always been too impatient to take the time to sketch. Sitting in my cell it was amazing to learn that I could in fact do it well. It was the coolest picture I've ever drawn. (And I'll probably never do one like it again.)

After a while I realized I had two options: I could make jail a really shitty experience or I could make it a positive thing, as much as it could be. I looked at my life to figure out why I was there and what I needed to change. I asked myself why in so many ways.

That was the upside of jail. I would have much rather done that soul-searching under a tree or in some rad cabin in Montana. When I knew I was leaving, that picture I drew of myself was the last thing I took off the wall. I still have it and I'll always keep it. I'm looking at it now and it's like smelling something from childhood: It brings me right back—a little too efficiently—to my cell. I hope the statute of limitations is up on this, but I took something else when I left: I took my jail shoes. They're black with a piece of gray rubber on the toe that says "L.A. County Jail." To this day, they're my constant reminder of where I never, ever, ever,

ever, EVER want to go. And they sit right where I can see them every day—in my studio.

You want to talk about powerlessness? Check this. I had been in the slammer less than a week, and loud and clear, I hear some inmates down the hall shouting, "Hey, Tommy!" I'm like "Hey, what up?" Those guys had a TV in their cell and they tell me how they're watching my wife hanging out on the beach holding hands with "some surfer dude" on *Entertainment Tonight* or some shitty Hollywood news bottom-feeder show. Whatever.

I never saw the guys who kept me up-to-date, but those cons were like the fucking *Enquirer,* informing me of every way my life was turning into one big pile of shit. They were there when Pamela was on *Jay Leno* and Jay asked her in a really condescending way, "You're not going to get back with Tommy, are you?" Jay's audience booed and thanks to my fellow prisoners, I got the play-by-play. Pamela told Jay, "No," she wasn't getting back with me.

Imagine being locked up and hearing, through your fellow locked-up fuck-ups, that your wife is moving on. If that isn't going to teach you that you're no longer driving the bus down the highway that you think is your life, I don't know what is. It fucking *sucked* and at the time I wanted to see what was going on, but thank God I didn't have a TV. That box would have been in a thousand pieces, along with the bones in my hand and probably other parts of me that I'm glad are still intact.

To tell you the truth, what I've just told you is the least of what I saw and what I learned in jail. It changed me—how couldn't it? One of the saddest things I noticed in jail is that there are so many disturbed people incarcerated who have no outlet to learn about anything or get motivated to better themselves in any way. The libraries in jail are wack. And if there is any place that could use a supply of meaningful books, that's it. There are maniacs in there, locked up, with no information to learn about the world, which guarantees that they'll be exactly the same when they get out. Good luck to you if you're in jail and you want to change. All you can get access to are old stupid books that say nothing. The library cart was full of fiction—and there isn't a place more in need of nonfiction than jail. Fantasy means shit when true reality is all around you.

I was fortunate enough to have books shipped to me during my stay. And all I kept thinking when I got out is that maybe some of those guys, had they had the right resources, stood a chance to change. It wouldn't help all the convicts, but having real books to read would help some of them—and if the taxpayers' dollars went to that, it might make a difference.

What I saw in jail was more insane than anything I've ever seen anywhere. And it changed me—I was in solitary, but there was a hole in my wall that my neighbors could pass things through. Even if you can't see anyone else, you are connected, a part of a community whether you like it or not. I learned that inmates are the most resourceful people in the world. They make homemade wine that they call "pruno" out of juice, sugar packets, bread, and yeast. They put it in a trash bag and let it sit for a couple of weeks. When it's ready, you hear a huge cry, all down the cell block: "Pruno!" The pruno would make its way around, delivered by the trustees. These were the lucky inmates—they get chosen to sweep the floors, clean shit, and serve the food, and they'd use their advantage and access to steal whatever the other inmates needed. Put it this way: If you're friends with the trustees, you could get whatever you want. They'd change all the time though, because they always got busted. When the pruno was ready, they'd bring it down in a plastic garbage bag and hold it under the door. I'd pull the bag from underneath the door and they'd push on the other end, sending the liquid and the whole package through the inch-wide crack at the bottom of the door into my cell. The first time a batch of pruno was ready, I heard someone way down the cell block yell, "Send T. Lee some of that motherfuckin' shit!" It tasted like ass, dude, but it would get you *fucked* up. Sometimes the wardens would come down and bust the guys making the pruno. And then we'd all have to wait another couple weeks for the next batch to ripen.

There were so many motherfuckers in jail who didn't give a fuck about what was going to happen to them. If you're caught smoking weed or cigarettes or doing heroin in jail, you get another year added to your sentence. Most of the guys didn't really give a shit about that. I'd be sitting there in my cell, being offered everything—and you can get anything you want in jail. A joint would come through the hole in my wall and I'd say, "Fuck that, dude. I'm outta here in a few weeks." Guys would take one cigarette and make four little pinner cigarettes out of it. It was crazy to get one whole cigarette. I hadn't had a cigarette for weeks in jail and then one day, all of a sudden a little rollie—that's what we called them—comes under my door. I look out my little window and there's the trustee who chucked it to me. Unfortunately, I don't have a light. The guys in the cell next to me told me how to make fire *MacGyver* style. They told me to chew the wood of my pencil and pull out the lead, and then stomp on my plastic razor to get the two blades out. I was then instructed to put the blades in the electrical socket, wrap toilet paper around the pencil lead, and touch it to the blades. It lit up in my hand and I torched my miniciggie. I stood on my bunk, blowing smoke up the vent. I was loving it—until I realized that I could stay in jail for another year if I was caught. I threw that thing down the toilet fast.

I learned so much crazy stuff in jail. You can make a dagger out of newspaper if you roll it up tight enough and sharpen it against the floor. You can take the roller ball from the deodorant you're given and if you rub it on the floor long enough you can make dice. You melt the black combs you're allowed to mark them up. Once you've got dice, you can gamble.

When I was in jail, all I wanted was to get out. I sat and thought about why I was there and what I would do to make sure I never got there again. So many guys in there didn't care though. They didn't think they had anywhere else to go. They got fed every day, they had a place to sleep, and let me tell you, there were more drugs available in there for free than there are on the street.

The trustees came by offering heroin, pills, everything. There's a hospital in jail, so every drug on earth was available. They'd ask me what I wanted but to me it always felt like I was being set up. One day, the chief warden pulled me into another room and told me that a couple of the trustees didn't dig me and wanted to poison me. He just wanted to let me know.

After I was in there for a while, there was one day when I looked out of my little twelve-by-twelve-inch window and saw the guards carrying away some stiff, dead, blue-lipped motherfucker. You can't really ask what happened when someone dies in jail because no one says anything—not the inmates, not the wardens, no one. It was like it never happened.

If that wasn't insane enough, the whole time I was in jail, I signed more autographs than anywhere else I've ever been. I found out that there are a lot of fucking Mötley fans in jail, which is pretty scary. Each day, the wardens would take inmates from different wings of the jail out for a walk and as they'd pass my cell, slips of paper would fly under my door, asking me to write a note to guys' girlfriends, brothers, or to whomever it meant something.

I'm not sure how many of you can relate to this, but the day that you know you're getting released from jail is the best day of your life. You know you're getting out, and you wait all fucking day to hear your name announced over the speakers: "T. Lee, roll it up," which means roll your shit up and get out. You don't know what time it's going to happen, so you just wait. When your name is called, all your homies start shouting, "Yeah! Dude, rip it, good luck! Don't come back!" As I was leaving, I looked back, knowing that all of them are going to be there for a long time. They're still there, I'm sure, and that's tragic.

I learned a lot in those four months and I'm glad that I wrote a lot of it down. I left with a whole folder full of notes. Those journals are filled with some crazy, crazy shit because I was spinning out like bald-ass tires on a rainy day. I came out of jail a different man because I met myself, someone who had been chasing a dream without looking in the mirror for far too long. In that way, and only in that way, it was an enlightening experience. I finally found out who the fuck I really am.

I didn't answer all my questions about life, and I may never—does anybody? I did answer a few of the big ones (thank God). For what it's worth, I read a lot and I'm going to list the books I read. They seemed like the answer to everything. They changed my life and if you're out there, and you're fucked, feeling lost, feeling like you need some guidance, feeling like you need to find your own truth, this is my gift to you. What works for one person might not work for everyone, but treat this like a smorgasbord of spiritual information. It's a buffet—make a plate, taste it all, take as much as you like of each dish, and when you're ready for seconds, create your own recipe. You will get it wrong at first, you'll burn it, you'll undercook it, but don't stop, that's life. Get back in the kitchen and prepare to ask yourself, "How hungry am I?"

There were many that moved me, but this is T. Lee's twelve-pack, in no particular order:

1. *The Wisdom of James Allen: Five Classic Works Combined into One*, James Allen
2. *Conversations with God*, Neale Donald Walsch
3. *Awakening the Buddha Within: Eight Steps to Enlightment*, Lama Surya Das
4. *In the Meantime: Finding Yourself and the Love You Want*, Iyanla Vanzant
5. *Dirty Jokes and Beer*, Drew Carey
6. *The Artist's Way: A Spiritual Path to Higher Creativity*, Julia Cameron
7. *Awakening the Buddhist Heart*, Lama Surya Das
8. *Meditations from Conversations with God*, Neale Donald Walsch
9. *Please Kill Me*, Legs McNeil
10. *Hammer of the Gods*, Stephen Davis
11. *Tuesdays with Morrie*, Mitch Albom
12. *Raising a Son: Parents and the Making of a Healthy Man*, Don Elium and Jeanne Elium

Conversations with God meant the most to me. There are times in every-one's life when a certain book or song will land at exactly the right time. This was mine. I was so moved by it that I wrote to the author at the ad-dress I found in the back of the book. He wrote back to me and sent me a signed copy of his new book. His words changed my life—I would even say that his words saved my life. Don't worry, Oprah, I'm not going to start the Tommy Lee Book Club or anything, but if all you people out there have the time to read a book (which I guess you do because you're reading this one), read a book that you find meaningful for one hour a day—it is a great gift that you can easily give yourself. Hell, if that book is mine, I'm flattered. Reading is like vitamins for your soul. A good book can change your life as much as a perfect piece of music or an amazing painting. It can take your world and show you parts of it you might be missing. And don't you want to know as much about being a human as you can?

I don't know, but it seems to me that people don't do anything unless something is broken. Trust me, I'm one of them. When you are in a bad way, you start looking for answers. You go to a shrink, you get reli-gious. You can call it soul-searching or whatever you want, but taking the time to ask yourself the big questions isn't a part of the regularly scheduled program.

Those who have a child or a demanding job, or *fuck*, just trying to get the bills paid and get a nice comfortable life for themselves know how fast the days, weeks, and years go by. Finding time for yourself is a challenge, as dumb as that sounds. I learned the hard way that everyone needs to make time for themselves, even if it's just a few minutes. Do it. More im-portant, it's the only way you'll know who you are, how you feel, and dis-cover what you really want out of life. If you don't have those answers clear in your mind yet, don't worry, there's still time if you're still breath-ing. Time is all we have here, so make the most of it. If you need a regular reminder, check this shit out: www.deathclock.com. Get in touch with yourself so that you can truly, honestly, openly love and share the real you with whomever you choose. If you don't, that's a lonely life, my friends. You're walking through this world in a cell, just like I was, but it's worse — it's a cell you can't even see.

When I got out of jail, my good friend Bob Procop picked me up in a Bentley. I fucking love those cars. There were paparazzi everywhere outside, so we ran and jumped in the ride, and I'll never forget driving down the road looking around at the world for the first time in four months. It freaked me out: stoplights, traffic, people crossing streets. It seemed like everything was so crazy, going so fast, that it made my heart pound and filled me full of anxiety. Everything that was once familiar to me seemed alien. My man Bob had a fresh pack of Marlboro Lights in the car. I lit one up and hands down it was the best cigarette I've ever had.

We drove down Pacific Coast Highway after finally getting out of downtown L.A. and then I started looking at the beauty all around me. The scenery was way too much — the stars, the ocean, the sky, the trees. If you haven't cruised PCH, let me tell you, it's heaven: a winding road right on the ocean with cliffs and mountains to one side and God's swimming pool on the other.

Bob was taking me to his beach house that he'd filled with bubble bath and a bunch of chicks. I love him. I hadn't taken a bath all summer. We get there and it's on. I'm sitting there with four amazing-looking women in the hot tub, stars above us and bubbles below. I remember turning my head away so no one could see me crying. Finally, I was out of that fucking shithole.

It was the first time I had been around any people at all and I didn't know how to act. Somewhere in there I forgot how to talk to people. I had nothing to say to them; I really didn't know how to be. Everyone congratulated me on getting out, it was great, but all I wanted to do was go home. Bob understood, so he took me home. Pamela had taken the kids and moved out. The place was empty.

I have another friend named Bob,* who held down my fort while I was away. He let me into my home and I stood there in awe. I walked through every room in the house as if I'd never seen it before. Only this time it was different. My family was gone, my kids' toys weren't all over the floor, the closets were empty, and so was I. We had called it the Love Palace. And now it felt like a drafty ruin.

I wanted to escape. I didn't want to think about what I was feeling. All I wanted to do was sleep: sleep in my own bed. You don't even know, and I hope you never do, now all I wanted was to rest and not be roused by the sound of jangling keys, slamming doors, and announcements barked over the fucking PA system. The two Bobs could see how bad I wanted to be alone, so they left. They (and I) were ready to celebrate my release, but I knew my sentence was far from done. I had to be downtown at the probation office the next morning. Fuck, yeah, I wanted a drink, a party, you know, the whole nine. But that wasn't going to happen. My party was lying down in my *own* bed. I had slept way too long on a piece of shit one-inch-thick-trying-to-be-a-mattress cot that smelled like the lid on a rancid can of fuck.

I was all kinds of spun out after jail. Everyone called like crazy—my answering machine was smoking. I sat there and stared at the thing and didn't know what to do. It felt good to hear people congratulating me and wishing me well, but as much as I wanted to I couldn't call them back. I just wasn't ready.

After a few days the Bobs had a group of people come by just to say hello and I totally hated it. I hadn't decompressed yet. I just remember wanting everyone to go home and feeling like shit about it. I just wanted to be alone. I needed time to slowly resurface and I had no idea how long it was going to take. I thought, "Damn . . . I just want to sleep for weeks."

---

* Neither of these Bobs should be confused with the aforementioned Bob Ritchie who dated Pamela Anderson after she and Tommy were divorced. No, that Bob is altogether different.

14

STATE OF METAMORPHOSIS

a.k.a.
MY NEW METHOD

When I got out of jail, I planned to leave the Crüe because, after twenty years of the same thing, I had to do something else as soon as possible.

I wanted to go everywhere that no one expected me to go. I thought about my next move every day I was in jail. I had so much to say and I was gonna fucking rock it. Sitting in there, with nothing but time on my hands, a million melodies and lyrics came to my head, which, as noted before, I recorded on my home answering machine after a friend set it up to accept collect calls. My bills were fucking *insane.*

Nikki came to visit me in jail and talked to me while I was behind glass in shackles. Nikki and Mick were the only two bandmates who came to visit me. I told him right then, before I was even released to do the final Mötley tour, that I was leaving. When I first told Nikki, he looked at me like I was on crack. I couldn't expect him to get it—he wasn't sitting around, alone, thinking about his life for four months. As I explained it, he began to understand. He could see that I had a lot on my mind and that I had to work it out on my own.

I agreed to do Mötley Crüe's *Greatest Hits* tour, but I told Nikki that

I planned to bring my portable studio with me. When the tour was over, I was going to do a solo project. Every night after our gig I went back to my room and stayed up until three or four in the morning working on music.

I wrote a phrase that became my motto, and it goes something like this: "Music never talks back to me, music never argues with me, music is my best friend, music doesn't put me in jail unless I get naked onstage, music makes me happy, and music makes me sad only when I want it to. Music is my memory, and music is my wife. Music is my life partner, the only one who will never *ever* leave me." It's true. I make music—it's my language, it's the best way I know how to say what I want to say.

After the Mötley *Greatest Hits* tour, my new sonic assault was ready and so was I. I pulled in all the shit I was listening to and loving. *Methods of Mayhem* was a creative free-for-all—something that I'd been dying to do. It was time to mix it up. *Fuck*, I'm a drummer, I love everything with a beat, from Earth, Wind & Fire to DJ Shadow, from Josh Wink to the Beastie Boys to Rage Against the Machine, from the Wu to DMX. And there's more, of course. I could go on for days. I wanted to do something different and my motivation was music that inspired me from all genres.

I was free now and on my own to mix it all up—rock, hip-hop, techno, industrial—fucking rhythm for days. Some people just weren't ready. To them, I was an eighties rock drummer turned wigger. I didn't grow up in the 'hood, I wasn't in a gang, I didn't sling rocks on the block. Never said I did. Why does singing with rhythm and loving hip-hop mean I'm trying to be all gangsta? Fuck off, y'all. Whatever. Really, truly, honestly, I've got no interest in being involved with anything unless I love it. Listen to "Welcome to Planet Boom," which came out in 1994 on the Mötley album *Quarternary*. I was already fucking with hip-hop beats and rhythmic vocals back then. I've been rocking samples, video, retarded drum spectacles, and whatever took shit to the next level for years.

Methods of Mayhem was a completely natural evolution for me. I didn't care if I fell flat on my face, I did what I was feeling. I had been a fan of everything from the Beastie Boys to Nine Inch Nails for far too long. Rock and hip-hop together have always been so cool, I had to fuck with it.

Dance music was kicking my ass too. And I finally had the chance to mix it up. I can play piano, I can play guitar, but first and last I'm a drummer. Hip-hop, if you ask me, is the verbalization of rhythm. It's like playing drums with the English language. Why wouldn't I mess with that? Why wouldn't I make something funky?

I argued that point in every interview I did after the *Methods* album came out in 1999. But it was hard for many people, after seeing me play drums in a rock band for so long, to see me up front singing, playing guitar, and making music that didn't sound like Mötley Crüe. There were journalists who just went for it to the point that I had to say, "Look, I'm not going to fight with you, but you've got to realize who I am. I'm a drummer; I'm moved by beats. My whole world revolves around rhythm. How can I not write music that is founded on that?" Everything I do, I do to a beat, whether it's playing guitar, driving my car, or making up a new handshake with my kids. N!%%@, please, I'm a rhythm man.

At the same time, I love melody, and when I write songs they're also all about melody in one way or another. Aside from the first Mötley record, which was all Nikki, I did a majority of the songwriting with him. Most of the hits that people know us for are due in part to me. And as rock as Mötley ever got, there was always a melody in there. I grew up with Cheap Trick, and if you want to hear melody and rhythm and pop you can't deny, listen to them, right now. That power pop tradition had a huge effect on Mötley and the way I approach a song.

After working with the same three guys for more than twenty years, I couldn't wait to collaborate with other artists. I wasn't going to fuck around: I contacted every artist I wanted to work with directly. I assembled Tommy's roster of all-stars: U God of Wu-Tang Clan; Lil' Kim, the nastiest girl in the world; my man DJ Mix Master Mike; George Clinton; the Crystal Method; and the F.I.L.T.H.E.E. Immigrants, an L.A. underground rap group y'all need to check out. I just thought, "Fuck, I'm going to make a crazy new record. We'll figure out what it is when it's done."

Methods of Mayhem was a huge test, and it was a test I passed, a test which made me stronger. No matter what the critics or the fans who didn't like the album have said, I think it was probably the best work I've done. I stand by it fully and a lot of the hip-hop peeps I've met said they dug it too. And that was a huge compliment.

People who like to be spoon-fed would be confused, but I did not care. There's a track called "Metamorphosis" that lays it all out. I wrote it in jail, and it was a turning point in my life. I wanted to write a song about how things change from one form to another: seeds to flowers, love to children, babies to adults, songs to memories, marriage to devotion, guilt to blame, and how I could be a son to my father and a father to my sons. When I sang those words all the changes I made in jail made sense.

There's also a track called "Anger Management," and the inspiration there is obvious. The song "New Skin" was my farewell to the shitty parts of my past that dragged me down. Here's the chorus: "Like a snake shed my skin leave my past where I've been . . . Can you feel what I feel? . . . To hold on must be killed don't cry over what's been spilled . . . Can u feel what I feel?" *Methods* was my experiment, my Frankenstein.

I expected some fans to not get it at all. There are always those people who want their favorite artists to keep making their favorite album over and over again. After prison, I gave less of a fuck about that than ever. It was cathartic for me to write those songs because I took the lessons I'd learned in jail and put them out there for everyone to hear.

What I wasn't ready for was the reality of dropping back into the music circus while I was on probation. There I was, touring with my band, playing our new shit, and getting drug tested every single day on tour. When we rolled into town, there'd be a taxi or limo waiting for me at the hotel that took me to the nearest clinic where I would pee in a cup while a nurse watched. That cup of urine would be shipped back to Los Angeles for analysis—and if they found a trace of *anything,* I was going back to my studio apartment at County, L.A.'s premier correctional living facility. It wasn't the way I was used to touring. Plus, I've never been a pee-on-command kind of guy—except when playing fireman. Living on a bus with the maniacs in my band, who partied every single night, wasn't easy. They'd forget that I couldn't be around huge clouds of weed smoke and more booze than Daytona Beach at spring break. Headlining our own *Methods of Mayhem* tour was hard, but it was nothing compared to the summer we spent on Ozzfest. Every single person and every fucking place I looked was WASTED.

I got off that tour without getting into trouble and there's only one reason for that: music. I had a full portable studio built into the back suite of my tour bus. We ripped everything out to fit all the equipment in. It was Tommy's Nest, Tommy's Happy Place—and I needed to go there the second I was offstage to hide from all of the debauchery around me. I'd spend most of my nights after those shows back in my room or on the bus making music.

My life being my life, things were never straightforward, even when it seemed like everything was in line. A major trademark lawsuit arose after the album came out and we were on tour. Of course it did. A company called TT Sounds Good put out some sample CD *Methods of Mayhem* that producers use for loops and special effects in the studio. They sued me, claiming I stole their title. Dude, I've had the word "mayhem" tattooed on my stomach since back when those cats were still shittin' yellow.

It's good that I'm a Libra, because Libras are able to see both sides of a situation. For the astrologically unaware, the Libra symbol is the justice scales. Anyway, I could see where TT was coming from, getting all sue-happy, seeing dollar signs everywhere. Sorry, that's just my opinion. I'll let you decide. Trademark law—I know a fuck of a lot about it now—dictates that if you release something like an album or a book, you have a trademark over that name for the body of work. Seems to me like a collection of samples and sounds isn't exactly thematic. It's a collection of sounds and special effects—we're not talking *Led Zeppelin IV*. Anyway, the record company lawyers settled without my authorization—because they didn't need it—but I was told by a juror that if the case had gone to a jury we would have won. During a recess toward the end of the proceedings, I was sitting in a restaurant in New York with the lawyers from my record company, going on about how we can win, when all of a sudden I see one of the team go over and shake hands with the guy who was suing me. The record company lawyer—someone supposedly on *my* side—just cut a deal to hand the other side a shitload of money. I almost started slugging my legal team right there over their fucking overpriced entrées. They probably billed me for those too.

Losing when I knew we could have won wasn't the end of the insults of course. My record company at the time, MCA, pretty much went out of business. In the late nineties, all the labels were folded into massive conglomerates that control almost all the music that is put out today. It happened fast, people were fired, no one gave a fuck about the stuff or a lot of the artists, and when the lights were shut off at MCA, guess who got slapped with the lawyers' bill in the summer of 2003? Yep. Whatever. I'm glad I had a cold bottle of Jäger on hand that morning. As a famous German philosopher* once said, "What does not kill me makes me stronger."

---

* That would be Friedrich Nietzsche (1844–1900).

15

STATE OF SOCIETAL DEBT

a.k.a.
ANGER
MANAGEMENT
AND
COMMUNITY SERVICE

One condition of my release from jail and probation period was that I immediately enroll in anger management classes and complete 450 hours of community service. I'm not complaining about it, even though it wasn't easy and at the time I thought it was more than I deserved, considering that my peers in anger management had committed seriously violent crimes and done damage to themselves and others that I couldn't even dream of. Looking back now, that doesn't matter: I learned a lot about myself and that's all I care about.

Now for those of you wondering about anger management, or those

of you about to start anger management (What up, Jack White?*), I'll tell
you as much about it as I can. There's a verbal bond you make when you
join an anger management group that swears confidentiality over everything you and your group share. I can't tell you what was said but I can tell
you that the meetings were weekly and lasted two hours. Mine took place
in downtown Los Angeles at 6 P.M. and I was convinced that they were
scheduled then so that all the members were completely irritated and full
of road rage by the time they walked in the door. For anyone who is lucky
enough to have never been caught in rush-hour L.A. traffic, let me tell
you, it's like trying to swim laps in the La Brea tar pits.

Here's the drill: If you show up late, you don't get credit for the class,
which made that car ride even more of a test of your temper. Being late
was great—you could leave if you wanted to, but that wasn't going to help
you at all. I was late a few times and I always stayed, hoping to get credit
for good behavior. I never did, and that made me really fucking angry.
Thank God I was learning how to deal with that.

I had to log fifty-two hours of anger management in all. That would
have taken me twenty-six weeks, which is roughly six and a half months if
I weren't constantly called out of town for work. With my schedule at the
time, playing on the Mötley *Greatest Hits* tour, recording and touring
with *Methods of Mayhem,* and then recording and touring my solo
album, *Never a Dull Moment,* it took me three years to graduate. And that
made me really, *really* fucking angry. Thank God I had learned enough
about powerlessness by then to let it go. He had become my new best
friend, Mr. Powerlessness. We still hang, we converse, we know each
other well. And we're sure not to spend too much time together—just
enough.

---

* On March 9, 2004, Jack White of the White Stripes pleaded guilty to a charge of
aggravated assault stemming from a fist fight in a Detroit bar with Jason Stollsteimer, the
singer of fellow Detroit city rockers the Von Bondies. Stollsteimer made disparaging
comments about White in the press and White claimed that he regrets the incident but
was raised to believe that "honor and integrity mean something and that those princi-
ples are worth defending."

I also got another gift from the program: the inspiration for the song "Anger Management" on the *Methods of Mayhem* album. It's still one of my favorites to play live because it's really heavy and it's therapy. I always feel better after I play it because it embodies the best way to get my anger out: doing something physical and expressing my anger constructively. It brings me back to the time when I couldn't control myself and allows me to see all over again how I've changed. And that makes me really, really, *really* fucking happy! Woo-hoo!

I finished my 450 hours of community service in 2003, completing all the conditions the court had demanded of me, and after almost five years, it ended the terms of my probation. And that made me really, really, really, *really* fucking happy! When you're on probation, you must show up in court with your lawyer before the judge for progress reports every three months. I was surprised and glad that last day because after some legal maneuvering by my lawyer and support from Denise, my probation officer, the judge reduced my sentence from a felony to a misdemeanor. I'm glad he did, but I have to tell you that being a felon for a while has its benefits. Before my sentence was reduced I got a note in the mail requiring me to appear for jury duty. I mentioned it to my lawyer, Barbara Berkowitz, asking her the proper procedure for rescheduling something like that. My legal guru just laughed at me for a full minute and said, "Tommy. Sweetheart. *Hello?* You are a *felon.* You are not allowed to do jury duty. You know how they ask you if you have a record or if you have any prejudice against the legal system because you've been to jail or accused of a crime? Well, that's you. And enjoy it, because that is the *only* break you get for being a felon." Oh, well, I'm a felon no more. Still, I've got this strange feeling that when I show up for jury duty as a nonfelon, I'll be one of the first ones to be booted out of the jury pool.

Being a felon had that one perk, but community service had *a lot* of them. I did charity work like giving away clothes to the homeless in the wintertime and serving food at a few missions during the holidays, and I also worked with Magic Johnson at Christmastime giving away gifts to kids who wouldn't have gotten any otherwise. We were at his movie theater in L.A., where there were movies for them to watch while we served them ice cream and popcorn. The appreciation in their eyes was amazing to me. I had helped adults who had fallen on hard times before and that was one thing, but witnessing the happiness in those children's eyes was something else. They were truly, truly grateful and it warmed my heart. I also did some clerical work for CAAF—Children Affected by AIDS Foundation, the American Cancer Society, and the ALS Foundation. Picture me in an office. Let me tell you, I can input information into computers pretty well now, and I know my way around a photocopier—I made hundreds of leaflets and letters in addition to stuffing envelopes. The whole time I thought about Rob Schneider on *Saturday Night Live*, playing the Makin' Copies guy.

When I was on the *Never a Dull Moment* tour we did a show in South Korea, and while I was there I wanted to do something to give back to the incredible people in our armed forces who live their lives so far away from our country. I'm so grateful to those men and women out there protecting us that any way I can give back is the least I can do. I inquired about playing a show for them on the base, but they really weren't set up for that. They decided that they'd just have me pay a visit instead. When we got over there though, the political climate in the area had grown dangerous and civilians weren't allowed on the base.

Since I couldn't tour the facility in South Korea, the military diverted me to Pearl Harbor, Hawaii. It was incredible to be in such a historical place, where I was allowed to stay in the admirals' quarters, and let me tell you, those big-cheese brass cats live large: Their rooms are like phat-ass hotel suites. During the few days I was there, I was taken on tours of different ships and nuclear submarines, and I met a bunch of really cool servicemen and women. I loved talking to them and learning about their day-to-day life. I was so happy that some of them had copies of my CDs, that I could sign stuff for them, and that what I do had touched them in some way. Seeing a lot of them standing there with my music in their hands, whether it was Mötley or my solo stuff, really moved me: My music had meant enough to them that they packed it in their bag before they left home. To physically see that something I was part of was also a part of them, whether it inspired them, reminded them of home, gave them strength to get through the day, or just pumped them up to be out there serving our country—fuck, that was an honor. It meant the world to me. In some strange way, I felt like I was a part of their experience and I was proud—I somehow felt like I was fighting with them.

I'm lucky enough to say that I really saw the ins and outs of how a military base and all the ships in our navy work. There were certain rooms I wasn't allowed to go in, but I saw the torpedoes being loaded onto the submarines, the control rooms—everything. I looked through the periscope and that thing is so powerful, you can see anything, in full detail, from miles away. Picture the biggest zoom lens you can buy as a consumer and you're not even close. All I can say is that the control rooms look all green and full of flat screens like they do in the movies. I couldn't believe that some of these people live underwater for six months at a time. There's only so much room in a submarine, so the crew shares beds and they have to sleep in shifts. And they don't sleep on what I'd call a cot—their beds are more like fold-down shelves with blankets. I can't thank them enough for being out there doing what they do, so I'll thank them again: Thank you! It was an overwhelming day: I was in awe of everyone I met and everything I saw.

I was blown away by all these young kids, just out of high school, willing to give their lives to protect the rest of us. I met young married people who are both in the navy, stationed on different ships, and are apart for six months or more at a time and communicate through email—and can't tell each other where they are because revealing their coordinates is a high security risk. At one of my progress reports, we informed the judge I had done that tour and I almost felt guilty when he counted it as a few days off my community service. To me, it didn't feel like work at all; it was a privilege.

I learned to feel the same way about the work I did with the Tree People. It's an organization that replants trees and plants up in the mountains in the Hollywood Hills, as well as picks up trash in parks, sprinkles fertilizers, moves mulch, digs ditches, and does whatever it takes to maintain the greenery on public land. There were days when I didn't want to go out and get all dirty, but by the time I got there, I'd always be really glad I was there. I love trees, so the chance to have quiet time in nature, working with my hands, caring for the earth, and giving back to the universe in some small way, felt right. I learned a lot about native foliage in California, pines, oaks, their root systems, and all the plants that make up the ecosystem. It did wonders for my mind. I told all my friends how great it was and sometimes people like TiLo, the rapper from *Methods of Mayhem*, or Gerald, my life coach, would come with me and put in four or five hours. Those hours outside, digging in the dirt, were essential to my healing and growth. It was meditation for me and I need that in my life. I wasn't mad though, when my internal monologue was interrupted for the right reasons. We were usually working in parks where I stood a really good chance of spotting a hot girl walking her dog. Reflection is great, but nothing makes my day brighter than a hot girl strolling by in warm weather.

16

STATE OF MUTUAL APPRECIATION

a.k.a.
TESTIFY!
TOMMY TESTIMONIALS

The following opinions were gathered from a wide array of famous and nonfamous individuals who have inspired me. Some know me personally, some don't. Some will never know how they've touched my life through what they do.

Thank you to those who testified on my behalf. And to those who didn't, eat a hot bowl of *dick*. I'm going to list everyone whom I wanted to hear from, because all of you who aren't in this business called entertainment need to know how much bullshit goes on. There are concentric circles of publicists, managers, agents, and little people with big egos who have nothing better to do than cock-block to feel important. We asked everyone on this list to offer between one and one hundred words that came to mind when they heard my name. The excuses you'll read about why their client wasn't available are retarded!

It's comedy to me, so I've included all of it, with my comments, for your reading pleasure.

Trent Reznor: Tommy is the definition of a fucking rock star. Charismatic, charming, volatile, somebody you want to invite over but might stain your carpet, a great guy and a fucking great drummer.

Pink: Tommy Lee is one of the fuckin' hottest musicians left. He's managed to stay above the tides; he's an awesome fuckin' drummer . . . and he's hot.

Check this out, people. Here is a direct transcript of a conversation between my writer, Anthony, and Mike Tyson's secretary, who he said sounded like she had been enjoying the senior citizen discount at the movies for years now.

A.B.:   Hi. I'm just following up on a letter I sent to your office from Tommy Lee.

Lady: Oooh. Tommy Lee? The rock star?

A.B.:   Yes.

Lady: Well let me write this down, deary. Where's my pen?

A.B.:   (waiting) Okay.

Lady: It's here somewhere. Ohhh . . . where is that pen?

A.B.:   (waiting)

Lady: Okay, I found it. Okay. So you're calling for Tommy Lee.

A.B.:   Yes, he's working on his autobiography and he would love to get a testimonial from Mike Tyson.

Lady: Okay. (She spells everything out.) So Tommy is working on an a-u-t-o-b-i-o-g-r-a-p-h-y. Oh no, I need to scratch that out (she starts over). So Tommy is working on Mike Tyson's autobiography?

A.B.:   Um, no, he's not doing that. Tommy is working on his *own* autobiography and would love a *testimonial* from Mike Tyson.

Lady: Okay (spells everything out again). So Tommy is . . . working on *his* autobiography and wants to get testimony from Mike Tyson.

A.B.:   Yes, a *testimonial.* Mike is an inspiration to Tommy and he'd like to know what Mike has to say about him.

Lady: A t-e-s-t-i-m-o-n-i-a-l.

A.B.:   That's right.

Lady: Okay, deary. . . . Thanks again.

A.B.:   So, um, will he do it? *Click* (sound of dial tone).

Larry King: Tommy Lee is an American rock legend. He's highly talented, always controversial, and there is no doubt you pay attention when he enters a room. The real question is, Would he bother using the door?

Pharrell Williams of the Neptunes and N.E.R.D.: He's a great drummer with a lot of style. He keeps his chops up in terms of technique and his style in drumming; his chops are very sharp. Also, "Pour Some Sugar on Me" can be played in the middle of any hip-hop party. I love that.

MAN, THAT'S AWESOME
THAT PHARRELL PAID RESPECT.
I'VE ALWAYS LOVED HIS SHIT,
EVER SINCE "WHEN DOVES CRY."
OH, WAIT, MY BAD.
PHARRELL IS THAT PRODUCER GUY
FROM ATLANTA WHO DATES JANET JACKSON.
THE LITTLE GUY, RIGHT?
DISCOVERED KRIS KROSS. NICE.
THANKS, BRO.

I'd like to apologize for meeting Steve-O from Jackass when he was an impressionable eleven-year-old. When I see footage of him snorting wasabi, blowing chunks, or regurgitating a goldfish, I feel guilty and somewhat responsible for creating this monster. Without further ado, here's Steve-O:

HOW TO MEET YOUR FAVORITE
ROCK STARS
by Steve-O

I was eleven when I got my first Mötley Crüe album and it seems like, ever since then, I've had a major fascination with "sex, drugs, and rock-and-roll." When I was twelve, I had my walls covered strictly with Mötley Crüe posters and I devoted art projects at school to re-creating Mötley Crüe logos. I was thirteen when the Crüe came to my town (Toronto at the time) on the *Girls, Girls, Girls* tour, and, the day before the concert at Maple Leaf Gardens, I saw on the news that the band was in town and had gotten into some sort of trouble. It immediately occurred to me that they must be staying in a hotel, since the concert wasn't until the next day. I decided to find out what hotel they were at. I figured that the band members wouldn't check in under their own names (assumed or given) and guessed that they would check in under the name of their manager. A check of every album sleeve revealed only one name for their manager and no separate names for a tour manager. The name was Doc McGhee and, as soon as I knew that, I began to call every hotel in the yellow pages, starting from the very top of the list. My mom was in the kitchen, where I sat on the phone, and she was complaining that I was tying up the phone line too long. My father was watching a football game in the living room, but he had never seen his son so motivated and committed to accomplish anything, so he told my mom to back off and let me continue my mission. I sat there calling hotels for, literally, hours. It turned out to be a number at the bottom of the pages-long list that patched me through. This guy

answered the phone and I asked if he was Doc McGhee. He told me
that he was Doc's brother, Scott, and before he could say anything else
I blurted out, "As in Mötley Crüe!?!" Slightly frustrated, Scott asked me
how I got the number. I explained to him what I had done, I truly
sounded like a little girl on the phone, being that I hadn't even hit pu-
berty yet. When I got done telling Scott what I did, he told me that the
Crüe had taken a bus to Ottawa for that night's show and that he was im-
pressed by my initiative. About the Maple Leaf Gardens show, he asked,
"How'd you like it if I put your name on the list for a couple backstage
passes and tickets? I can get you in the fifth row." There's no explaining
how stoked I was at that point. That was October 24, 1987.

My dad wouldn't normally have been so proud to take me to a heavy
metal concert, but for the passion of my efforts that got us there, he really
was and that made me feel great. When we got there, we waited in line
with all these photographers and reporters for our passes—it was awesome. Sure enough, I was on the list and we got everything Scott had
promised. The concert was rad. I especially liked the beginning of the
drum solo with the cool drum kit, when Tommy Lee's beats were timed
with Nikki Sixx's gulps of Jack Daniel's. Nikki drank like fuckin' half the
bottle and poured the other half on the crowd; it was so rad.

After the encore, the arena emptied quickly, but I wasn't going anywhere. My dad and I had to wait for a while to be allowed backstage but
when we were, Nikki Sixx was one of the first people I saw. Maybe they
told him there was an extra stoked kid he should talk to, because it
seemed like he came straight to me. I talked to him for a minute, got a
couple of autographs, and my dad took a picture of us. Then I saw
Tommy Lee and he seemed as stoked as I was, he hung out with me for a
while, even after signing autographs and taking a photo. It was the best.
We hung out with Scott McGhee too. My dad and I were actually the last
people to leave. Vince Neil walked out of a private room and right past us,
without a word, right before we left.

The next day I got sent home from school to change my Mötley Crüe
concert shirt; I was proud of that. I was proud of everything about meeting

Mötley Crüe. There wasn't anything I really wanted to ask or say to them, but meeting them changed my life forever. It sounds gay, but meeting Mötley Crüe taught me that I can accomplish anything I set my mind to. It doesn't matter what you want, it simply matters how fuckin' bad you want it and that you never stop going for it until you have it.

Tommy,

    Thanks for asking me to give a testimonial for your book. We met in 1987 and it changed my life forever. I always say, "Mötley Crüe isn't a sound, it's an attitude." You were my hero because you behaved horribly badly, not because you're a great drummer. One night, when I was out on bail and facing eight years in prison, I was doing tons of cocaine, alone, and I amused myself by trying to track you down again. I posted a message on your message board or something and you wound up writing back to me. That was really fucking cool too. You could honestly say that I was contacting you for advice on my felony charges, but really I just wanted to get my mind off of them. You wrote me back and told me, "Dude, you're in almost as much trouble as I've been in." And that was the most rad email ever. I wrote you back with, "I don't know if that makes me feel better, or worse, but thanks man!" Since then, every time either of us has done something really funny, we've emailed each other about it and that's really rad too. That's about all I can give testimony about—let's get off our asses and film some legendary shit together so we can write more cool shit. Thanks bro,

                                                Steve-O

LESBIAN TESTIMONIALS

The following opinions were gathered in various Los Angeles locales, from Hollyweird to Malibu. The names have not been changed at the request of the lesbians.

Catherine: I thought Tommy seemed really sweet and tonight I met him and now I know he's really sweet. He just acts like a little boy. You know, he jumps up and down and he gets excited about everything. That innocence is fucking hot as hell. It's like he's a little baby, as wild as he is. It helps that he's adorable, but the hotness is way more about the way he is.

Lenny: Tommy Lee is so fine that I want to be him. I want to be him because if I were him, I would get all his chicks. He keeps it sensitive and he rocks, and since he's a drummer he has that, like, math brain. He is super-hot and sexy with his little shirts and his man muscles. And he's got a sweet, sincere smile to go with his realness. I love him, and later tonight when I fuck my girlfriend I'm going to make her call me Tommy. I'm going to call my girl Pamela, Mayte, or whoever he's with. Fuck it, I'll call her all of them.

Lenny's girlfriend: I'll be whoever you want, baby. Why don't you just say, "What's your name again?" Then we'll switch. I've got to be Tommy too.

Lenny: Fuck yeah, it will be good. My turn to be the bitch.

Jozie: * Here's the thing. I'm a man-hating lesbian but I love Tommy Lee. He really should feel very excited to know that. He's got amazing tattoos and his little nipples are pierced. I get angry because guys don't hold up the same degree of personal hygiene that girls do. But if you look closely, you'll notice that Tommy shaves his arms, which is very, very hot. That wins him many, many points. Tommy's got hair on his head and not on his back. That's cool — that's how it's supposed to be.

---

* Jozie was the hottest dancer on the *Mötley Crüe Greatest Hits* tour in 1999. Tommy adores her for many reasons, among them, that she can ably and accurately urinate while standing. Tommy discovered this Jozie fun fact backstage one night when she sidled up next to him at the men's urinals and let it fly.

Tommy: I like to keep it where it's welcome.

Don't worry, I've saved the best for last. Here they are, my best friends, the elusive and way too cool, including the answers, if any, that were given by their representatives in response to our request.

Lenny Kravitz

Madonna

Christina Aguilera

P. Diddy

Method Man

Bob Costas

Angelina Jolie: She will not be able to participate. Sorry.

Martha Stewart: I received your recent email to Erica Schwartz requesting a testimonial from Martha Stewart regarding Tommy Lee. Unfortunately, we will not be able to provide this testimonial, due to the volume of requests that we receive. Thank you for considering Martha for this project and if you have any additional questions, please let me know. Samantha Schabel

Julia Roberts

Elizabeth Hurley

Jim Carrey

Bill Clinton

Kevin Spacey

Al Pacino

Robert De Niro

David Bowie

Chris Rock

Jenna Jameson

Howard Stern

Robin Williams

Kid Rock

Richie Sambora

Prince
Naomi Campbell
Johnny Depp
Missy Elliott
Ronnie Wood
Keith Richards
Michelle Pfeiffer
Dave Grohl
Conan O'Brien
Carmen Electra: Carmen is going to be passing on your offer, but thank
    you for thinking of her and best of luck with the book! Take care,
    Nicky
Brad Pitt: I'm sorry but he's not available. Sorry it's taken so long to get
    back to you.
Adam Carolla
Snoop Doggy Dogg
Shaq
Hugh Hefner
Woody Harrelson

17

STATE OF LOSS

a.k.a.
SEPTEMBER 11, 2001

As my dad was dying, my mom took care of him every single day. He was bedridden and she would change him, feed him, bathe him, massage his body when his muscles were sore. To me, that is true love. She took care of everything. I just had to pull my mom aside one day and tell her how amazing she is and how amazing it was to see her be that way with him. I said, "Mom, you are still in love with him." And she just looked at me and said, "Yes, as much as always."

My dad died of multiple myeloma, cellular cancer that invades your red and white blood cells. It's treatable, but it's not curable. I spent a lot of time with him when he was sick and I'm glad I was able to. I couldn't stand seeing him spend his last days in a hospital bed at home surrounded by four stupid walls, so I rented a houseboat for five days where he could wake up in nature on the water every day. I wanted him to wake up and not see walls—just water, mountains, and blue sky. He deserved to smell the barbecue and have a fishing pole in his hands one last time, because fishing was my dad's favorite pastime. My assistant

Viggy* and I lifted him out of his bed and into his wheelchair, and rolled him out to the deck. We put his cowboy hat and some shades on him and there we were, fishing together one last time. He had the biggest smile on his face and I did too, even though inside I was crying because I knew, and so did he, that this was *it*. I felt lucky to have this time with him because I really didn't see him enough when I was younger. I really didn't see anybody but my bandmates from the time I was seventeen until I was thirty-eight. It was a gift to share my dad's last days with him and tell each other all those things we didn't say earlier in our lives.

Just before he died, I was with him, and tears start coming out of his eyes when he looks at me and says, "I'm not scared." I start crying too, and he says, "I've got amazing kids. I've had an amazing life. I'm ready. Don't worry about me, it's okay. This is okay, I'm ready to go now. I love your mother and I've loved my life. I'm ready now." We were crying together and I've never felt closer to someone and more heartbroken at the same time. He was also hallucinating from the medication he was on, so he was also talking to other people whom he was seeing. It was the most intense moment of my life.

My dad died at home, during the week of September 11, 2001. I'm sitting there in his room with him, just watching him die. On the television in the corner, I see the most insane act of terrorism in the history of mankind. I really wasn't sure what was real anymore. How do you prepare to lose your only role model? How do you do it while the world is exploding? I had never seen so much death and I hope I never do again. My life was changing forever while the lives of everyone around me, around all of us, changed forever too. With that one act, that one event, those fucking assholes tore a hole in the world and changed everything as we know it. I kept thinking of how deaths come in threes. I sat there for a week, looking at my father and the television, thinking about the three bombs that had dropped on my life.

---

* Viggy, also known as Big Vig, was born on May 21, 1969. He has been Tommy's drum tech and assistant since 1998.

Dad,

    We all miss you terribly, and Mom is so lonely without you. Don't worry, I'm okay, Dad, because I feel like you're watching me and with me all the time. I was sitting on the balcony writing lyrics last year and I knew you were there. A black crow landed just inches from me and started squawking at me. He wasn't mad, he wasn't scared, he was just trying to talk to me. I sat there, staring at him, and I asked him if he was you. He stayed for a while and we talked, and in my soul I hoped it was you. Was that you, Dad?

    I love you.

    Thank you for just being you, Father.

Love,
Your son, Tom

18

STATE OF SHOCK

a.k.a.
LIGHTNING STRIKES
NOT ONCE
BUT THRICE

By then I was numb; the first bomb that had dropped in my life was like Hiroshima. It was the tragic death of a little boy named Daniel in my pool. We were celebrating my son Brandon's fifth birthday, and it happened in the summer of 2001. The other two were soon to follow. That fall my dad passed away, and the Twin Towers fell, our country went to war. All of it was tragic, but the worst happened first: that beautiful little four-year-old boy dying at my house. It's still very hard for me to even think about, and sometimes it's impossible for me to even look at that side of the pool. I'm in the pool almost every day because I love the water, so he's never far from my thoughts. It never gets any easier and it probably never will.

It was the first birthday party I'd thrown for the either of the boys after Pamela and I divorced—it was my first effort as a single dad. The day was June 5, 2001. I'd planned a small get-together: my nanny, Melissa, handed out the invitations at school. People started showing up at about noon, and we had between thirty and forty people there, including kids and adults.

Gerald, the man who had seen me through all the changes I'd lived through since going to jail, was with me that day, helping out. We made all the preparations and once the party was under way, he relaxed by the pool with me and talked to me about life in the wise way that he does, teaching me to open my mind like no one I've ever met.

To get a picture of what happened that afternoon, I need to tell you about my pool. It really is amazing. It's more like a natural lake or pond than anything else. There is beautiful beige slate stone around the deck, and the bottom is easy on your feet and looks like tan and black sand. It winds around to the left and, like the rest of my yard, there are trees and plants all around it. It has a beach entrance so when you wade into it, it's like walking into a peaceful ocean: It's very shallow and slowly gets deeper.

That afternoon Gerald and I are sitting at the table by the pool under the sun, taking everything in. People are here and there, and everyone is having a great time. All of a sudden we hear this woman scream, "Oh my God!" Gerald and I jump up and run to the beach entrance where a woman is pulling a boy out of the water. I see what is happening so I run to call 911. A friend of mine runs over and helps pull the boy out. He gets him on the deck and starts pumping his chest. As I tell the 911 operator what is happening, I'm watching Daniel throw up all over the place.

Daniel had been tearing it up all day, floating around the pool with his big water wings on. I'd seen him having a blast: squirting everyone with his squirt gun, swimming, splashing, and doing all the things a four-year-old loves to do.

I watch in disbelief as Daniel is pulled from the water and laid on the deck. I'm relaying instructions to the adults caring for him, shouting to them how to administer CPR. Everyone is hysterical. I'm yelling, "*Fuck!* Listen to me! They're telling me what to do!" I give the phone to Renee, a woman whose son goes to my son's school, and tell her to give 911 the address because I don't want to be on the phone—I want to go over and help.

Time stopped for me. It seemed like half an hour, but the paramedics probably showed up ten minutes later. There is a circle around Daniel and we are pumping his chest and calling his name, hoping he'll start breathing again, but he's still completely unconscious. All the other kids don't understand what is happening. I tell Melissa to take my boys inside because I don't want them to see this. The ambulance shows up and the EMTs bring out an oxygen tank and start pumping Daniel's chest, hoping to revive him. They know that time is of the essence so they load him onto a gurney and transport him to the nearest emergency room.

Daniel's parents weren't there at all that day: They'd sent him to the party with his nanny, a German guy named Christian. I'd met Christian for the first time that day, when he came up to me halfway through the party to tell me that he was going to the Wango Tango festival, a concert held each year in downtown L.A. He pointed out a woman across the pool and informed me that she would be responsible for Daniel for the rest of the day and that she'd also drive him home. I say, "Okay, as long as someone is watching him, that's cool." I recognized the woman he had pointed out, so I didn't worry. I thought she was a teacher's aide at our kids' school. All the kids at the party had a nanny or parent to watch them, I made sure of that.

As Daniel is being pulled out of the water I look for the woman who is supposed to be covering for Christian and she is nowhere to be found. As I'm on the phone with 911, I shout for her, over and over. I found out later that while Daniel was drowning she was taking her dog for a walk in my front yard. I fucking lost it—this is *not* happening. She's supposed to be watching him, he's in the pool, and she's walking her *dog?*

When she comes back to the pool and sees the paramedics she says, "Oh my *God!* Am I in trouble?" Fuck yeah, you are. After that she just turns and runs out of there with her dog. I point at her, shouting, "You were supposed to fucking watch him! Where the *fuck* have you been!"

Daniel's parents show up as he is laid on the gurney, and of course they lose their fucking minds. His father screams, "What the *fuck* happened?" The police are there by then and they have to restrain him. Daniel's mother is crying, doubled over, hysterical. I can't even imagine showing up to a party and seeing one of my boys lying there with paramedics all around him. I pray that I never do.

I have no idea how to approach them. I want to comfort them in any way I can. I want to tell them what happened. They are so hysterical—and I don't blame them. Daniel's father is so enraged and out of control that I know he won't hear me if I try to talk to him. I know that if I were in his shoes, I would be acting exactly the same way. He wanted answers—NOW.

I feel helpless, so I go inside to make sure that my sons are okay. The boys don't really understand what is going on at all. To them, this is Brandon's birthday party and all they want to know is when they can go back in the pool. They had seen a little bit of what had happened, and they ask me what is wrong with Daniel. It takes all I'm made of to hold it together. I tell them that Daniel swallowed too much water and that he'll be okay after he goes to the doctor. I want to believe what I'm saying too.

I talk to the sheriff for a long time, walking him around the yard and the pool, answering all his questions. I don't hear one word he says to me because all I'm waiting for is the phone to ring, hoping the voice on the other end will tell me that Daniel is okay.

My assistant, Viggy, went to the hospital with Daniel's family to help out if he could, while I looked after the boys and spoke to the police. Half an hour after they left, I hear the phone ring and I run to answer it. Everything goes into slow motion as I hear Viggy on the other end. I ask, "Is Daniel okay?" He is quiet for a moment and he doesn't have to say anything. I know what's coming next. "He didn't make it, bro."

I hang up the phone, I sit down, and I cry. My nanny is with my boys and I hope that they don't come looking for me. I pace around the room like a zombie, contemplating so many things that I hope no one ever has to handle: How can I tell my sons that their friend died in their pool? How can I even try to express my deepest sympathies to Daniel's parents?

I go to my bedroom and write Daniel's parents a letter. This is the letter no one *ever* wants to write. I'm a parent, so I can imagine what they are going through. Still, I really have no idea — imagination is one thing, reality is another. After I get through it, I fax it to them right away. I got no response. I understood. Later, I heard through friends of theirs that to them my letter looked like something that a publicist wrote, and that broke my heart. I really, really, really wish they had been there that day.

For an entire week afterwards, I stay locked in my room. I'm scared to come out, I don't eat, I don't do anything. All I do is watch the satellite transmitters rising up on the trucks in front of my house. I sit in bed watching the news feeds live from my street and listen to the helicopters buzzing above my house. I feel as if I'm being hunted down like a fugitive: My room shakes every time they pass overhead to snap another picture of my pool. All I can think about is that none of this can really be happening. I had spent the last three years doing my best to clean up the mess in my life and I had made myself a better person. I felt that all I had done, in one instant, because of one unfortunate accident, was meaningless.

My phone wouldn't stop ringing, everyone from my mom to friends I'd lost contact with were calling me. It was nice to hear all of them saying such wonderful things like, "We're so sorry, Tommy. Just know that it wasn't your fault and that we're here for you." I'm glad to hear all those voices, but I can't talk to anyone. I'm so sad that I could only leave my room to go to the kitchen to try to eat something every few days.

I don't know for sure, but I heard that the woman who pulled Daniel out sold her story to *The National Enquirer* for $10,000. *Fuckin' bitch.* When I hear this I call her and ask her if it is true. No return call — of course; she had already bailed. A friend of mine who knew her said that as soon as she got the money, she ran out of town. I read *The National En-quirer* story eventually. It's all about how she was in the pool and how she reached over and grabbed Daniel. The tabloids deal in the lowest common denominator—everyone knows that. Selling them a story about a crazy night out on the town is one thing. I couldn't believe that *anyone* would go so low to make money off a little boy's death. I was so disgusted with humans. *Fucking disgusted.*

I knew that I would never get over Daniel's death, but I was desperate to find some way to learn how to live with it. I wanted to restore some kind of balance to my house and to my soul. I spoke to Gerald a lot to figure out what I should do. He found a woman from the Chumash Indian tribe who came and performed a ceremony at the pool.

She had never been to the house before and had no idea where the accident had happened. Amazingly, it didn't matter. When she walks through the gate into the yard, she pauses for a moment, looks around, says nothing, and walks to the exact spot where Daniel was lying as we tried to save his life. She has a bag, and when she kneels down, she pulls out feathers, pouches of herbs, redwood bark—all the tools for her ritual. She burns things in a bowl, she chants, she moves, and she waves her hands in the air while she sings in her native tongue. I wish I spoke her language, because I want to know all those powerful words she said that day. I had drained the pool and refilled it, and she blesses the new water. I know that no matter what she did or what anyone does, nothing will erase the memory, but I feel that she can help us heal. I wanted my kids to understand what had happened so I had them with me while she did her ritual. It helped all of us to say goodbye and send Daniel all our love.

A few months later, it happens. *Boom*—lawsuit. I knew it was coming. Daniel's parents sue me. I think, "Fuck, this is it. I'm going down." I know that my entire history will be used against me and taken out of context. Every single surface judgment that anyone has ever made about me will be exaggerated. I am the perfect guy to place the blame on: the irresponsible, tattooed rock star with a history of bad behavior.

During the case, some members of the jury were older folks, and I kept looking at them thinking about all the tabloid headlines they'd probably seen about me. All I could do was tell the truth, be myself, and pray that they'd hear me, look past what they'd read, and recognize all the cheap tricks the other side's lawyers used to paint their portrait of me. Thank you, all of you, for doing so. After months of wrangling and another Bible-thick pile of legal documents, they decide that I'm not responsible for Daniel's death. Standing there, hearing that decision that day, I'm relieved but I'm not happy, because there is no victory in this situation. How can anyone win when Daniel is dead?

19

STATE OF YAKUZA

a.k.a.

入墨

(ENTER INK)

When my dad and mom were first married, they communicated with symbols and dictionaries until she learned English well enough. If that isn't love, I don't what is. I remember her handing him pictures of chickens to let him know that we needed eggs while he flipped through the Greek-English dictionary trying to find the word.

I went to a dream analyst named Dick Wiener a few years ago.

THAT GUY'S NAME
IS AWESOME!

The first time I went to see him I had long sleeves on and we had a good talk. The next time I went I was wearing short sleeves so he saw all my ink and wanted to know all about it. When it came time for my third appointment, I couldn't find his number and I couldn't remember his address. So I called information and asked for Dick Wiener. The operator started laughing and said, "I have two Dicks." I said, "You do? Damn!" She goes, "I have a Richard Wiener and a Dick Wiener." I'm all, "Yeah! Dick Wiener, that's the guy. Could you give me his address?"

Dick Wiener told me that the tattoos are my form of communication. I told him all about my life, all about my parents, and he told me something fascinating: I learned how to express myself in symbols from watching them. He said that at a really young age I internalized my mother's experience and made it a part of me. He said that what I put on my body is what I want to bring into my life and what I want to say about myself. He's right: I've got koi fish tattooed on my arm and I have a koi pond, I've got a cheetah, and someday I'll have one. Most of what I have on my body has manifested itself in one way or another in my life.

I've got a lot of tattoos and I've got a thing for them—that's retardedly obvious. I've already said this, but my first one was Mighty Mouse breaking through a bass drum. He's got a pair of drumsticks in his hand, he's on my right shoulder, and he's pretty faded. But he's still rad. I got him right when I started Mötley because Mighty Mouse was my childhood hero. He always saved the day, he was a good guy, he was a role model who did the right thing, and at the end of every episode, he always got the chick. He'd wail on the bad dude, dump him in jail, shine that guy's evil plot, and then go scoop up his lady and fly off with her. What a pimp.

When I went to get Mighty Mouse, Nikki Sixx was with me. He was the reason I was there, so he had to come. He was definitely the guy that kicked off tattoos in Mötley. I didn't know anybody with tattoos other than him. Younger readers, check this out—back then, most rock bands didn't have tattoos. Nikki started the trend in our band and definitely set the trend for all the dudes who copied us.*

I got Mighty Mouse inked onto my body at Sunset Strip Tattoo. A guy named Kevin Brady did it, and it still looks great. Kevin did most of my stuff. Wherever the fuck you are, Kevin, hey, man, you're getting your props right now, bro. Thanks. And good luck.

Mighty Mouse was my start because he summed up my childhood to me. After I began hanging around tattoo shops though, I immediately gravitated toward the Oriental style. It was peaceful, easy to look at, color-ful, and so beautiful. To me, adding tattoos to my body was like buying art. But it was better because art hangs in a house or a museum and tat-toos are fucking on you, with you, right there with you, every minute of the day. I started adding more almost immediately. When I looked in the mirror at that first one, I thought, "Wow, that's really beautiful, but I'm out of balance." I started putting them here and there on my arms, on my legs, trying to get it all to balance out in my head. They're totally addic-tive, like potato chips—there's no way I'm having just one.

If there is one word I want tattooed on my body it is the one that means pleasure and pain at the same time. I don't know what that word is, I don't think it exists. Maybe that word is "tattoo" because a tattoo hurts like fuck while it is happening but I'm thinking, "My God, when this is over it is going to look amazing." I've got the word "tattoo" on my wrist. And it fucking hurt like hell. Wrist skin is sensitive, please believe.

My tattoos were done at separate times in many places, but I don't think of them as individual pieces anymore. They've become one big work of art.

---

* Rose Tattoo, a hard rock band from Sydney, Australia, were together and inking them-selves as much, if not more, than Mötley Crüe in the early eighties. Tommy heard about them back then, and when he saw a picture of Rose Tattoo's lead singer, Angry Ander-son, Tommy's response was, "Woah, hey! That guy is craise!" Anderson was already coated in ink, head to toe.

I've never been with a woman who is covered from head to toe in tattoos. That would be amazing because when I see pictures of it, I think it's hot as hell. I would study her body like a Bible. I met a woman in Japan once on the bullet train* who had her back completely covered. The Japanese Mafia, the Yakuza, have their women tattooed. She was definitely one of them: She was in a beautiful dress and was surrounded by some tough-looking dudes. It was probably a pretty stupid thing to do, but I showed her some of my tattoos and made a gesture like I wanted to see hers. She didn't say a word, she just got up kind of nervously and led me to the space between the cars. She let down her dress straps, covered her breasts, and let her dress fall to her waist. Her entire back was covered and it was one of the most beautiful things I've ever seen. She had it done in that incredible traditional Japanese style, and it depicted a Geisha girl dancing.

So any sane, tattooed lady, please apply, there is a position to fill here in Tommyland, and help is wanted.

One of the most amazing experiences I've ever had was getting tattooed in Japan. People will argue about where the art originated, and I don't know, but I tell you, that night, it felt like I was being inked at the source. I was sitting there with Yakuza members, being tattooed according to their tradition in one of their secret spots. We were drinking sake, lying on mats, with the tattoo artist in the traditional position with his legs crossed hammering the ink in manually. Nikki and I were there together, looking through the guy's artwork while an interpreter told the artist what we wanted.

---

* The Japanese bullet train, or Shinkansen, is a network of high-speed people movers that connect Tokyo with all of the major cities, as well as the city of Fukuoka on the island of Kyushu. The system was inaugurated in 1964 and completed in 1975. Today's trains achieve speeds of close to 200 mph and are as clean, efficient, and hyper-modern as the rest of urban Japanese culture. Most Shinkansen arrive at their destinations within the second of their scheduled time. A yearly tally of the entire network's lateness (and you can be sure the Japanese do measure this) will yield discrepancies that amount to something like a whopping twelve seconds—that includes every train, on every line, for the entire year. Craise.

We worked for that session, let me tell you. We had begged our Japanese promoter, Mr. Udo, to take us to a Yakuza artist for years. He just kept saying "Oh, no, no, no, no" every time we went to Japan, but finally he caved. Pretty early into the night I figured out what he was freaked out about.

We were picked up in a van with blacked-out windows so dark we couldn't see where we were going. A couple of bald guys get out of this thing and open the door. You could tell right away that under the tight-collared shirts they are wearing, they are tattooed from head to toe. It's heavy. They drive us to their clubhouse, but if my life depended on it, I couldn't tell you how to get back there.

When we arrive, I notice right away that the guy tattooing has no pinky. He's got this huge callous in the web between his forefinger and thumb. As he tattoos us, by hand with a bamboo stick, we communicate with him through our interpreter.

It got more bizarre. Nikki and I are getting tattoos and one of the bald-headed guys who picked us up comes in and says something funky in Japanese. Then he whips out his dick. Dude, I'm lying there on the fucking mat and he's standing right above me with his dick out. Plus, in this whole Yakuza tattoo scene that we're in, they take a mixture of cocaine, novocaine, and water, soak it in a washcloth and rub it on your skin as a topical anesthetic. After they rub it on your arm, you feel nothing. So there I am, looking at some bald guy with his dick out, while home-cooked numbing juice soaks into me, and a guy with no pinky pokes my arm with bamboo. Nice.

The guy with his dick out, by the way, pulled it out to show off what he'd done to it. I'm looking at it and thinking, "He must have some disease, what the fuck is wrong with this guy's dick?" He has bumps all over it. I ask the interpreter what the *fuck* is going on with this guy. He tells me that the guy has pearls in his dick. They do this thing where they take a bamboo stick that's as sharp as a knife, make an incision, and put a pearl in the shaft. Once that heals, they do it again. This guy was fully loaded — he had more speed bumps than a school zone. His dick must have been

worth a couple grand. They say when you fuck with pearls all up in your dick skin, it hits the girl's clit, right up on the top side where she likes it. It was the ultimate human dildo, attached to a bald tattooed Japanese guy. For a minute there, I was like, "Woah, hey. Maybe I should get one."

DUDE, NO WAY.
I GIVE PEARL NECKLACES, MY MAN,
I DON'T WEAR THEM.

That night was far more traditional than the day I got some switches inked on my elbow in Dallas, Texas. The Crüe was touring *Generation Swine,* and John Corabi was our lead singer then. Crabs was extremely hungover that particular day so we did the sensible thing and went to Benihana's to drink and drink and drink and drink. Dimebag—that's Darrell, the guitar player from Pantera—is with us and he decides that we need to swig Hulk Blood, a mixture of Midori and sake. It's a shot, and of course we order many. Corabi is so hungover that real soon he's fucking wasted. The man's liver is on crutches. At this point, Corabi is still so fucking happy to be in the band that he religiously wore the $5,000 pair of leather pants we'd bought him. (I think he slept in them.) So there he is in hot-as-fuck Dallas, wearing his leather pants, wasted as hell. It's the middle of the day, we're drunk, and we need something to do. We go to a tattoo parlor and Dimebag gets "Hulk Blood" inked on his leg. I get my "kill" and "reset" buttons, and Corabi gets the same thing. His are on the outside of his left arm, mine are on the inside of my left elbow. They are my out when shit gets too fucked for words. I concentrate on what effect I want it to have, and push the button. I "kill" sparingly. It's huge—I only blast that one when someone needs to die and I can't do it myself because I don't want to spend the rest of my life in jail. It's all I can do when I really want someone to go away and I'm okay with that. "Reset" is used more frequently. It's what I do when I'm hungover, tired, you know, when

I've got to reset. It's for those times that are just, "Oh God, please. God, please reset this, I need to come back." I've got to be careful about the "reset" switch too, because it's easy to accidentally bump it and use up one of those valuable chances.

We got tattoos that day in Dallas, but we weren't done. The three of us decide we need to water ski and go out on our friend's boat. It's about one hundred-something degrees and we idiots meet Rex, the bass player from Pantera, at the lake. Corabi passes out on a park bench next to where we hopped on the boat. We left him there in his leather pants, just all Drunk Guy. He must have taken his shirt off at some point because when we got back to scrape him up, dude was sportin' the most fucked-up sunburn I've ever seen. It was classic. In a few short hours he'd turned into Mr. Blistering Drunk Guy. Crabs got a tattoo that day, but even if he had sat for eight hours with some cat who specialized in red he never could have made that fucker's skin look the way it did.

If anyone reading this is thinking of getting a tattoo, stop for a minute, take the design home, and live with it—don't get it that night. This is art for life—it's no impulse buy. Think about it a good long time, plan it out, find the right artist for the right tattoo—they're all out there, so do it right. Whatever you do, for the love of Jesus Christ and all that's holy, don't get a girl's name tattooed on your body. It's a curse, it's taboo, it's the beginning of the end. It's like naming the fish in your aquarium—as soon as you do, you've got a floater on your hands. Girls come and go, but what you're putting on your skin isn't going anywhere. And if you're thinking about lasering that fucker off, good luck. It's twice as painful, twice as expensive, and it doesn't work. Trust.

20

STATE OF ENGAGEMENT

a.k.a.
MAYTE

I met Mayte after the *MTV Icon* show they did for Janet Jackson. We were at the after-party when my assistant, Viggy, noticed her. Viggy had worked for Prince for five years, so he knew who she was. I'm drinking champagne with Jermaine Dupri

DON'T YOU MEAN PHARRELL, BRO?

When Viggy tells me he'll be right back. I see him plow through the crowd to the middle of the dance floor to say hi to this beautiful girl. I'm like, "Go Viggy!" I go back to rippin' it until a minute later when Viggy slugs me on the shoulder, turns me around, and introduces me to Mayte. She looked stunning, as amazing as she always does. I babbled at her, "*Wow*. Nice to touch you. You are *gorgeous*." It was a pretty stock greeting. I kissed her on the cheek and watched her go back to the dance floor. I thought she was still married to Prince—lucky fucker. A little later Viggy asked me why I didn't talk to her longer. "Dude, she's Prince's wife." Not

anymore, he told me. *"Fuck!* Where is she, dude? Go get her!" Viggy found her and God bless him for doing so.

I've got to be real here: Mayte does not have the kind of name that is easy to get right. Here's how you say it: *My-tay.* I made Viggy say it a few times over in my ear so I wouldn't fuck it up when I met her again. It was loud in there, and homie had to scream it for a minute until I got it right.

I already knew about Mayte before I met her; she was Viggy's fondest memory of working for Prince. She was always cool to him, he'd gotten to know her well, and he'd been telling me how sweet she was for months. He had been on a mission, playing Cupid, telling me how we would be perfect for each other. Viggy isn't a small man, he weighs in at about two hundred plus and is six feet tall—we don't call him Big Vig for nothin'. Big Vig looked like Moses parting the Red Dance Floor when, for the second time that night, he grabbed Mayte and brought her back to my table.

It was awkward. Mayte and I had already met but there we were saying hello to each other again. I just stared at her like a homeless man looking at a steak. I thought she was incredible, but in my mind, she had been married to Prince—what the fuck would she want with me?

A few days later she called Viggy to ask him if I'd be interested in writing some music with her. I was excited, and maybe I was naive, but in my heart, I thought nothing else of it. She came over with her sister and we hung out in the studio, talked about music, played each other stuff that we loved and stuff that we were working on. I had never worked with a girl before and I was inspired right away. There was something sexy about connecting on that level with a gorgeous member of the opposite sex. At one point during the day, her sister left to do an errand, and Mayte and I took a walk out to my koi pond where we sat and talked for hours. We talked for so long that working together became secondary and getting to know each other took center stage. We had one of those conversations that stop time: We had so much to share that neither of us felt the hours passing by. We felt so comfortable, there in one of the most special, peaceful places in my house, that we let everything out. She shared her joy and pain: She was recently divorced from Prince and she'd lost a child just after birth. We talked about life and marriage. I've been a Prince fan for so long that to hear what he is really like was crazy. Both of us were adjusting to major life changes—my divorce from Pamela and the custody battle over our kids was about to begin. It had been a long time since I'd met someone I could discuss my life with so honestly and naturally.

That day I realized how small our world is. Back in 1994, I recorded "Welcome to Planet Boom." It was my very first solo effort and it was all about rhythm. I couldn't believe it when she told me she didn't know anything about Mötley, but instead *that's* how she knew who I was. I remembered hearing once that Prince used to play that song all the time. (I freaked when I heard that one of my favorite artists loved my song!)

Mayte and I bonded right from the start. It felt natural when we spent time together, so we started to see each other a lot. I had always wanted to be with a woman who could share my love of music. Mayte sang, she danced—*fuck*, can she dance—

I'D JUST LIKE TO ADD A HELL YEAH TO THAT! HER DANCING IS CONTAGIOUS. . . . EVERY TIME I SEE IT, I JUST HAVE TO DANCE TOO!

and she loved being with me in the studio, writing and creating until the sun came up. I'd never experienced that before and I was *lovin'* it.

During the first year of our relationship, I was going through a heap of shit. Mayte had no idea what she was coming into, but she was so supportive that there is no way I can ever thank her enough. She lived with me and lived in my house through some of the worst shit I've ever dealt with: custody battles, probation, and all the emotional fallout from my breakup with Pamela. All that shit was open wounds that I was trying to

sew up. She was amazing with my kids—she treated my boys like they were her own. She loved them and they loved her—they still ask about her, all the time. She was the only thing that kept me going most days, and I feel completely unable to put down here in words how much that meant to me. Most women would have bailed after learning what my day-to-day reality was like at that time and how hard it was for me emotionally. It was ugly. Thank you, my Lit.

Mayte and I had an amazing relationship. We helped each other heal and grow. We also had a lot of fun together. We had our own language in which we talked like a couple of strange Europeans. She's Puerto Rican, so she did that accent to the fullest, and I'd answer her in my best slimy Greek Guy imitation. People didn't know what the fuck was up with us. I'd say, "Hhhello My Leetle. What arrrre ju doingk?" She'd say, "Nuthingk, Paapi. I waantt to suhhk jour dickkk."

For my fortieth birthday, Mayte threw me an amazing party. She did it in my favorite place, the place where we first got to know each other, the place I call the Garden of Truth—my Japanese garden. It was a surprise and I had no idea. She did it right. I wasn't home that day, so she picked me up, blindfolded me, and handed me a watermelon martini—the official house drink in Tommyland. As she drove us up the long winding road to my house, I knew where we were going and I became Mr. Bummer Surprise-Party Guy. "We're going up to the house, right?" I said. She tried to keep the mystery alive and said, "No, we're not! No way." Believe me, I know the roads around my house better than the cats who repair them. I was like, "Oh. Here we go, we're going through the tunnel!" She'd say, "No, we're not!" And I'd say, "Okay, one more turn and we're there!" When we got there, Mayte led me down to the garden, while I kept saying things like, "So we're walking by the pool now, right?"

It didn't matter that I knew where we were. When we got to the garden I couldn't believe my eyes. She had transformed it into the best present I could imagine: an outdoor sushi restaurant full of my closest friends. I had told her that I had always wanted to do that. She heard me and made that dream come true. There were tables all around the koi pond, candles, the sushi chef doing his thing, and familiar faces as far as my eyes could see. I had it all: I was in my favorite place with my favorite people. What more could you want?

My birthday party was a lot smaller than Puff Daddy's—thank God. Mayte and I went to that one, and if you haven't read any of the magazine or newspaper articles about it, let me tell you—it was crazy. He threw it in Morocco and chartered two 747s to fly hundreds of his closest friends in from New York and Paris. Mayte and I went with my friend and coproducer Scott Humphrey, and we realized we were in for it right away. We're taxiing down the runway, and Puffy gets on the PA and says, "Once we get to forty thousand feet and this motherfucker levels off—it's *on* y'all!" And on it was. Champagne, the Hen, boom boxes, dancing—all of it—and his mom is on the plane!

Everyone is feeling Irie,* even the stewardesses, and at one point I think: "If I see the pilot walk back here and party up I'm gonna freak!" It reminded me of the Crüe on our private flights but with a helluva lot more people. This was the Nonstop Hip-hop and We-Don't-Stop Airbus to Africa.

After ten hours on the soul plane we finally land in Morocco and the big red carpet is rolled out for us motherfuckers. We exit the airport and we see everything that is Marrakech: camels, snake charmers, men playing those long, crazy Middle Eastern trumpets, belly dancers, and drummers everywhere. The first thing I heard was women singing in traditional Muslim style: that strange yell that is somewhere between a chant and a yodel. All of us pile into a shitload of Mercedes limos that are lined up, waiting to take us to the hotel, while Puffy cruises to this crazy palace he had all to himself.

It was a four-day party. There were a few pre–birthday party parties,

---

* *Irie* is a Rastafarian term that connotes positive feelings and all things good. Rastafarianism is a religious movement that began in Jamaica in the 1930s that is based on Biblical prophecy and the teachings of Marcus Mosiah Garvey. For a firsthand Irie experience that no words can describe, book a vacation to Jamaica immediately.

the birthday party, the day after the birthday party party, and the after-party for the day after the birthday party. Somewhere in there, everyone spent a day at a lake riding camels, Jet Skis, four-wheelers, horses, chicks—just ripping it up and eating barbecue. There were models from New York and Paris getting all crazy all over the place. Puffy was walking around in one of those Moroccan white linen suits, taking it all in. (Everyone had bought one by the end of the trip. Mine is upstairs in my closet. It's almost like a dress, or a muumuu. Nah, I guess it's more like a tent. Now I know what girls feel like when they wear a dress with no underwear—it's fuckin' cool.)

YEAH IT IS.
YOU KNOW I LOVE MY FREEDOM.
LET A BROTHER BREATHE!

Mayte, Scott, and I spent a day walking around the souk, which is the huge maze of an open-air market that is fucking crazy. We were having a great day—until I got bit by a monkey. This guy comes up to us, pimping the little guy for money. Morocco is a Third World country, so people make money however they can. I love monkeys because we had one in my house when I was a kid, so I was psyched. When I go to touch this monkey he grabs my finger, puts it in his mouth, and chomps down on it, hard as *fuck*. Oh, damn. I'm thinking about all of the diseases going around Morocco and how I've probably just gotten all of them. I was lucky, that fucker didn't break my skin. I couldn't believe it when the guy asked me for money! I wasn't going to pay for a monkey bite. That's fucked up.

Mayte and I were together for two years. She moved in with me and we shared everything. I asked her to marry me in 2002 on New Year's Eve. We were at my house with my sister and her children, Mayte's parents, and my boys. After we ate dinner, as it got close to midnight, I couldn't wait any longer. I asked her father if I could marry his daughter and he gave me the go-ahead. I hadn't planned to do it that night, but I got so excited that I couldn't wait. I took a Gummi Bear ring from the kids' candy jar and put it on her finger. I promised her that I'd get her a real ring, told her that it would be something special, but I had to know if she'd marry me. She said yes.

Everyone was happy, everyone was hugging, and everyone was drinking champagne. We had cans of Silly String and we shot it all over the place. It felt so right: Mayte is amazing, she was my best friend, my partner, and she brought so many new things into my life. She has a huge, warm, loving family and I loved being around that. They have a tradition around the holidays—they make pastellas. They're wrapped in banana leaves and made of plantains, yucca, pork, garbanzo beans, and stuff I don't even know about. It was amazing to watch Mayte and her family tear up the kitchen, making a huge batch of those things. They're delicious. Of course they are—they're made with love.

While Mayte and I were together, I recorded my most recent record, *Never a Dull Moment*. She was supportive, she had ideas, she was an honest critic, and she helped me in so many ways. I love that record and I'm proud of it—it was an evolution for me. I was able to express myself more honestly than I ever had, because I knew myself better than I ever had. I was truly on my own this time: There weren't many guest stars, it was just me. To make that leap with my best friend and lover by my side was a first for me and it was amazing. I would play her songs, she'd be excited to listen, and she had great ideas of how to make it better. We wrote songs together—another first for me. I felt that everything I was doing was in the right place. Mayte *got* it. My ex-wives supported what I did but they weren't musicians. Maybe I expected them to understand what they really couldn't—music wasn't their language.

Mayte sung on that album and when I toured she danced in the show. She was hot as fuck—she *is* hot as fuck! She had showed me a video of her dancing with Prince, and I freaked. Mötley had had dancers, but let's face it—they were more like strippers. Mayte is a real dancer. Our

friend, Brian, a choreographer, came down to rehearsals and worked out a routine with Mayte. I put together some crazy beats for her to dance to and we arranged a light show to highlight her dancing. I loved playing a show with my girl every night. I loved sharing the high you get after a show with the woman I was sharing my life with. It was the first time I'd been on tour with my girl. And most girls would be jealous of so much shit that happens on tour, but Mayte wasn't. Every night I'd go to the front of the stage with a camera that was hooked to the big screens behind me. It was the Titty Cam because I'd only point it at all the girls flashing their tits. If that wouldn't piss off the average woman, I don't know what would. Mayte didn't care—actually, she fucking *dug* it. She'd either be down in the audience filming all the crazy chicks with her own camera, or she'd be at the side of the stage checking out the video Breast Buffet.

I don't think Mayte ever got over losing her first child. She had always wanted to be a mom and that was the only problem we had in our relationship. She really wanted children right away. The timing was terrible for us: She was talking about having children while I was fighting just to keep mine. I had never thought about having any more children than my boys. For a minute I thought that it would be rad to have a little girl. Then I thought about how protective I'd be when she became a teenager. I thought about her going on dates with guys and how motherfucking horny teenage dudes are—fuck, how motherfucking horny *all* dudes are. I didn't like the thought of that one bit—until I figured out how I would handle it. When the guy showed up to take my daughter out I'd pull him aside. "Whatever you do to my daughter, I'm gonna do to you," I'd tell him. "You kiss her, I'm kissing you. You suck her titties, I'm gonna suck your titties. You fuck her, I'm fuckin' you."

WOAH, WOAH, HEY, DUDE!
NO WAY!
I'M NOT GOING IN THERE!

I felt a lot better after that.

I DIDN'T!

The straw that broke the camel's back came one day when I was sitting by the pool studying a deposition, preparing for an appearance in court the next day. It was the middle of the trial surrounding Daniel's death, and I was taking the stand the next morning. Mayte came and sat next to me because she wanted to have "A Talk." Again, bad timing— really bad. We had been engaged for more than a year and Mayte wanted to know where the relationship was going, when we were going to get married, and when we would start a family. A part of me thought that she was being really selfish and that turned me off. The other part of me didn't blame her. We had been in limbo for a while, mostly because of the drama going on in my life. Her biological clock was ticking and her life was on hold: I couldn't give her everything she needed and deserved. I told her that if she wanted to go she should because she should be in a relationship with someone who could give her what she wanted. Right then, there was no way I could be that guy. She asked me why I asked her to marry me. I said, "Because I love you." Sometimes that isn't enough.

We had been through so much bullshit together—bullshit that had nothing to do with our lives together but that affected us to the point that we started fighting a lot. Please believe, you do *not* want to fight with a Puerto Rican woman—*you will lose*. There wasn't any solution for us: She wasn't happy, I wasn't happy, and neither of us would budge. We broke off our engagement in the summer of 2003, and I'm happy to say that we're still friends. It is hard for me sometimes, because in my heart I think that if we had met at a different time and place in each other's lives we would have been together forever. I'll always love you, my Little.

21

STATE OF BEGINNER'S LUCK

a.k.a.
T-BONE'S WINNING STREAK, LAS VEGAS, JULY 2003

I went to Vegas in the summer of 2003 with a bunch of my friends. We went to The Palms hotel, up to the Ghost Bar, which is at the very top of the place. It's got this amazing deck with a clear piece of Plexiglas in it so that you can see the street, hundreds of feet down, while you dance. We're partying up there and it's fucking retarded. Later we go back to the Hard Rock casino to gamble. I'm not a huge gambling guy, mostly because I don't know how to play most of the games. My friends want to play craps, which I've never played before. But I don't care! I take two hundred bucks out, throw it down, and pick up the dice. My friends are like, "Dude, just roll the fucking dice. But no matter what, do *not* roll a seven. You roll a seven, you crap out, and we're fucking *done*." I roll the dice. *Boom!* Everyone at the table is all "Yaay!" Everyone wins. I have no idea

why or how. I just know I did something right. I don't know how to bet or where to place my chips, so one of my boys bets for me. And I roll again. *Boom!* Again, the whole table blows up. They're yelling, "*Fuck! No way!*" I hit it again somehow.

Twice in a row would have been good enough for me, but dude, I keep on going. I roll the dice for almost an hour without crappin' out. I must have had a fucking horseshoe up my ass that night. Everything was just right. I would roll whatever my boys said we needed. We need an eight? *Boom!* They'd put a thousand dollars on the table, and they'd tell me to roll a six. I'd be like, "Six? Okay." And I'd roll it.

By the time I was done, the combined winnings at that table were $101,000. My friends loved me. The strangers who won loved me. The hotel hated me. The host from the Hard Rock came up to my room in the morning to inform me that security watched the tape several times because they thought I had been cheating but had decided that I hadn't. How could I cheat when I'd never played craps before? According to him, never, ever in the history of the hotel has anyone ever rolled the dice nonstop for almost an hour. I thought that was awesome and I asked him if I could get the tape. It was the most epic night that will never, ever happen again. I'm not even gonna try.

22

STATE OF ADORATION

a.k.a.
FANATIC

I love my fans, I always have. They keep musicians going, and if it's going well, they keep musicians eating too. Mötley always made as much time as possible to sign stuff, just hang out for a minute, whatever we could do. I can't even tell you how many times my manager, or security, or road manager has thrown me over his shoulder and carried me to the bus or plane or wherever because I was signing shit or taking pictures until I was in danger of fucking up the schedule. There are times I'm not into doing stuff of course, but you know, if any bit of music I've ever made means that much to people that they want to shake my hand, talk for a minute, or just have my name on a piece of paper, fucking bring it on—that rules! Sure, sometimes I do just want to get through the grocery store and buy my kids their Capri Sun juice boxes, get some steaks, and bail, but I'll always try to stop to say hello. Of course some of these well-wishers just want an autograph to go sell on eBay. I've learned after all these years to pick them out a little better—they're the ones who have no idea about my music.

I see it all: Some people want to tell me all about their lives, some people want to hug me, push me, and get all kinds of physical.

So if I could take a moment here and lay down a rule to my people out there, I just want to ask you all to please understand that when I'm with my little Monkeys, please just say hey from afar and let us be. My time with them is precious, and I want it to be all about them. Those are the times when fans are not the first thing on my mind. I'd like to think that although I've had a pretty unique life, I'm led by common sense. And common sense says that if someone is hanging out with their children, it is family time! I don't care if you're famous or not, if you're a parent spending time with your children, no one has the right to interrupt you. I'd like to add that a meal is sacred, people. No matter how much you love your favorite entertainer, don't bother them while they're eating. We need to eat, and we love food as much as you do. So let us do it in peace.

I've had people walk right up to me while I'm feeding my boys out in public—which is a double whammy fan no-no: interrupting family time *and* meal time. At those moments, yes, I'm still Tommy Lee, but before that I'm Dad. The worst kind is a fan who has the balls and the lack of brains to come up and disturb me, then isn't the kind of fan who's going to go away quietly. Nope, that guy or girl doesn't only want an autograph or a picture, they want to talk to me like they know me. They want to tell me about that show in Boston that changed their lives back in 1989. I mean, that's great and all, but right now, I'm just trying to get some ketchup on the boys' fries, okay?

The worst it's gotten for me was the time I was taking a shit—just trying to drop a log—and a piece of paper with a pen on top of it came sliding sideways under the stall wall. I just hear, "Dude, could you sign that?" You're fucking kidding me! I'm *dumping*, dude. I'm busy, I'm stocking the lake with brown trout. It was everything I could do not to grab some poop, slop it on there, and send it back. But I didn't. I couldn't. I just signed it, slid it back under, and went on with my business. By the time I got out of the stall, the cat was gone. I was desperate to see who he was. That cat had the biggest balls on the planet—he *defines* fanatic.

I'm cool hanging with fans as long as no one gets too crazy. I go to local bars to play foosball and video games, and just have a few rounds with the regulars. I'm definitely not on some ego trip and I'm not at all trying to be trendy and cool—you should see where I hang out. Considering some of the situations I've ended up in, I should probably roll with security, but I usually don't.

I'm not tripping, y'all, really—I've got the mad fan love, but there are some fans I just don't understand. I was in Bora Bora on vacation not too long ago. It is by far the most romantic place in the world. It's not the kind of place where anyone cares who you are: It's so free that no one bothers anyone because the place inspires this natural high that I've never experienced anywhere else. The ocean, the trees, the sand, the raw beauty, is all so insane that the people there are completely in heaven, feeling lovely and forgetting about the rest of the world for a while.

That last time I was there though, I'm on the beach, just chilling, and out of the corner of my eye I see a guy coming my way. I think "Uh-oh . . . oh, no . . . Oh, *damn* . . . okay, here we go." He's carrying a book and I know what book it is when he's still fifty yards off. It's *The Dirt*—of course it is. Here he comes. Okay, fine. I'm ready.

"Hey Tom! Hey man! Hey, what's goin' on?"

"Nothin' dude. Just chillin'."

I'm thinking, "Oh, shit. Of all places for this to happen. *Great.*" He starts talking to me, telling me he's on his honeymoon and when he comes up for air, I congratulate him. Then he starts telling me about his wedding. After that he drops the fanatic bomb: He says, "Hey man, I don't mean to bother you, *but*, could you sign this?" No problem, dude.

Okay. I've gotta say this because it's been chappin' my ass for years. Whenever people *anywhere* say they don't mean to bother you, they are *fucking lying.* They're lying like a rug in a flophouse. They're lying like politicians on the campaign trail. They're lying like a married man on a business trip. They're lying like a computer nerd in a singles ad. They're lying like that girl who says she never does this on the first date. They're just fucking *lying. All of 'em—always.*

And they ask you to believe their lie anyway. If they really listened to themselves, they would realize that they just said, "I really don't want to bother you." And if they heard that, maybe they'd already know what I'm thinking: "Well . . . if you don't want to *bother* me, then *don't.*" But they *do* want to bother me, and hey, man, that's cool. It could be worse. *No one* could be asking me for my autograph.

Anyway, so I'm on the beach and this dude asks me to sign his book, which, as I predicted, is *The Dirt*, the autobiography of Mötley Crüe. I'm thinking to myself, "You're on your honeymoon, and right now you are standing in the most beautiful place on earth and you're reading about *Mötley Crüe?* Woah." That's crazy. This guy is just married and he's more interested in learning about some of the gnarliest rock-and-roll debauchery that's ever been. I sign it and say, "You brought this on your *honeymoon?* Are you out of your *mind?* Where is your *girl?*" He told me that his girl was back at the hotel doing her own thing. Woah. Hey. Dude, that's not good. While he kept going on about how amazing the book was, I kept thinking about how his poor newly wed wife must be wondering why he was reading that book on their honeymoon. Then again, maybe she bought it for him to inspire him to new heights of nastiness. You never know these days; people are weird and love comes in all kinds of craise. Even I'm confused.

So I signed it, on one condition: that he find something else to read while he's in Bora Bora. I said, "That's not really a beach kind of book to read, my man. But I'm really glad you like it." He wasn't having that at all. He said something like, "It's perfect for right now. Everything I need to know is in here, bro." I found that totally fucking scary. I guess to some people a lot of drugs and retarded excess is postnuptial bliss. Whatever. God bless the freaks. I wish those two and all the rest of you well, wherever you are.

23

STATE OF MEDICATION

a.k.a.
IT'S NOT YOUR MOTHER'S ROBITUSSIN

I have a Jägermeister* machine in my house. That's a good thing most days, but sometimes it's a problem. For example, when my girl is upstairs waiting for me in the bedroom and the loud *bzzzzp* sound of the dispenser sells me out. It's not something I like to share, but on the night of my fortieth birthday, after every guest had left and the house was finally quiet again, I thought, "Fffhuck it, one more shhot befhore I go tuh bhed." There I am,

---

* Jägermeister is a 70 proof liquor made from a blend of over 50 herbs, fruits, and spices. Legend has it that it was inspired by the story of Hubertus, a valiant young warrior who lived in the seventh century, lost his princess to ill health, and apparently during a deer hunting trip encountered a massive stag wih a cross floating between his antlers. This was, keep in mind, before Jägermeister was invented. Here are a few popular Jäger-fueled drinks for the curious. They are, at the least, fun to order: Redheaded Slut, Suck, Bang and Blow, Liquid Cocaine, Sex with an Alligator, Blue Smurf Piss, Shut the Hell Up, Oatmeal Raisin Cookie, Instant Death, and Little Green Man from Mars. Consult your local bartender for more information. And consider yourself warned.

on my knees, head tilted back, sucking the nozzle, holding the dispense button in, gulping a river of Jäger. In my peripheral vision I see Mayte, just standing there, shaking her head, with her arms crossed, watching me. *Busted.* I say, "Hiii bahby." She says, "What are you *doing?*" I say, "I thinhk I drhopped mhy kehys over hheare . . . sohmewhere. I'm just down hhere on the flhoor luhhking for them." She looked at me and said, "Happy Birthday, baby. I'm going to bed."

Never mind that story, the point is that I know what to do with Jäger-meister. What I *don't* know is why my better ideas haven't been put into action yet. Jäger goes with everything, please believe. Jägermeister coffee is a personal favorite. Just whip up your usual coffee and hit it with a shot of Jäger. You won't regret it. And there's more: You can make Jäger desserts: Jäger root beer floats, Jäger chocolate sauce, Jäger ice cream sundaes. And I've got plans for the hot dog stands. Dodger Stadium needs to know that every dude in that whole place would *kill* to buy a Jäger Dog. They could make the Jäger into some funky jelly paste and shoot it into the middle of the dog back in the factory. When it gets stuck on one of those hot dog merry-go-rounds, it's *on.* It won't be as cold as I like it, but it won't matter because when dudes bite into one of those doggies and snap the weenie skin, *BOOM!* There's three shots of Jäger right down your throat. It's self-contained—there's no mess because there are no shot glasses to clean.

With the state of the world as it is, it wouldn't surprise me if I found Jäger fruit punch in little juice boxes at the store. The label would probably suggest serving it at those times when your kids have had too much sugar to turn the volume down on the little guys. They've got all kinds of mood-altering drugs for kids already. I'm sure we're not far away from Flintstones chewable Prozac. Jäger is made from poppies, right? That shit's natural.*

---

* Yes, Tommy, it is, for the most part, natural. Aside from the caramel coloring and several additives, the ingredients in Jäger are as natural as the flowers that decorate God's green earth. Understand that these synthetic elements are essential: They keep the Jäger fresher and, by extension, the Jäger drinker happier.

I mean, *fuck* Jell-O shots—have you ever had frozen Jäger? The colder the better, trust me. Why are there no Jäger pops in my freezer right now? That's a Jäger to go. It's the Jäger you can take anywhere. And your girl can suck on it, all the way down to the stick. And on those nights when you've had too much Jäger, that pop will have your back. You and your girl have dessert and a dildo . . . all in one frozen treat!

I want to take it further. Jäger potpies, that's what I'm talking about this winter. A Jäger broth, carrots, peas, potatoes, and meat marinated for days in Jäger. Forget the after-dinner drinks. Why wait when you can have them now? Jäger tastes like cough medicine, so it's *got* to be good for you. Listen, Meister Jägermeister, we should collaborate on some of this shit. You got my number? You can find it in your frequent-flier program files— I'm enrolled. Whew, damn, all this writing has made me tired. Actually I feel kinda sick. I feel like I've got a cough. I'll be right back. Time for my medicine. *Bvvvvvvvvvvvzzzzup.*

24

STATE OF MELODIC MEMORY

a.k.a.
FILL YOUR HEAD
WITH MUSIC

I was fourteen or something close to that when I really got hooked. It happened right down the street, at my friend's house. His older brother was the one on the block with the records, and I remember sitting there in his room with my friend when that guy dropped the needle. That was *it*—I was *done*. That guy had a fuckin' kickin' JBL/Pioneer system and he was blasting Zeppelin, and the only way I could make sense of everything I was feeling was to say to my friend, *"Dude,* your brother *rules!"* I was still a little kid then and that guy turned his bro and me on to Led Zeppelin, Black Sabbath, Van Halen, Cheap Trick, Ted Nugent, and Deep Purple. What a fucking gift. I was like, "Oh my *God,* this is fucking *insane!"* He'd play a song for us and I'd start jumping up and down, yelling, "Play it again! Play it again!" I'm still like that. When I think about how much time has gone by since then and how much music I've heard and how much music I've made, I'm so happy to say that the way I experience powerful music has not changed a bit. When I hear a song that gives me goose bumps, I play it over and over again until I've absorbed every bit of what's going on. I play it until I burn it out. It's a good thing technology has moved beyond records because I'd have a graveyard of worn-down, bald-ass vinyl behind my house by now. A great song hits me on so many levels. I hear it as a musician first, dissecting the chords and parts, analyzing the production, the effects, and how the final product was crafted. It's like a puzzle that I love working on and that I have to understand. After I've put all the pieces together—which might take several weeks—I hear it as a fan. And as a fan, I take in the song or album's full impact: the message the artist is trying to get across and the emotion involved. Music at its most basic and its most complicated is simply just communication. It is communication on many levels, from the heart to the mind to the soul. I hear rhythm first—of course I do, I'm a drummer. The rhythm locks me in first most of the time, then the bits of the song that reflect my life in some way. If a song is truly amazing though, it doesn't have to have a message, feel, or vibe that has anything to do with my experience of this world. If the singer, the guitarist, or the band as a whole bare their soul well enough in those three, four, five, or six fucking minutes, they will reach me. If the lyricist and the musicians are really, honestly, laying it down, I can *feel* it. And that is what music is all about: telling stories, no matter what they are, that hit the listener in 3-D: mind, body, and soul.

If a song is real—whether it's pop, rock, rap, r&b, reggae—any style can touch the entire world if it's real. It hurts me that the state of music right now is so fucked up. Music has become an industry of copycats put out by the labels for profit. Everyone sounds the same, and everyone looks the same. I don't know if it's the powers that be or the artists themselves, but when I look around, it seems to me that all the hip-hop dudes are wearing basketball jerseys from their favorite teams and that's it. That looks cool and all, but damn—this is entertainment. Change it up, dudes! The rock dudes are the same, and so are the pop stars. Music is such a versatile art form that everyone can be different, sound different, look different, and tell very different stories—so why aren't they? And hey, what happened to the rock star? There doesn't seem to be any new rock stars out there, no one captivating and strange and alien like there used to be, like Led Zeppelin and David Bowie. Whatever.

It's hard for me to talk about music, because when something is so much a part of me and so important to me, it's hard to capture the feelings in words. I'm just going to list a few of so many bands and albums that have moved me then, now, and still will tomorrow.

SIGUR ROS

That band sends me back to the womb, and it's scary. I had Christmas dinner at my house this one time with my ex-fiancée Mayte and some friends. I was cooking and hosting, and after we'd all eaten and were just chilling out, I put that album on and I can't even describe what happened next. All of a sudden I'm walking around my house in a trance. I laid down on the floor and curled up like I was an infant. I couldn't talk and I couldn't move—all I could do was listen and be still. There's some kind of amazing subliminal science going on in their music and I don't know what the hell it is. They are from Iceland and they don't sing in English, but there's a message there, if you want to hear it, that sounds like a complex and weird mix of angels and noise. If you tap into the vibe they create, you will go on a journey, wherever your mind will take you. That Christmas, it really hit me and I had no idea where I was anymore. I left my body—I mean fully left—and I was right at home, the place I know best. For a band to take me, or anyone, that far away from what they know the best is an incredible achievement. That night, when the music hit me, all I could do was lie down and feel the floor and listen. I wasn't sleeping, I wasn't sad—I still don't know what I was: I was simply in the space they created. One of the greatest things about their music is that they called the album *Untitled*. It leaves everything open, letting the listener paint the sound canvas however they want to. The songs don't have titles and the album art work doesn't have clear pictures or anything else to root the music to an image or an idea. It is up to the listener to decide what the music is all about. That is what froze me up and stopped me in my tracks. It sent me into myself, very powerfully and immediately. It's an incredible thing to accomplish, because their art isn't a performance, it's an invitation to be a part of what they've made. I was happy to be invited and I got way too into it. Mayte shut it off because she thought I was heading somewhere far too weird, and she was worried that I'd never come back.

LED ZEPPELIN

My only regret in this life is that I never got to meet or see my hero John Bonham beat the shit out of a drum kit live. By the time I would've been able to see Zeppelin in California, Mötley was just getting off the ground. And after that I was on tour full-time and never had the chance to see him before he passed away. He was the greatest fucking drummer I've ever heard. If only I could have seen him, if only there had been some way while he was alive for me to tell him or, in any other way, pay my respects to the effect he's had on my life—I don't know what I'd give to be able to do that. Probably far too much. I don't even know what to say. How can I tell anyone what his drumming did to my life? He fucking rocked me and he defined how I think about rhythm. Bonham made me realize exactly what drums had the power to do.

Rock-and-roll when it's great is a complex monster. It's dynamic, a unit full of parts, like all amazing music: There's the singer, there's the guitar player, and a lot of people only pay attention to them. But you know what? I don't care what anyone says—those guys aren't the ones moving the house. The drums and beats do that, people. And that goes for whatever music you listen to. Drums are the base: They're tribal, they're primal, and they are the earliest form of music we know. Drum beats come from the rhythm that starts us off in this world, the first music we hear—our mothers' heartbeat in the womb. Drums and rhythm are as simple and as complex as that. When you see 60,000 people going off, whether it's at a rave, a rock show, a rap show, or a freakin' parade or ceremony of whatever kind, I guarantee you the proceedings begin and end with the beat of a drum. That is the source. When I heard how Bonham did it, I freaked the fuck out. I can't even begin to fully capture how I felt when I first rocked the house, or what it is like, sitting on my drum throne in a stadium, arena, or even a little club, with a kick-ass bunch of players waiting for *me* to start the fucking fire. That's what a drummer does, and it's a powerful position. Once you know you're good enough and once you really *know* what you can do back there, and once when you've got an arsenal of songs to tear it up, it's incredible. You look out into the crowd and you just think, "I've got *all* you motherfuckers right now. Let's rip!" There's been moments when I can't believe it. I've watched entire arenas bouncing in time. And you know, my bandmates might do their thing, but it's something fucking else to look out there and watch the people moving their bodies to what I'm doing. They're not bouncing to the lyrics, they're not bouncing to the guitar, they're bouncing to the drums. I guess I got off the subject. Hey! Guys! Mr. Page and Mr. Plant, and Mr. John Paul Jones! If you do another Zep tour anytime soon, please call my ass— you won't be disappointed!!!!

VAN HALEN

I'll never forget hearing their cover of the Kinks's "You Really Got Me" on the radio and thinking, "Daaaaaaamn! No fuckin' *way!*" I really couldn't believe it when I heard "Eruption." Eddie's guitar solo and tone was so fresh to my ears—it was nothing I'd ever heard before. I lost it just like every guitar player and rock fan on the planet did. Their first record changed my life. Then I saw them live at Long Beach Arena, and there I was standing on my chair the whole fuckin' time trippin' out on how this unreal band served everyone the heaviest shit around at the time. Thanks dudes! That was a great night for me: I snuck out of my window, jumped off the roof into the tree next to it, climbed down, and hopped in my friend's car. And I stood on my seat in the arena rocking the fuck *out* all night.

CHEAP TRICK

Cheap Trick opened up for Mötley in 1986 for nine of our U.K. shows. We were really hitting our stride, and I couldn't believe it—to me, it was insane that *we* weren't opening up for *them*. They were my heroes. Dude, I sat out on the side of the stage every night watching Cheap Trick, my favorite band of all time, play—and every night I was amazed, speechless, and just like, "Woah." It wasn't even their heaviest period—back then a lot of my heroes were doing pop. Trick had just released "The Flame," Robert Plant was doing the Honeydrippers, and Bowie was doing his pop thing. Mötley was in the middle of our craziest shit, but even then I could understand how those guys, who'd all been through a bunch of shit, wanted to do something new, more mellow, and mature. It was so cool to see Cheap Trick in that phase of their career, totally able to shift gears into their old stuff too, and hold it all together because they're such amazing bad-ass players. And they were on that tour as they always are, every single night. Guys . . . if you only knew how much you've inspired me with your melodies and songs. Words escape me. Again . . . thank you. All I can say is go see them—they're still touring and as bad-ass as ever.

SNOW PATROL

One of my new favorite bands—wow! To me they are a blend of Radiohead and Coldplay. You all *must* hear them—you'll be thanking me later.*

---

* Their most recent album *Final Straw* (A&M Records) is available on the Internet through Amazon.com, at Circuit City, Wal-Mart, and local record stores (who could use your support in this age of digital music piracy) near you now. The album is a departure from the band's earlier indie albums (of which there are three), which focused more on lush instrumentals than traditional song structure and storytelling. The latest album, as well as the band's live show, is thrilling. Tommy plays it constantly and though he loves it all, his favorite songs are "Same," and "Run." I particularly like the song "Tiny Little Fractures" and one evening played it forty-five times in a row.

THE FUNK

My love of funk was the one thing that separated me from a lot of my bandmates and friends growing up. In the late seventies and early eighties, unless a dude was a drummer, or black, most rock guys had no love for the funk. To me, that music was the black equivalent of the rock I was listening to. It is so musical: There are horns; guitars; amazing, soulful singers; and players that kick ass. I couldn't stop listening to it: It had great rhythms, it was sexy, you could dance to it, and you sure as hell could fuck to it.

GOD BLESS THE MASTERS OF FUNKY! HIT ME! IT'S HOT IN THE HOT TUB! I JUMP BACK, KISS MYSELF! HAAEYY! GIVE THE DRUMMER SOME!

Funk was the original hip-hop—it was party music, it had a story, and sometimes it had a meaningful social message. I listened to a lot of funk when I was practicing the drums. I'd sit in my room with my headphones on learning funky beats for days, weeks, months, and years. It gave me more of a swing than the other rock drummers I knew, and I've used the lessons from the hallowed halls of funk ever since. And anyone who says rock-and-roll and funk aren't cousins is crazy. I used a fill from the Gap Band's "You Dropped a Bomb on Me" in "Girls, Girls, Girls." If you don't believe me, go listen to both of them right now.

So without further ado, here's a list of thanks to my funk professors:

Prince
Ohio Players
Gap Band

Digital Underground
Parliament-Funkadelic
James Brown
Joe Tex
Sly and the Family Stone

ELECTRONIC MUSIC

It's such a huge, diverse genre I don't know where to start. Fuck it, let's start at the start—with my definition: Electronic music is made by machines, designed by maniacs out there in Gizmology Land (one of my favorite places to be!) who have found a way to make machines capable of doing whatever you want them to. I couldn't believe it the first time I was shown that a computer could do what I wanted to do to music. I kept thinking, "What? I can program this thing to do whatever I want? Are you kidding me?! Let me at it!"

I first recorded with computers in 1984, when I was writing songs for the *Girls, Girls, Girls* record. That's where "Wild Side" came from. I played a chunky guitar riff and chopped it into sixteenth notes on the computer—because I could. When I heard the result I freaked! And so did my band. That was it—I was hooked. That said, the technology at the time was the biggest reason not to be into it at all. I used an Apple IIci and if any of you computer geeks like me out there remember that ancient piece of shit, it was hell. It took forever because by today's standards it was as powerful as a really good calculator, and it had shitty sound cards. It was totally wack—but I did not care! Manipulating sound like that was a whole new world to me, and I've been discovering how big that world is ever since and loving how it continues to expand.

The truth is, the human feel can never be replaced because a machine can not reproduce the imperfections, soul, and style of someone communicating feeling like only people can. At the same time, the rigidity of a computer cannot be reproduced either. When you mix both of them together, you create a marriage that yields something completely inspiring and original. It is a union of opposites that allows for so many possibilities and accidents. Whenever I've tried new things, like taking a new piece of gear out of the box and fucking with it without ever cracking the manual, I've come up with some of the coolest parts I've ever written. In my life, as in the lives of so many other artists I've spoken to, the coolest things have happened by trial and error—they've been those beautiful mistakes that were meant to be. To me that is the legacy of computers and electronic music. Computers have freed up imagination in all the arts, from movies, music, architecture, and design to every creative field you can name. If you can dream it, a computer can make it. And there's no limit to dreams.

Anyway, here you go. Here is a list of bands across genres, from industrial rock to dance music to hip-hop, that opened my ears and my soul to whatever new sound was created by smashing human and robot together.

Nine Inch Nails
Ministry
Orbital
Massive Attack
Mr. Oizo
Beastie Boys, featuring my man, Mix Master Mike
Basement Jaxx
The Chemical Brothers
Peaches
Portishead
Jay-Z
Missy Elliott
Josh Wink
Adam Freeland

Daft Punk
Aphex Twin
DMX
Eminem
Dr. Dre

HOW TO (SELF) LEARN DRUMS
BY TOMMY LEE

Get yourself some headphones and some cardboard boxes, trash cans and lids—hell, whatever you can destroy without consequences and just play, play, *play!* That's how I did it: I put on what I loved, listened, and did it! Here are a few of the albums that taught me what's what:

The Sweet, *Desolation Boulevard*
Led Zeppelin, *Physical Graffiti*
AC/DC, *Back in Black* and *Highway to Hell*
Cheap Trick, *In Color*
Kiss, *Alive!*
Parliament, *Mothership Connection*
Van Halen, *Van Halen*

I've done my best to dive deep and lay down my earliest influences. These made a huge mark—they got me started and it hasn't stopped. At this point in my life, there are way too many to list. I am a musician first and still a huge fan second—and I think that's even more important. I listen to just about everything, except country music (sorry, cowboys—my dad played that shit all the time and kinda wrecked it for me). God bless music and the people who make it. It was always there for me all the times I needed it. It was there for me no matter what was going on, no matter what went wrong, and no matter what I did. It still is and always will be! I will *always* love you, music, as you've always loved me!

25

STATE OF FAREWELL

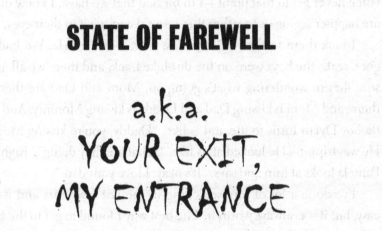

a.k.a.
YOUR EXIT,
MY ENTRANCE

At forty-one years old, I am at a very interesting point in my life, and I feel lucky to be here. I have learned, I have loved, and after knocking my head against walls of all kinds—some of which I built myself—I've discovered who I am and what I want out of life. And you'll never know what it is! Just kidding. What I want out of life is simple: I want happiness—the kind that keeps your soul warm even when the world around you is cold. I want peace, and I find that in my home and in my mind when I make time to meditate. I want love, and I have found it in so many places. I want family, and I'm lucky to still have my mother, my sister, and my two amazing children.

For our boys' sake, I'm happy that Pamela and I have put a lot of our differences behind us. We're finally able to enjoy what we started: the beautiful babies whom our love brought into the world.

Healing takes a lot of time and when you're impatient, it takes forever. She and I loved so intensely that when it blew up, it left scars, anger,

resentment—and don't get me started again on the lawyers' bills. Finally, finally, finally, she and I can look at each other and say, "What the fuck were we doing, dude? That shit was *retarded*." So many people who divorce never get to that point—I'm blessed that we have. I know our boys are happier seeing us together these days. I can see it in their eyes.

I took them to the X Games last year, with Pamela. We had crazy good seats, the boys were on the dirt-bike track, and there we all are. I'm sure they're wondering what's going on, Mom and Dad are there with them, and Mom is kissing Dad and Daddy is kissing Mommy. And my little boy Dylan turns to me and is like, "Daddy, you're kissing Mommy!" He was trippin'. He looked at us like, "What are they doing?" Right then, Pamela looks at him and says, "It's okay. I love your dad."

I've done a lot of soul-searching in the last few years and it wasn't easy, but it was always worth it. The best way I found to get to the bottom of how I am feeling at those moments is to write myself a letter. It gets my mind open until everything pours out. I'm going to share one with you. It was written as this project was undertaken.

Hey Tommy,

I'm writing to tell you that I'm not sure where I am anymore. I know a few things. I'll never move out of Malibu . . . until I'm ready to build my dream home in Bora Bora. I've been there six times and I will either build a second home there or retire there when I'm ready. Life is still really good for me in spite of all the drama—jail, the custody battles, the courts, the probation. In spite of it, I'm happy for it. I'm learning what I never took the time to learn. I've still got hurdles—a lot of them. Life can be so unpredictable sometimes. I'm really confused about relationships in general. Why do they start off so sweet and fresh and turn sour so quickly?

I've really been enjoying being alone for the first time in my life. I play music, I create music, I play with my kids, I answer to no one, and I come and go as I please. I've got the space to do more soul-searching and I really need to. All of us desire companionship, but not all of us need it. Those are two completely different animals.

To tell the truth, I feel a bit lost right now. I'm in my forties. I don't know if I have the energy to put into a relationship that may or may not work. So far I've been through two marriages, one annulment, and one engagement—and here I am. Why should I go down that path again?

Starting my book has gotten me thinking as I go over the details of my life. I'm reliving my past accomplishments and thinking about my future goals. I'm bringing my mistakes and my lessons out into the light. I'm realizing all over again how extraordinary my life has been.

That's it for today. And who knows what tomorrow will bring me, or what I'll do about it. Don't worry, I'll fill you in as it comes.

Be you, be safe, be good, be what you want, be what you are.

T.

This is the end of the ride, ladies and gentleman. Thank you for visiting Tommyland and I hope you enjoyed your stay. I'm sorry to say that all good things must come to an end, and this is where we must part. After the safety bar is released, the door will open automagically. Please take a look around to make sure you have all your belongings and loved ones as you make your way to the exit. For those of you first-timers, do come again, we're open all year. For those regulars who have a season pass, well, I'll be seeing you again real soon I'm sure. I'm staying, because after all, I live here.

Afterglow
(From the album *Never a Dull Moment*, 2002)

One love up above countin' your blessings, learning the lessons
That make you strong, doin' no wrong to no one
What do we do, how do we roll to hit the next level?
Do you wanna go?

EPILOGUE: STATE OF AFTERTHOUGHT

a.k.a.
THE AFTER-THE-LAST-CHAPTER CHAPTER

When we set out on this project, my plan was to take a picture of Anthony and me to celebrate the very moment we wrote our last word. Y'all are so lucky I didn't. We were scaring me. Remember Heaven's Gate? It was that bad. After months of purging my life's highest and lowest moments and weeks of staring at nothing but each other lit by the creepy glow of a computer monitor, we were ready for some fucking spaceship to land and for the little green guys to abduct us. They never did. They probably thought about it until they got a good look and whiff of us. We were on a mission and everything else—showering, eating three square meals a day, assuring concerned third parties that we were still alive—none of it mattered anymore. We had to deliver our message. We'd only remember what life was like before when we caught glimpses of the outside world on our way to restock the fort with the essentials: cigarettes, more cigarettes, liquor, frozen pizza, the occasional fresh vegetable, and more liquor.

Don't worry, it's all okay now. We're done, thank God, because we

Although the author(s) stated that the aforementioned stinky self-portrait was not taken, here it is. Therefore, they (we) lied.

reek like a marinating loaf of *wrong*. The test results haven't come back yet, but I don't think any permanent damage was done during this experiment. We're no more insane than we were before, right? Hey, Anthony, we're no more insane than we were before, right? "We're insane! Yaaay! Yaay, we're insane! Yaay!" Dude, I said, we're *not* insane. "We're insane! Yaaay! We're insane!" Well . . . maybe Anthony is. We'd better go, he's not looking so good and he thinks he's Special Ed from *Crank Yankers* right now. We're out of here. Goodbye! And *good luck.**

---

* Tommy and I would like to send our condolences and fondest feelings to our English editor at Simon & Schuster, who, citing the psychological damage and emotional duress incurred at our hand during the editing of this book, quit his position two weeks before the closure of the project. We're sorry he was unable to hang in there, and like two victims of Stockholm Syndrome,* in this case, in reverse, we miss him dearly.

   * Stockholm Syndrome is a psychological condition through which the abused bond to their abusers as a means to endure violence. The name of this condition stems from a bank robbery that took place in Stockholm (duh) in 1973. The robbers kept four hostages captive in the bank vault for six days, after which the victims became attached to the perpetrators, raising money for their defense and testifying on their behalf at the trial following their capture. The human is an interesting creature, indeed.

PHOTO CREDITS

P. ii: Photo courtesy of Isabel Snyder.

P. 5: Photo courtesy of Isabel Snyder.

P. 6: Photo courtesy of Dara Blumenhein.

P. 11: Photo courtesy of Tommy Lee.

P. 42: Photo courtesy of Tommy Lee.

P. 86: Photo courtesy of Tommy Lee.

Pp. 112, 113, 140: Collage photos all courtesy of Tommy Lee.

P. 209: Photo courtesy of Tommy Lee.

P. 262: Photo courtesy of Anthony Bozza.

P. 263: Photo courtesy of Tommy Lee (laptops in studio).

Flipbook animation by Syndrome Studio, www.syndromestudio.com.

Photo Insert
Tommy Lee Smoke 1999, photo by David LaChapelle, 1999.

Tommy Lee, live drum shots, all courtesy of Tommy Lee.

To'Up Illustration by Eli 5 Stone, 5stone.com.

Tommy writing, photo courtesy of Justin Jay.

Tommy in studio singing, photo courtesy of Tommy Lee.

Tommy crouched on monitor, photo courtesy of Tommy Lee.

Tommy screaming with knit hat on, photo courtesy of Isabel Snyder.

Tommy playing guitar/blue lights, photo courtesy of Dustin Jack.

Tommyland sign at party, photo courtesy of Tommy Lee.

Tommy/Pamela costume party, photo courtesy of Tommy Lee.

Tommy naked, photo courtesy of Tommy Lee.

Still photo from "Hold Me Down" video, photography by Dean Karr.

Tommy giving the finger, photo courtesy of Isabel Snyder.

Tommy blue photo with cowboy hat on, photo by Brie Childers.

Tommy with P. Diddy on red carpet, photo by Justin Jay.

Tommy shadow with horns pointed up, photo courtesy of
Isabel Snyder.

ACKNOWLEDGMENTS

Endless love to my writer Anthony "fo-shozza" Bozza, I want to thank you for helping me purge the truth and make some sense of my life on paper to share with this world. Trust is a big issue with me and it was difficult to open up and trust that you wouldn't do what so many others have done to me. I thank you!!! Working with you on this book has been quite the experience—you get me, and I get you!! We've shared so much . . . you know more about me than anyone and we're not even fucking!! . . . hahah! . . . Finally . . . I now have a little brother.

Big ups to my editors Luke Dempsey and Suzanne O'Neill, my publisher Judith Curr, and all who worked so hard on this epic tale at S&S/Atria. Love to Erin Hosier, my book agent, for keeping us all in sync. . . . We got one hell of a book on our hands y'all!!

The true loves of my life Brandon and Dylan Lee (yes, one day Dad will try to explain all this to you boys). I love you Mom and Athena. Mom, we all miss Dad. . . . I look forward to the day when we all see each other again in heaven. I hope some of this stuff in this book doesn't freak you out—god at this point I would imagine nothing freaks you out anymore, and if it does or I have caused you any pain, I'm sorry Mom! . . . I never meant to, and please stop reading those damn tabloids!! Athena, my dear sister, we've not always been the closest but know in my heart you're the only sister I have and I love you so much.

Thanks to my awesome team for believing in me with their guidance and patience through some crazy ups and downs. . . . I love you guys. . . . Without you so many things would not be possible: Carl Stubner, my music and career manager, who guides the talent flow and locks in the deals; Barbara Berkowitz, my lawyer, who fights in the trenches and always has my back. Gerald Wil Rafferty, Ph.D., my life coach, who always gives me great advice (some of which I actually follow), you will never know how much calmness and hope you gave me when I was at my lowest point in life; you're truly an angel. Corey Wagner, the hands-on man at Sanctuary, who somehow manages to just get it done. Thanks to David Weise and Christel Layton, who worry about all the details and pay my bills for me and helped clean up some real messes. Thanks to my agents, Mitch Rose and Erin Culley-LaChapelle, and all at CAA for your music and film bookings. Blain Clausen, Nick Lawson, and Jeff Fioretti at Sanctuary . . . thanks guys for all your hard work.

Super love and kisses to Alecia, Heather, Mayte, and Pamela; Diane Copeland . . . my love is endless for you! . . . You are my best girlfriend and sister, my lovely spiritual angel who stayed with me when not many did—all the late-night phone calls, the books, cards, and letters you sent. I'll never forget the hours you spent with me crying and comforting me in the most uncomfortable time of my life. . . . I'll also never forget all the times you set the phone down near the stereo and let me hear something that I was missing so bad . . . music! I love you Diane . . . *muuuuuah!!*

Thanks to David LaChappelle, Isabel Snyder, Dean Karr, Brie Childers, Dustin Jack, and Justin Jay. Thanks to my webmaster J.J. "Mr. Gizmology" Bugajski and his team for all your hard work and an amazing website. Artist Todd Gallapo for your dedication with my two great album covers and this book cover. Eli 5 Stone, thank you for the killer illustration "To-Up"; you're a talented tortured artist (aren't we all) who I hope will find peace soon. Thanks to James and the badasses at Syndrome for the stickman flipbook animation. Thanks to Dale Hoffer for the transcription and to researcher Lindsay Goldenberg. Much love to my musical soldiers who have rocked the world with me. . . . Scott Humphrey, more than a music producer, a music collaborator, and my best friend; Viggy, J3, Will, Marty, DJ Aero, Perk, Chris, Kai, and Tilo. Love to the Mötley Crüe dudes Nikki, Mick, and Vince, with whom I have spent twenty-plus years, and even with all the madness we built a huge career together that has gone down in history. A special shout out to all the fans, who over the years have supported all my musical journeys . . . thanks for letting me entertain you. . . . You guys fuckin' rock!!

Love to Melissa Croland for your friendship and helping me with my baby boys whenever I need it . . . you rock girl. Love to Bob Suhusky, who kept my home safe while I camped out in L.A.'s finest gray bar motel and handled all those personal voice mail messages. Thanks to Scott Blum for your wisdom and ideas that never seem to end, you are a think tank, no doubt, and most of all your friendship. Steve Duda, thanks for the twenty-four-hour tech support and knowledge and friendship you have shared with me. Jason Harley, for all those very special nights in the kitchen tasting those amazing meals and also teaching me how to better my cooking skills. Tommy Rose, my driver and homeboy, who no matter what is always there to pick my ass up. Also thanks to Alter for teaching my kids and me how to spray paint graffiti on my garage walls, you fucker. Also a huge thanks to all the people who keep my home, Tommy-land, the happiest place on earth!!

I want to thank YOU the reader for your support and interest in my life . . . enjoy the book. . . . I really, really, really enjoyed living it! . . . It's been bananas!! Just because your name may not be here doesn't mean I have forgotten about you. It's just that the list is endless . . . you feel me?

Tommy Lee
www.tommylee.tv

AND OF COURSE
A BIG FUCK YOU GOES OUT TO . . . WELL,
YOU KNOW WHO YOU ARE!

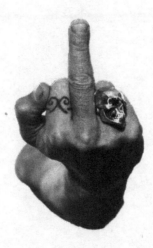

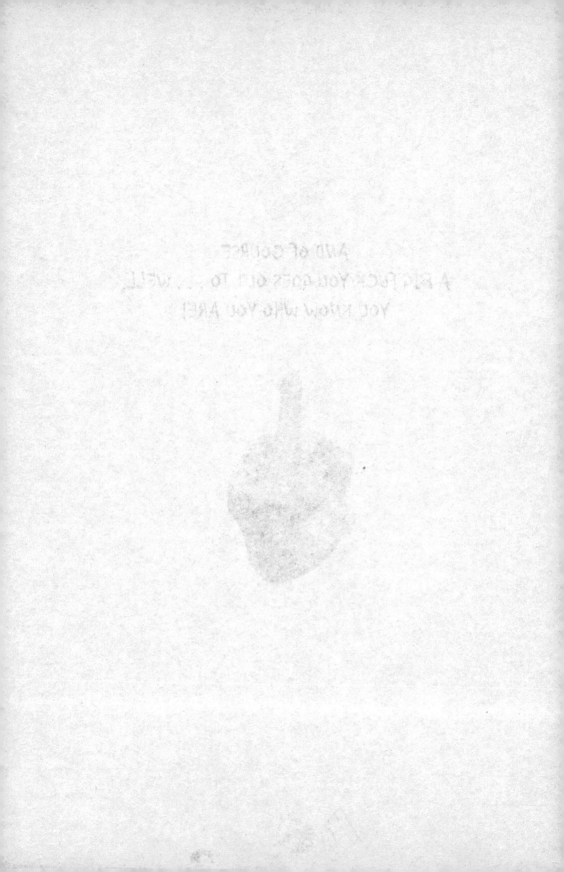

NOTES

NOTES

NOTES

NOTES

NOTES